CUTTING
THE CORD

Vern C. Lewis, Ph.D. AND

CUTTING THE CORD

Bruce Narramore, Ph.D.

**Tyndale House
Publishers, Inc.
Wheaton, Illinois**

Scripture references, unless otherwise noted, are from the *Holy Bible,* New International Version, copyright © 1973, 1978, 1984 International Bible Society. Used by permission of Zondervan Bible Publishers. Scripture quotations marked NASB are from the *New American Standard Bible,* copyright © 1960, 1962, 1963, 1968, 1971, 1972, 1973, 1975, 1977 by The Lockman Foundation. Used by permission.

Front cover photo copyright © 1990 by Robert Cushman Hayes

Library of Congress Catalog Card Number 90-70006
ISBN 0-8423-7544-9
Copyright © 1990 by Vern C. Lewis and Bruce Narramore
Printed in the United States of America

96 95 94 93 92 91 90
9   8   7   6   5   4   3   2   1

CONTENTS

PART I

LIVING WITH TEENAGERS

There is a time for everything, and a season for every activity under heaven.

ECCLESIASTES 3:1

CHAPTER ONE CHANGING TIMES

The mother of three adolescents spoke for many parents when she remarked: "The two most difficult times of life are when you *are* a teenager and when you *have* a teenager." For many parents that is true. Certainly no stage of childhood carries more potential for anxiety than adolescence. Almost from the day our children are born, older friends warn, "Just wait until they turn thirteen!" Other parents, and even some "experts," describe adolescence as a period of near-insanity when teenagers lose their rationality, become obnoxious or rebellious, and cause parents unrelenting misery.

Newspaper, radio, and television reports don't help as they depict the frightful condition of the younger generation. They tell us one of every five teenagers in the United States is a problem drinker of alcohol.[1] Well over half experiment with marijuana and other, heavier drugs. Up to one out of every twelve U.S. teenagers have made some kind of suicide attempt.[2] Three thousand teenage girls become pregnant in the U.S. every day and more than half a million babies are born to American teenagers every year. On top of this, fighting and negativism often peak during the early years of adolescence, and many previously agreeable children become moody and oversensitive.

For many, adolescence clearly is a time of turmoil. For all, it is a time of change. Teenagers are passing through dramatic physical and emotional changes that require major adjustments in their ways of thinking about themselves and others. They are no longer protected children living secure within their parents' limits. They must test out their ability to think for themselves and experiment with life outside the home. They must learn to compete with their peers. They must come to grips with their maturing sexuality. And they must accept greater responsibility for their lives and for their futures. Each of these changes can create fear of the unknown. Taken together they can be overwhelming, confusing, or discouraging.

Would you say your own teenage years were a carefree, no-conflict time of life? Or were those years punctuated with alternating periods of excitement, apprehension, discouragement, jealousy, and irritation?

In workshops on rearing teenagers, we often ask parents if their teenage years were their happiest or their most difficult time of life. At least five times as many parents call the teen years their most burdensome time rather than the most enjoyable.

Teenagers aren't the only ones who can find adolescence difficult and perplexing. Parents have to do their own adjusting. It isn't easy knowing how to react to a teenager's emotional ups and downs. It isn't easy consoling a teenage daughter who has been devastated by a broken friendship. It isn't easy dealing with an angry, sullen son or a depressed daughter who doesn't feel like talking. And it isn't fun when a child who was happy and agreeable suddenly starts challenging or arguing with everything we say.

I[3] will never forget our son Richard's first day in junior high school. He came home more negative and argumentative than he had ever been in his life. He was on his sister's case for one thing after another and was griping about everything his mother and I had to say. It was almost as if someone had given him a lecture saying, "Now you are an adolescent. You are supposed to go home and have a bad attitude." After we had a little talk, Richard settled down, but it was obvious to us all that he was moving into a new phase of his life.

Changes in our teenagers can be complicated by our own stage in life. Most parents of adolescents are approaching middle age—or are well within it. We are beginning to take stock of our own lives. We know the effectiveness of our parenting is about to be tested. We are forcefully reminded by our children's approaching departure that life doesn't last forever.

Single parents are facing the struggle of rearing children and supporting a family by themselves. Remarried parents are trying to blend an array of personalities and perspectives into one functioning family. And curiously, many parents are facing some of the same issues their adolescents are encountering. For example, just as teenagers are trying to find their way in the world beyond the home, mothers who have devoted their lives entirely to their children now consider moving outside the home for a job or finding a new source of meaning for their lives.

Widowed or divorced parents may be dating and looking for a mate at the same time their sons and daughters are. And some mid-life adults are reconsidering their careers at the very time their teenagers are exploring all the school and work options open to them. This means we may be rethinking and reorienting our own lives at the same time our adolescents are rethinking theirs.

When you couple this unique period of changes with the foreboding statistics on teenagers, it is no wonder many parents are convinced they are in for a tumultuous time from the day their sons and daughters step foot into adolescence. But this is only one part of the picture. Parenting adolescents can be a rich, rewarding, and enjoyable experience.

Teenagers Can Be Fun

Most teenagers are interesting, entertaining, and even funny.
Their lives are filled with drama, challenge, and intrigue. If you
can catch them long enough to talk, you can enjoy deep and
rewarding conversations. Teenagers don't have to be watched
every minute like young children. Once they or a friend obtain a
driver's license, they don't have to be driven all over town. They
generally cause fewer discipline problems than when they were
younger. They are more able to help with big projects around the
house. Getting them to help, of course, still presents a problem,
but they are physically and mentally able to do much more than
they were a few years earlier.

What is more enjoyable than watching your teenager jump
excitedly into new activities? What is more rewarding than seeing
your sons and daughters tackle new challenges and learn to feel
more like competent men and women? And what is more fulfilling
than seeing your children gradually grow up and assume their
role in adult society? All of these changes can make the adolescent
years one of the most enjoyable times for parents. Watching a child
leave childhood and grow into a mature adult is like watching a
beautiful butterfly coming out of its cocoon.

Your children's adolescent years can also provide you the opportunity to develop deeper and more mature friendships with your
sons and daughters. If things go well they will share some serious
and important concerns about their lives. Although you will
always be their parents, you also have the opportunity to become
great friends and to share meaningfully throughout the years to
come. When your sons and daughters have families of their own,
you may have the privilege of sharing meaningfully in their
children's lives.

Many parents have the added opportunity of seeing their teenagers mature spiritually and make their childhood faith their own.
Each of these developments brings fulfillment and joy to parents
who have looked forward to the day that their children would
become responsible and happy adults. That is why the Bible says,
"Sons are a heritage from the Lord, children a reward from

him. . . . Blessed is the man whose quiver is full of them" (Ps. 127:35).

Birth Pangs of Adulthood

Thirteen-year-old Lori is a typical early adolescent. Her mother complains that Lori has become "impossible to live with, is never satisfied with her looks, and is moody and negative about everything." On top of that, "she can't keep her feelings under control," and when her mother asks her to do anything around the house, she flies off the handle and accuses her mother of being unreasonable.

Lori is struggling with the most important task of the teenage years. She is trying to grow out of her childhood dependency on her parents, establish her own identity, and become an independent adult.

For years Lori has been told what to do, what to wear, what to study, and when (and often what) to eat. Being stubborn and refusing to cooperate are her ways of saying, "I can think for myself! I don't have to do it your way! Stop treating me like a child!"

Lori has had enough of childhood and wants to start becoming independent. But like most early and middle adolescents, she isn't able to express her needs calmly. She can't casually walk up to her mother and say, "Mom, let's have a talk. I'm thirteen now and need to start growing up and thinking for myself. When you keep telling me what to do, I feel like a child. Could you please start letting go a little and allowing me to make a few more of my own decisions?" Instead she loses her temper, pouts, and fumes, or gripes about it. These are the only ways she knows to tell her parents she is ready to become an independent person and start moving away from her mom and dad.

Twenty-year-old Mark is on the opposite end of adolescence. A part-time college student, he alternately fails his classes or just squeaks by. He lives at home and parties until two or three in the morning on weekends. He ignores his parents' requests to come in at a decent hour, has quit two jobs within six months, and occasionally uses drugs. When Mark's parents try to talk to him about his problems, he blows up, tells them he is old enough to make his own decisions, and stalks out of the house in a huff.

Mark's anger and irresponsibility reveal his difficulty with leaving childhood and becoming adult. Like many late adolescents, he demands the right to set his own hours and do as he pleases, although he lives at home and expects his parents to pay his bills. He wants the privileges of adulthood without the responsibilities. He is trying to maintain the illusion that he is mature while he is still being taken care of by his parents.

Although Mark's parents nag and criticize him and tell him he needs to be more responsible, they continue to let him live at home and they pay his bills. Unknowingly, they are helping perpetuate his irresponsibility. The best thing they could do for Mark would be to require him to take a job or go to college and make passing grades, or else move out on his own. Any of these options would give Mark the nudge he needs to give up his prolonged dependency and move on toward adulthood. If Mark's parents don't hurry up and help him move beyond this "stuck" period of his life, he will carry his crippling dependency and irresponsibility into marriage or other adult relationships where they will create needless anguish.

Like Lori and Mark, most adolescents have to struggle at least a little to bid farewell to childhood. In fact, both the exciting possibilities for growth and the potential problems of the teenage years come out of this effort to become more independent and mature. Your teenagers' increased responsibility will be made possible by their maturing ability to make decisions for themselves, to decide their own likes and dislikes, and to put a certain amount of emotional distance between themselves and you. Unfortunately, some arguments, moodiness, and rebellion will probably grow out of the same effort to grow up.

Emotionally leaving mother and father isn't easy for young people. It requires major revisions in attitudes toward themselves and others. It means gradually turning away from parents as the major source of love in order to prepare for loving adult relationships with others. It means turning away from parents as the major source of security and comfort so they can start caring for their own needs. And it means no longer relying on others to be the authorities who set moral standards in order to form their own values and commitments.

This is why parents and children naturally have mixed feelings about the teenage years. We are excited and enthusiastic about some upcoming changes but uncertain, or apprehensive, about others.

Extended Adolescence

In earlier times the transition from childhood to adulthood was much briefer and more clearly defined. In a tribe in Papua, New Guinea, for example, male adolescents go through a ritualistic transition to adulthood when they reach twelve years of age. Villagers chant the following verse as the young adolescents crawl beneath the legs of men of the village and are hit with sticks and burned with glowing embers.

> *When you live under your mother's leg*
> *You do what you like*
> *You have what you want*
> *You ask for food and you receive it*
> *You ask for water and you receive it*
> *You come and cry*
> *You want a big fish*
> *Your mother cooks it for you*
> *But now, now you come under your father's leg*
> *Now you pay*
> *For being treated so softly at home*
> *A new time begins for you*
> *When you must know—*
> *That you are a man!* [4]

This initiation rite is a painful milestone that marks a great transition in their life: yesterday a tantrum-throwing boy, today a bold man. Missionaries who have observed this custom attest to the sudden change of attitudes and behavior this rite produces. They are less clear about the ritual's effects on the young males' emotional life and their ability to relate with sensitivity and respect to each other and to women of the tribe.

The Bar Mitzvah in Judaism has long been a much more gentle and uplifting ceremony for incorporating youths into adult society. On the first Sabbath after a boy has turned thirteen, he is honored at a ceremony marking his entry into manhood. For the first time in his life, the young man is asked to read aloud from the Hebrew Torah before the congregation. After the reading of the Torah, the boy's father pronounces the customary blessing: "Blessed be he who has relieved me of the responsibility of this child." From that time on, the boy is considered responsible for his religious acts and has the privilege of being counted among one of the ten men necessary for *minyan,* the minimum number required to hold a public worship service.

In previous centuries, the Bar Mitzvah often coincided with the beginning of a vocational apprenticeship, when young men started to learn a craft or a profession from a village elder. Taken together, these two events marked dramatic changes in status and activities for Jewish boys. With the disappearance of apprenticeships, the rapid changes in culture, and recent lengthening of years in adolescence, the Bar Mitzvah now marks a much less dramatic change. It still, however, offers Jewish boys one clear rite of passage toward adulthood.[5] It draws a line saying, "Before this I was a child. Now I am more adult and responsible for my values, choices, and beliefs."

For most Western adolescents, advancing from childhood to adulthood has become a lengthy trek along an unmarked trail. Compared to earlier cultures, it is much more difficult to become adult in the twentieth century. Like Mark, the young man mentioned earlier, many live-at-home late adolescents have no definite responsibilities to press them into adulthood. The skills needed to be a productive member of society today have become more and more complex and demanding. Formal education often extends well into the twenties. Vocational possibilities are endless, and the array of social, spiritual, and political choices is overwhelming. Coupled with the financial advantages of living with parents, these forces are making the period of adolescence longer and more difficult.

No generation in history has seen such an extended period of adolescence as have Americans in the last half of the twentieth century. Turning eighteen, joining the army, taking a job, and completing high school or college serve as "mini" passages. But none of these steps sends such a dramatic message to society that a new adult has arrived as did earlier, more formal rituals and practices.

This elongated adolescence creates positive and negative possibilities for you and your teenagers. On the one hand, it provides plenty of time to nurture and equip children for adulthood. This is good, since our frighteningly complex world requires skills and character strengths seldom needed in earlier times. On the other hand, this lengthened adolescence can delay the onset of responsible adult living and increase the likelihood of misunderstandings and conflict between you and your teens.

A Road Map for Parents

Helping your teenagers become more adult and independent is a little like preparing a ship to leave the harbor. Before heading out to sea, the ship is secured to the dock by giant ropes while it takes on fuel and makes preparations for the voyage. If it leaves the home port before taking on adequate supplies, its voyage is doomed to fail. But once the ship has been loaded for its journey and the engine put in gear, it had better be cut loose from the pier or a disaster will occur.

Like a ship prepared to leave the harbor, your twelve- and thirteen-year-olds have been tied to their parental pier long enough. If their childhood years have gone well, they have taken on a good load of emotional fuel by the time puberty shifts their gears of adulthood into motion. Now you must help them cut the cords[6] that have bound you together or they are likely to tear down the dock on their way out of the family harbor. If you help them make a smooth exit onto the sea of adulthood you can count on some occasional happy returns to home port in the years to come. If you don't, you may be in for years of conflict and frustration.

In order to leave home successfully, your teenagers need a good supply of two types of psychological fuel. First, they need to have taken in years of parental nurturance that produces an inner sense of being loved and an ability to relate intimately to other people. Second, they need to have stored multiple memories of small, successful voyages on which they tried out their abilities to float apart from mom and dad. Those memories provide the foundational confidence that they will need to cope with life outside the family harbor. These fuels represent the two most basic emotional needs of all human beings. We all need to be loved and to be able to relate intimately to other people, and we need a clear sense of our identities as separate people and of our own competence to function in the world.

In the pages that follow, we will tell the story of your adolescents' personality development through the eyes of their twin needs to be nurtured and to become independent from you. We will do this by tracing the progressive challenges adolescents will face at each of the four main stages of adolescence—pre-, early, middle, and late. We will show the conflicts or struggles that are likely to pop up at each stage of their journey and discuss what you can do to help them navigate successfully. In this way we will give you a kind of navigational chart or road map for parenting adolescents.

This book differs in three ways from many books for parents. First, our major emphasis is on what is normal. One of the most frustrating things for parents of teenagers is not knowing whether their sons' and daughters' sudden changes of attitude are normal. Are your teenagers being purposely obnoxious or are they simply going through a phase? Are your daughters excessively boy-crazy or are they within the normal range? Are they seriously depressed, or is their moodiness temporary and to be expected? By seeing what is typical for teenagers at various ages we hope to help you relax a bit and realize your teenagers may not be as different as you think.

Second, this book focuses on the reasons your teenagers act and feel the way they do. We try to take you beneath the surface of your sons' and daughters' sometimes frustrating and confusing attitudes and actions to the underlying causes. Once you understand those causes, you will find it easier to be sympathetic and to help them through this sometimes difficult time of life.

Third, this book is designed to be preventive. Although we offer specific suggestions for handling negativism, moodiness, refusal to take responsibility, dating, school, and other problems, our main goal is to help you avoid difficulties before they start or solve them before they get out of hand. Each stage of your adolescents' journey brings them face to face with new challenges and developmental tasks. Parents who know what to expect at these stages find it easier to help their sons and daughters navigate those potentially dangerous waters.

The remainder of Part I outlines the contours of the journey your teenagers will be taking. Chapter 2 introduces you to the parallels between that journey and the trip your children took in growing away from you during their first few years of life. Chapter 3 presents several principles for understanding and guiding teenagers of all ages. Part II (chapters 4-13) discusses the developmental tasks and the predictable struggles teenagers face during each of the four stages of adolescence. After presenting the typical challenges your sons and daughters face at each of these stages, we devote a chapter or two to specific guidelines for parenting adolescents at that age.

Once we have surveyed the entire landscape of adolescence in Parts I and II, Part III (chapters 14-20) considers several of the most frequently asked questions by parents of teenagers: questions about how to let go of your teenager, how to help them cope with their maturing sexuality, how to detect and avoid the potential tragedy of adolescent suicide, and how to cope with post-high school or college young adults who haven't yet left the nest—or who have returned after an abortive effort to make it on their own.[7]

NOTES

1. Beverly Beyette. "Alcohol—The Gateway Drug for Teens," *Los Angeles Times,* Dec. 27, 1988.
2. A. Spirito, L. Brown, J. Overholser, and G. Fritz. "Attempted suicide in adolescence: a review and critique of the literature," *Clinical Psychology Review,* 1989, 9, 335-363.
3. Although Dr. Lewis and Dr. Narramore have coauthored this book they have chosen to write from the more personal and readable first person singular "I" instead of the awkward "one of the authors." Unless otherwise noted, all personal and clinical illustrations in a chapter are by the author first footnoted. This illustration is by Dr. Narramore.
4. Michael Somare, in *Papua, New Guinea* (1975). Published for the Office of Information by Robert Brown & Associates Pty, Ltd., P. O. Box 3395, Port Moresby, Papua, New Guinea.
5. In more recent times, a similar ceremony and status (Bat Mitzvah) is conferred on Jewish girls.
6. We would like to thank Mrs. Jan Meyers of Bible Study Fellowship for her suggestion of *Cutting the Cord* as the title of this book.
7. Dr. Narramore has written a companion volume, *Adolescence Is Not an Illness,* which offers specific suggestions for handling such problems as peer pressure, discipline, dating, alcohol and drug use, money and conflict resolution (Old Tappan, N.J.: Revell, 1989).

For this reason a man will leave his father and mother and be united to his wife, and they will become one flesh.

GENESIS 2:24

CHAPTER TWO CUTTING THE CORD

If you are the parent of an early-adolescent son you may have found yourself wanting to tell him, "Stop acting like a two-year-old." And if you are the parent of a middle-adolescent daughter you have probably seen her feeling stubbornly independent one moment and helpless the next—much as she acted when she was about a year and a half old. These similarities are not coincidental. In fact, they hold an important key for understanding adolescents.

Adolescence can be understood as a kind of second birth. Just as unborn babies must leave their mothers' protective womb to live, teenagers must leave the protective womb of the home. Just as newborn infants must have their physical umbilical cords severed to separate from their mothers, adolescents must cut the psychological cords that have bound them to their parents.

Just as the umbilical cord that was once the unborn baby's lifeline to survival can choke life if it is wrapped around the unborn baby's neck, the emotional ties that have been the reservoir of your adolescents' love can begin to restrict and choke them if they aren't loosened at the appropriate time. And just as infants go through predictable stages of development with predictable feelings and reactions, adolescents pass through similar stages.

There are so many remarkable similarities between your adolescents' attempts to separate from you and the struggle of young toddlers to separate from their mothers that we will begin our story of adolescence with a brief look at your sons' and daughters' first three years of life. Once you understand the steps infants and toddlers go through in developing their initial sense of identity and autonomy, you will find it easier to understand many of your teenagers' struggles and reactions. In fact, we think you will be surprised at how much your teenagers can act like two-year-olds at certain stages of development!

When Teens Were Toddlers

Psychiatrist Margaret Mahler, during the 1950s and 1960s, shed light on the developmental stages of human beings by extensive studies of infants. While comparing the mother-child relationships of normal infants with those of psychotic infants, Dr. Mahler observed some startling differences.[1,2] Normal infants bonded closely to their mothers in the first few months of life. Then after a few months of nurturing closeness they gradually started separating from their mothers and developing their own sense of individuality.

In contrast, psychotic infants either failed to form an intimate attachment to their mothers or, after forming an attachment, weren't able to move away from their mothers and become separate individuals. Since they were unable to attach securely or separate on schedule, the psychotic children failed to develop a strong inner emotional life. When they grew older they were unable to perceive their world accurately and develop normal attitudes toward themselves and others.

In the healthy infants, Dr. Mahler noticed four stages of development beginning with an almost complete union with the mothers at the time of birth and ending with a clear sense of individuality at about three years of age. Adolescents pass through similar stages but on a much more mature developmental level. During infancy, children first become aware that they are physically separate and independent from their mothers. During adolescence they struggle to become psychologically independent. During both stages children encounter some relatively specific developmental hurdles that must be cleared in order for them to break away from past dependencies and learn to stand on their own feet.

In both infancy and adolescence, the growing person experiences the same two needs: the need for a loving attachment to another human being and the need to separate and find one's own distinct identity. In the rest of this chapter we will introduce the major stages infants and toddlers go through in separating from their mothers and the similar stages your teenagers are likely to encounter.[3]

The Roots of Intimacy: Birth to Five Months

During the first three months of life, infants have very little awareness of the outside world. Most of their movements are simple reflexes and their time is largely spent eating or sleeping. Since they aren't ready to cope with the world around them, infants go through something of a three-month "grace period," when they are completely dependent on their mothers and for most of that time relatively unaware of the outside world.[4] Even at this early age, however, infants are learning about their world. They scan their mother's face or fix their eyes on her. Mother's responsive cooing and engaging eye contact have a calming influence, and infants soon begin to equate her presence with safety, nourishment, and care.

Toward the end of the first three months, healthy infants experience an increasing awareness of the outside world.[5] They start responding to the appearance of faces even though they do not yet recognize those faces as separate people outside themselves. During this time, the baby cannot distinguish between his body and the mother's, which produces a sense of oneness with her. This oneness is so complete that babies literally do not know that they exist as separate persons. Both their emotional and physical existence are merged into their mother's.

Although infants come into the world with different temperaments, tolerances for pain, activity levels, and propensities for moods, their emotional lives are closely bound up with their attachment to their mothers. If mother is tense, the baby tends to be tense; if mother is relaxed, the baby is usually calm; if mother is angry, the baby experiences that irritation.[6]

During the first five or six months of life, mother serves as the infant's complete protector. She is so tuned in to her infant's subtle communications of discomfort that she hears those messages without words and meets their needs with a calming influence. She is so close that she, too, experiences oneness as the baby meets some of her maternal needs and she reciprocates. In fact, most mothers are so preoccupied with their infants that they withdraw much of their interest from other people and activities. Friendships become less important and their own career or their husband's work recede into the background.

Your children's success in coping with both adolescence and adulthood will be greatly influenced by the quality of attachment they experienced during those early months of life. Infants who attach securely to happy mothers are off to a good start. They are more likely to feel comfortable with others, to trust, and to establish meaningful relationships because they have a foundation for emotional closeness. Even if they run into serious problems or family breakdowns later, they are better able to cope because they have the strong foundation for health that was laid down in their earliest period of development.

Infants who fail to bond securely to their mothers during these early months are likely to struggle with close relationships in later life. They may resist intimate friendships, restlessly seek love from a series of sexual partners, careen through several chaotic marriages, or simply go through the motions of closeness without any true intimacy. Some become antisocial; others grow up seeking endlessly for someone to cling to or emotionally merge with in order to fill their inner emotional void. But once they find someone, they are so clinging or demanding that they are in danger of smothering their partners and frightening them away.

Donna[7] was this kind of "clinger." She came to a university counseling center seeking help with her relationships with men after her boyfriend of six months dumped her. He said their relationship was "too intense" and that as a sophomore he didn't want to get too serious yet. Donna was crushed but recognized this as a pattern in her life. During the past two years she had three other relationships that ended the same way. Each time she hit it off well with a young man but after a few dates she started feeling more serious than he did. She became jealous if he talked to any other girl and she wanted to spend all of their free time together.

Donna's counselor, in talking with her, learned that she was adopted. She spent her first two years of life in three different foster homes. Although she received good physical care, she lacked even one stable mother figure to whom she could attach securely. When she was three, Donna was adopted into a fine family, but her earliest needs for bonding were never met. She was fearful of being separated from her adoptive parents and was quite dependent. Throughout childhood her feelings were easily hurt. In junior high she was jealous when her girlfriends spent time with other friends, and she had crushes on one boy after another.

When Donna started dating, every relationship quickly became intense. Boys initially liked her because she was warm and affectionate and seemed to admire them greatly. But when Donna became possessive and demanding, she frightened them away. They started feeling they had no freedom or space to make their own decisions. Sixteen years after she lost her mother, Donna was still trying to fill that deep emotional void. Her mother's total absence, and disappointment with one surrogate mother after another, made her too dependent and demanding to experience enjoyable dating relationships.

Other infants have less extreme problems attaching to their mothers. Some fail to bond securely because of inborn constitutional factors or the mother's severe illnesses. Others have trouble because their mothers were too anxious to parent them calmly or because their mothers experienced prolonged periods of postpartum depression. But whatever the cause, problems in bonding securely to the mother can make it more difficult to relate securely to others in the future.

The Dawn of Individuality: Five to Ten Months

After infants experience the blissful comfort of being one with their mother, they are ready to start separating from her and to begin their long journey to adulthood. This process begins in earnest during the fifth or sixth month of life and continues strongly for the next couple of years.[8] It is this process of separating from mother and developing a sense of personal identity that has important parallels with adolescence. Teenagers separate on a more mature developmental level, but the four major developmental stages over the period of five months to three years of age have a lot in common with the four stages of pre-, early, middle, and late adolescence.

From about five to ten months of age, infants are engrossed in discovering that their bodies are different from their environment, and that their arms and hands are different from detached objects such as toys, a crib, or mother's face. This marks the beginning of the infant's sense of self or personal identity. Dr. Mahler labeled this the phase of *differentiation*, since infants are engrossed in finding out how they are different or distinct from their environment. During this time, infants realize that their mother is distinct from other people, and mother receives preferential smiles when she appears. They also start pushing away from mother more forcefully and frequently. They want to hold their own bottles or begin to motion or move in the direction of something they see and want.

Later, before puberty, ten- to twelve-year-olds go through a similar period of increasing awareness of their differences from others. They develop a heightened awareness of their bodies and their distinctiveness from the opposite sex. They start thinking and acting differently from their parents. These preadolescent changes will be discussed in chapters 4 and 5.

The Practicing Period: Ten to Sixteen Months

Once infants develop their initial self-awareness, they begin separating from their mothers more aggressively. They crawl away short distances, sit upright, and begin to walk. Since each of these activities help ten- to sixteen-month-old toddlers continue differentiating themselves from their environment and practicing being separate persons, Dr. Mahler labeled this the *practicing period*.

Remember the excitement on your one-year-old's face as she toddled away from her mother and began exploring on her own? She was practicing at being separate from you. Practicing toddlers are like cars with very small fuel tanks. Children this age regularly go to their mother to receive an emotional refill and then drive away to explore their worlds. But before long, they get near empty and come running back for another emotional refueling. If mother is consistently available when they come in for a fill up, toddlers gradually develop a sense of emotional security. Knowing that mother is available when they need her, they learn to stay away for longer periods of time. But if mother isn't available when they come in for emotional refueling, they can become frightened, lonely, or depressed.

The development of language in your children's second year of life intensifies their efforts to distinguish themselves from mother and practice being separate. Soon after learning *mama* and *dada* (or something engagingly like it) toddlers start saying *me* and *mine*. This lets them own things and know what belongs to whom. Chances are, *me* and *mine* soon become their favorite words. In fact, do you ever remember seeing a toddler reach out to another child and say, "Yours!" and give his toy away? Rarely. In this stage and the next, toddlers are so busy finding out that they are separate people with minds of their own that they are not inclined to share anything. They label things with words and hold onto things in order to establish their separateness, and they aren't about to surrender their dawning identity by yielding their prized possessions. Only after they learn who they are and what they own will they feel secure and strong enough to share with others.

At about thirteen or fourteen years of age, most early adolescents go through a practicing period of trying their wings, a bit like ten- to sixteen-month-old toddlers. They start reaching out and excitedly exploring their world. But like the toddler, they don't yet know their limits and some of life's realities! Junior high crushes, first boyfriends, and experimenting with cigarettes or alcohol are all efforts at practicing something adult. But like the toddler who accidentally pulls a lampstand over on his head, early adolescents may not be aware of the potentially dangerous consequences of their behavior. They may also go through a phase of real selfishness or possessiveness before they learn that being adult means being able to give, not just having the power to acquire and keep one's own possessions. These parallels will be explored when we come to early adolescence in chapters 6 and 7.

The Reapproaching Phase: Sixteen to Twenty-four Months

After a period of practicing being separate, both toddlers and early adolescents move on to the next developmental stage: the *rapprochement* or *reapproaching* period. This period is characterized by increasing independence mingled with occasionally strong feelings of dependency and need. Sixteen- to twenty-four-month-old toddlers, for example, typically become much more independent and assertive. They play alone for longer periods, do more things for themselves and often first learn to say, "No!" Even though these older toddlers are moving further away from mother, however, they return often to take on more emotional fuel or to share their experiences and be encouraged or affirmed. If mother isn't available when they return for emotional refueling these older toddlers can also become very anxious or depressed.

When Beth was twenty-one months old, her mother went into the hospital for four months and her aunt who had been her only baby-sitter suddenly died. When Beth's mother returned from the hospital, Beth was initially quite withdrawn. Then she attached herself to her mother and followed everywhere she went. Through-out kindergarten and elementary school, Beth returned home each day and painstakingly quizzed her mother on her day's activities. One year when Beth could see her home from the classroom window she became upset each time her mother left the house. At fifteen years old, Beth continued to shadow her mother. She spent no time with friends, always wanted to help her mother around the house, and showed a serious lack of confidence to do things by herself. Thirteen years after the tragic loss of her aunt and her mother's illness, Beth was still trying to quell her fear that no one would be there to give her emotional support when she returned home.

Sometime between fifteen and eighteen years of age, middle adolescents go through a reapproaching phase similar to the sixteen- to twenty-four-month-old toddler. They move further away from parents. They start driving or dating or taking part-time jobs. They stand increasingly on their own. But they can also experience increasing anxiety and depression and a lot of mixed emotions. Middle adolescents can act stubbornly independent one minute and incredibly dependent the next. They can love you one minute and hate you the next. And they often want to spend time with their friends or to be left alone, but when they need you, they need you. They feel abandoned or depressed and lose confidence if you are unavailable as a home base for encouragement and support. This and other dynamics of middle adolescents are discussed in chapters 8 through 11.

Putting It Together: Two to Three

The last period of early childhood development occurs from approximately age two until three. During this year the same children that have gone through the tumultuous second year of life—with their stubbornness and their vacillations between independency and dependency—begin to stabilize their personalities. They become less fearful, their emotions are more stable, and they are content to play alone or with others whether mother is present or not. They seem to have accomplished their initial break from dependency on mother and learned that they can stand alone. Their frequent use of "No!" reflects their growing confidence and is a way of further solidifying their independence as a separate self. It is their way of saying they can think for themselves. Independent people can say no.

Since a child's unique identity, as one who can stand somewhat on his own, comes together at between two and three years of age, Dr. Mahler called this the stage of *consolidation*. The three-year-old's increased ability to be alone without panicking grows out of his newly acquired ability to keep a mental picture of his mother in his mind even when she isn't present. Until two years of age, young children do not have a well-developed memory bank of parental pictures. That is why they can't leave mother for long without becoming frightened. For them, to be out of sight is to be out of mind.

Remember how your toddlers often panicked when you were just around the corner or down the next aisle at the market? They were afraid you had vanished or left for good. And remember when your fifteen-month-olds played peek-a-boo? They covered their eyes with their hands and thought you couldn't see *them*. Their mental processes hadn't matured enough for them to realize that even when they couldn't see you, you were still present.

Although infants start developing their memories of themselves and others in the later part of the first year of life, they are not able to keep clear and lasting memories of parents until they are nearing three years of age. By that time, most children develop both a good sense of their own individuality and a relatively stable mental picture of parents. Realizing they are separate people with powers of their own, and having a solid memory of their parents, they are ready to start living more independently.

By three years of age, most children have also learned to take care of many of their own needs and wishes. They can find their toys, feed themselves, or do other things you used to do for them. This reinforces their dawning independence and gives them courage to be even less dependent on mom and dad. They still need our loving care and availability, but they are on the way to the time when they will be able to leave the harbor of home.

A little like three-year-olds, late adolescents (ages seventeen to twenty-one) also go through a period of consolidation. They show increasingly mature behavior. They have a greater ability to handle frustration. Their memories of themselves and others are more stable. Their emotions become more controlled. Their love-hate relationships often start to subside. They take their first job or move away to college, and their character solidifies. They still have a lot of maturing to do, but the major contours of their lives are pretty well established. Parenting late adolescents will be discussed in chapters 12 and 13.

The Expanding Years

During the rest of the first decade of life, children continue developing their personal identities. They experiment and they watch and imitate their parents and others. They learn the skills of reading and writing and communication. They come to love daddy as well as mommy. They develop their feelings about mas-culinity and femininity (their gender identities) by interacting with their mothers and fathers. And they develop social skills, especially with their same-sex friends.

Through all of this your children have the same two needs—the need to feel loved and comfortably close to you and the need to increasingly become their own separate person. If one of these is more important in the early years, it is the need for loving support. In adolescence the need for consistent, supportive love remains vital, but the need to gradually separate and become more independent becomes increasingly the more important goal.

Table I summarizes the stages of early child development and their adolescent parallels.

TABLE I

Infant Age	Infant Stage	Parallel Child or Adolescent Age	Parallel Child or Adolescent Stage[9]
0-3 months	The Autistic Stage	No similar age	No similar stage
3-5 months	Oneness with Mother	3-10 years	Oneness with family
5-10 months	Differentiation or Distinctiveness	10-12 years	Preadolescence
10-16 months	Practicing	13-14 years	Early adolescence
16-24 months	Reapproaching	15-17 years	Middle adolescence
24-36 months	Consolidation	18-21 years	Late adolescence

Infancy and Adolescence

Seeing the parallels between the developmental processes of early childhood and adolescence sheds light on the reasons some teenagers have a tougher time with adolescence than others. Children who pass comfortably through the first decade of life bring a sense of inner strength to adolescence. They know who they are and what they can do. Since they have bonded well during the first several months of life, they have a basic trust in others and a relatively strong sense of their identity as separate people. They have learned to relate confidently to others. They aren't hypersensitive to rejection. And they don't need to cling dependently to others to make up for earlier deprivations. They also

26

don't need to avoid close relationships because they don't fear being engulfed by an overcontrolling or intrusive parent. And having secure identities, they aren't riddled by anxiety because they have the inner resources they need to face the tasks of adolescence.

But what about children who enter adolescence with weak or insecure identities? What if they failed to bond securely to their mothers in the first year of life or had trouble relating to others? What if their mother was so tense and anxious that she couldn't let them happily explore their expanding world? Or what if they suffered persistent parental overcontrol during the first few years of life when they should have been learning to make decisions for themselves?

These adolescents will have a harder time. Their social and dating relationships may turn into a tangle of crushes, hurts, idealizations, or resentments. They may be unprepared to say no in the face of peer influence because they have habitually followed others. They may be so fearful that they can't fit comfortably among their peers. Or they may become stubborn or rebellious in order to cope with their fears of being overwhelmed by controlling people.

Problems in those early years of life won't doom children to a conflict-filled adolescence or, worse yet, a disturbed adulthood. But, other things being equal, difficulties in the earlier stages of life do accentuate the normal struggles adolescents face.

Chapter Highlights

Your teenagers' attempts to shape their independent identities have important parallels with toddlers' and young children's efforts to separate from their mothers. Like toddlers, teenagers need to feel secure within the safety of their families. And like toddlers they must grow out of their dependencies in order to become mature and independent. Understanding these similarities will help you know what to expect from your sons and daughters at each stage of adolescence. It will also help you know how to handle some of their otherwise perplexing attitudes and actions.

NOTES

1. Margaret Mahler, Fred Pine, and A. Bergman. *The Psychological Birth of the Human Infant* (New York: Basic Books, 1975).
2. Psychotic children are characterized by a gross inability to relate to other human beings, severe distortions of perception, and the absence of personal boundaries or a concrete sense of one's self.
3. Peter Blos was one of the first to describe the parallels between the separation processes of infancy and adolescence in *On Adolescence* (New York: The Free Press of Glencoe, 1962).
4. Since very young infants give little indication of any real awareness of external objects or people, Dr. Mahler labeled the first three months the "autistic" or "self" stage.
5. Researchers such as Daniel Stern (*The Interpersonal World of the Infant,* New York: Basic Books, Inc. 1985) now believe even very young infants have a greater capacity to recognize others and make autonomous movements. In either case, the first three months of life are characterized by a relative lack of ability to recognize the outside world.
6. Since this merger with mother is the most prominent feature of this stage, Dr. Mahler called this the *symbiotic* (or *oneness*) stage.
7. Personal and clinical illustrations in this chapter are by Dr. Lewis.
8. These ages are rough approximations and all children move through these stages on slightly different schedules.
9. These approximate ages are for girls. Boys are usually a year or two later through early or middle adolescence.

*By wisdom
a house is
built and
through
under-
standing
it is
established.*
PROVERBS 24:3

CHAPTER THREE
UNDERSTANDING YOUR ADOLESCENTS

For several months before her preadolescent daughter reached her thirteenth birthday, Marsha jokingly told her, "Laura, you can't turn thirteen until I'm ready!"[1] Like Marsha, many parents fear they won't be ready for their children's adolescent years. They seem to think teenagers are a special species that require a whole new strategy of parenting. Fortunately, that isn't true. Most of your sons' and daughters' basic needs remain the same throughout their lives. The ways you learned to help them mature as children will serve you well during their adolescent years.

Understanding a few characteristics of teenage development, however, will help you to avoid a lot of frustration and misunderstanding. Before we begin our journey through the four stages of adolescence, we want to introduce you to those important principles.

A Divine Design

Genesis 2:24 gives a foundational concept for understanding teenagers: "For this reason a man will leave his father and his mother and be united to his wife, and they will become one flesh." Notice the three stages in this verse. First, children are with their parents through their growing years. Next, they deliberately leave the parents. Finally, they are united to an adult mate. God intended children to move from a period of complete dependency on their mothers, through a period of separation when they seek to establish their identities as independent individuals, to a period of mature independency. This last period is marked by the ability to enter into intimate relationships with others while still maintaining one's unique identity.

Children must be loved and nurtured for many years in order to grow up and become healthy adults. Their close attachments to their parents provide the safety and protection they need to grow emotionally. But once those nurturing needs are met, leaving their parents becomes as important a part of growing up as staying close was in early years.

Growing out of the dependent relationships of childhood frees teenagers to stand on their own and to start looking at life through their own eyes. It encourages them to discover their own abilities and gain confidence in using them. It allows them to become more flexible and do some things differently than you do them. And it gradually enables them to accept new responsibilities without caving in or running to someone else for help.

If teenagers don't give up their childhood ways of relating to their parents and others, they will carry some very inappropriate patterns into adulthood. In their marriages they may feel hurt if holidays aren't spent with their side of the family. They may resent spouses who don't work or play or communicate or spend money like their parents did. They may get into conflicts over disciplining children because their parents "didn't do it that way." They may be inflexible because they don't have enough emotional distance from their parents to see life in new ways, think for themselves, or construct new loyalties to their spouse and children. Or they may struggle with alternating feelings of dependency and anger toward their mates because they haven't resolved their own dependency conflicts with their parents.

These and other painful results of failing to cut the emotional umbilical cord of childhood dependency will become clearer as we examine the various stages of adolescence. For now, however, we simply want to underscore this foundational principle: the Creator intended our children to go from a lengthy stage of dependency, through a period of separation in which they establish their own identity, into a period of healthy adult interdependency. This third stage includes the capacity to relate intimately and mutually to others. Many experiences of adolescence make much more sense when they are seen as efforts to complete this God-given process.

Even Jesus Christ went through the progression from dependency to independency. He began life, humanly speaking, dependent on his mother. He gradually "grew and became strong . . . [and] was filled with wisdom."[2] He asserted his independence as a twelve-year-old by staying behind in the temple in Jerusalem when his parents returned to Nazareth.[3] And he eventually left his parents for his life's calling and intimate relationships with his disciples and adult friends.[4]

Being both human and divine, Jesus was about his heavenly father's business there in the temple courts. Yet, as a human, his staying behind at the temple demonstrates the God-given principle that children must eventually separate from their parents. The timing and nature of Jesus' separation has two unique features. First, Jesus was coming into a fuller awareness of his deity and the life that lay ahead of him. Second, in Jesus' day, children tended to marry as soon as age fourteen or fifteen. Consequently, the age of his apparently abrupt separation from his parents is substantially earlier than is appropriate today.

Jesus' adult life also demonstrated the results of a successfully completed childhood and adolescence. He was able to stand alone in the face of incredible pressure at the same time he was able to be deeply loving and involved with others. This is the essence of psychological maturity—the ability to be an individual and to relate intimately and nondefensively to others.

Ages and Stages

The biblical principle of gradual development from dependency toward independency and the capacity for adult intimacy leads to a second guideline for understanding adolescents. Every stage of human development has one or more major tasks or challenges that are especially important for that particular period. Those needs or tasks must be met or finished in order for children to move successfully to the next level of maturity.

Horticulturists know that if a young tree does not receive enough nutrients and water during its first years it will never reach its full potential and productivity even if it is tended properly later. And physicians know that unborn babies whose mothers catch the German measles (rubella) during the first three months of pregnancy are likely to be born with birth defects or serious mental retardation. The same illness three months later generally doesn't have the same effect because the infant is farther along in his development. The same principle is true of our children's psychological development. At each stage of life, children have certain emotional needs and developmental tasks they must accomplish. If these needs aren't met or those tasks mastered, they have trouble moving smoothly into the next stage of their life.

Each developmental period brings new opportunities for growth, and each successfully navigated stage prepares them to enter confidently into the next stage of development. Each failure to develop the inner resources needed at a particular stage makes future adjustment that much more difficult.

Fifteen-year-old Beth, whom we mentioned in chapter 2, is a prime example. When her mother was hospitalized for four months and her aunt died, Beth was in a crucial stage in life. At twenty-one months of age she was just beginning to reach out beyond her mother and practice being separate, and she needed to learn that she would always have a nourishing harbor to return to in her need. But at the very moment Beth was reaching out, she lost both sources of her emotional supplies. Years later, as she tried to navigate her adolescent separation from her parents, Beth still battled deep fears of abandonment. She couldn't leave her mother because the last time she tried she was left completely on her own.

If Beth's aunt had died and her mother had been ill during Beth's first few weeks of life, these losses would not have impacted her the same way they did when she was a year and a half. At that early time, Beth wouldn't have known her aunt was missing, and a loving mother-substitute would have been nearly as good as her own mother because infants cannot tell the difference between a mother and a mother-substitute in the first several weeks of life.

In a similar way, Beth would have coped better if her losses had come after she reached three or four years of age. By that time, she would have had enough practice separating from her mother and approaching her again to build up an inner sense of security and trust. Her ability to hold a stable memory of her mother would also have matured enough for her to tolerate and understand her mother's absence.

Unfortunately, Beth's loss came at the very time of her greatest vulnerability to abandonment. Like Beth, our children need to master certain developmental tasks at every stage of adolescence.

Your Teenager Is Different

The stages your sons and daughters will pass through on their journey to adulthood are not rigidly time bound. Completely normal adolescents pass through them at different speeds and with different personality styles. Some race into adolescence at full speed as early as ten or eleven. Others don't become true adolescents until fourteen or so. Some move imperceptibly from one developmental stage to the next with little sign of conflict. Others change radically from year to year. Some are vibrant and happy through most of their adolescent days. Others battle periods of troubled confusion as they move from one stage to the next.

The ages we mention are intended only as general guidelines, not as rigid norms that necessarily signify delayed or distorted development.

For these reasons, the suggestions given here for parenting adolescents at different ages aren't limited to that age or stage. In fact, most parenting principles apply to all ages but take on special importance when teenagers face certain specific developmental tasks or needs. Preadolescents, for example, need special help in coming to grips with the emotional and physical changes of puberty. The sensitivity you develop with them then, however, can later help them as middle adolescents with their worries over dating and relating to the opposite sex. And the skills and sensitivities you honed to help early adolescents move away from you emotionally will be helpful in modified form when they take even bigger steps toward independence in middle and late adolescence.

As we trace your sons' and daughters' growth from one stage to the next, several suggestions will be offered for helping adolescents at each stage. But remember that those same principles are often helpful at other periods as well.

Six Adolescent Needs

Although each stage of adolescence brings unique challenges, several developmental hurdles run throughout the entire length of adolescence. In order to become healthy, well-adjusted adults, all adolescents must:

- develop their own distinct identity and a sense of their uniqueness and individuality
- progressively separate themselves from their childhood dependency on their parents
- develop meaningful relationships with peers and others outside the family
- crystallize their sexual identity and develop their capacity to relate well to the opposite sex

- gain the confidence and skills to prepare for a career, economic independency, and other adult responsibilities
- fashion their faith and value commitments and basic attitude toward life.

Your teenagers' attempts to establish their distinct identities, as an example, will be apparent throughout the entire period of adolescence. During pre- and early adolescence, they may use negative or argumentative tactics to prove they are individuals. During late adolescence they are apt to question or reject some of your spiritual or political convictions to accomplish the same task.

The same is true about their sexuality. Around eleven or twelve years of age, preadolescents become keenly aware of how they differ biologically from the opposite sex. At thirteen or fourteen, early adolescents practice their dawning sexuality by dressing more maturely and by idealizing or daydreaming about the opposite sex. By fourteen or fifteen many middle adolescents begin dating. And by late adolescence many teenagers have had at least one relatively serious, longer-term dating relationship. But in spite of the differences, at every stage of adolescence, your sons and daughters will be testing out their feelings about their masculinity or femininity and their ability to relate to the opposite sex.

This holds true for most of your teenagers' needs during the course of adolescence. These needs will appear in increasingly mature ways, but the underlying needs remain the same. For this reason, several variations of them will appear in more than one chapter. We will try to show the special forms those needs take at each stage of adolescence and the ways you can be most helpful to your teenagers at those ages.

One Step Forward, Two Steps Back

As your teenagers pass through adolescence, you should expect some alternating times of calm and conflict. Each time your sons and daughters are greeted by a new opportunity to separate themselves from you and become more independent, they may experience a surge of enthusiasm or excitement. But since they are facing a new and unfamiliar challenge, they may also feel afraid or overwhelmed. When this happens, they may temporarily turn back to the old ways they used to cope as children. They may pout or throw a tantrum to get their way or express frustration. They may withdraw and retreat or want you to indulge or protect or comfort them the way you did when they were children. Just as toilet-trained children may suddenly lose their bowel and bladder control following the birth of a younger sibling, teenagers too will occasionally regress to more childish levels of adjustment under the impact of new strains or stresses.

This means you should expect teenagers to occasionally act somewhat childish. Early adolescents may become as stubborn as they were at two. Middle adolescents will sometimes cry or feel like giving up just as they did at three or four. And even late adolescents will occasionally act as they did many years ago.

Because separating from you and tackling adulthood isn't easy, most adolescents rock back and forth between developmental stages a bit like a car stuck in the mud. When you first push it forward, you go only an inch or two. Then you let it rock back and gain momentum for a harder shove. After several efforts back and forth, it rocks far back—almost as though you are losing ground— but this provides the final momentum to push it over the hump. Your teenagers' occasionally childish times actually help them get ready to move ahead. Then, once they clear a developmental hurdle, they gain additional momentum and experience a strengthening of their personalities that ushers in a period of increased stability or calm.

If you think back on your adolescents' childhood years, you will probably remember these frequent cycles. For a few weeks or months your children seemed edgy or negative or upset by everything. But after a period of struggle, they eventually moved into a calmer phase. Then, after a few months or a year or two, that calm was replaced by another period of struggle, when your children were facing the challenge of the next stage of development.

Your teenagers will probably go through similar periods of quiet and calm. Those periods may be as brief as a few minutes or as long as a couple of years, but all adolescents must occasionally move backwards toward old ways of handling life as they prepare to surge forward again.

There Is a Second Chance

Your adolescents' back-and-forth experiences create an interesting possibility for new growth. By puberty, most children have settled into habitual ways of thinking and feeling and reacting. They have developed relatively consistent ways of relating to family members and others. They have found ways of maintaining their self-esteem. They have developed habitual ways of handling their emotions. And they have formed distinct ways of playing, studying, and working. In short, they have developed somewhat predictable personalities. This settling of their personalities is the end product of their first ten years of growth, and it makes the years just preceding puberty a time of relative stability and calm.

This calm, however, cannot last for long since it is based on childish ways of thinking about themselves and life. If your sons and daughters didn't break out of their childhood patterns, think of what they would be like. They would rather play than work. They would tend to follow blindly others' advice or standards. They would expect other people to take care of them. They wouldn't know how to hold a job or earn a living. And they would still expect someone to fix their meals and do their laundry. On top of all that, they wouldn't marry because some of the stability they experienced as six- to ten-year-olds was due to the fact that they avoided the opposite sex. As a result, unless they made a radical change in their attitudes, they would still be running around with their same-sex friends and marriage wouldn't interest them.

Something has to happen to propel six- to ten-year-olds out of those childhood patterns. What is it? The answer is adolescence. The biological and psychological changes of puberty start shaking up their young ways of thinking, feeling, and reacting. Changes in height and weight and shape and intelligence force them to rework their early ways of looking at themselves and others. These changes set in motion a cycle of growth unparalleled in scope, except for the first few years of life, and force a major reorganization of their personalities. It is these changes that account for the instability, unpredictability, emotionality—and eventual maturity—of adolescents. Although these changes can trigger upsetting and even dangerous actions, they also make it possible for your sons and daughters to find new ways of understanding themselves and living in the world.

We have all seen shy, quiet children blossom into confident, friendly, outgoing individuals during adolescence. We have seen demanding older siblings who loved to boss their younger brothers and sisters around become more sensitive and caring. We have seen jealous, possessive junior highers become more peaceful and contented by later adolescence. And we have seen brothers and sisters who fought and quarreled become good friends during middle or late adolescence—or at least by young adulthood.

We have also seen teenagers come to grips with their relationship with God or make major changes in their lives following a new spiritual commitment. In fact, the openness of most adolescents to search for God comes directly out of their need to find some way of understanding life and ordering their world. So, adolescence really is a second chance, an opportunity for teenagers to find new solutions to old problems and a chance for parents to do a better job than we may have done the first time around.

If your children had difficulty bonding to you in infancy or tended to remain overly dependent in their first years, for example, you can partially make up for that during adolescence. If you had difficulty expressing supportive love or overlooked your children's needs for encouragement and validation when they were young, you can focus on that now. If you have been overly anxious and protective in their first ten years of life, you can make a concerted effort to become more supportive of your adolescents' needs for confidence and decision making on their own. And if you haven't been talking over family decisions with your children and asking their opinions, now is the time to begin. In a real sense, both you and your adolescents now have a second chance.

How Teenagers Change

All parents know their teenagers change radically during the adolescent years, but the reasons for these changes are generally obscure. Those reasons do not lie solely in the physical and intellectual growth accompanying puberty. Those changes prepare the way for other transitions in your children's lives, but they don't generate them on their own. Four psychological processes actually account for the emotional growth of adolescents. Psychologists call these processes *differentiation, separation, individuation,* and *integration.* These processes will be described in even greater detail in coming chapters.

Differentiation is the process of becoming aware that you are mentally and physically distinct or different from your parents and others. It begins in the first year of life as infants begin to realize they are physically distinct from their mothers. In later life, differentiation involves learning to think and make decisions for oneself. Differentiation includes everything teenagers will do to become aware of how they differ from others. Most teenagers, for example, go through one or more phases of argumentativeness as they try to prove to themselves that they are different from you and can think for themselves.

Your teenagers' efforts to find their own distinctiveness will be reflected in the silent questions they ask themselves. At various times they will wonder, How am I different from my parents? How am I different from my friends? How am I different from the opposite sex? What is special about me? Is my uniqueness OK or not? As they successfully differentiate from their parents, they will increasingly be able to say, "I can think for myself. I am not a clone of my parents. I am different from others and I feel good about it."

For both infants and adolescents, becoming aware of their physical and mental differences from their parents is actually one part of a second psychological process leading to maturity. That process is known as *separation*. For infants, separation is the experience of emerging out of the totally dependent union with the mother and gradually gaining enough emotional and physical strength to be a separate person. It is a psychological process, not primarily a physical separation. For teenagers, separation is also primarily a psychological journey. It is usually accompanied by increasing physical distance from parents but is basically a process of disengaging from necessary childhood dependencies.

Your teenagers' need to separate from you emotionally will be reflected in nearly everything they do during their adolescent years. It will show up in questions they will ask themselves such as, Can I stop relying so much on my parents' love and care? Can I find ways of surviving in the world without my mom and dad? and, Can I find people outside of my family to share my life with?

Your teenagers' efforts to separate from you will begin shortly after they start proving they are different from you. They cannot stand on their own until they first know they have minds of their own that can disagree with you. But once they know that they can think for themselves, they want to try out their newly discovered abilities by putting a little distance between themselves and their parents.

Psychologists call the third main process adolescents undergo *individuation*. Individuation is the extended adventure of developing one's own unique and individual characteristics. Everything teenagers do to test out their abilities to think and work and play in their own way is part of their attempt to become individuals. Choosing their own clothes, friends, music, hobbies, and food are ways of saying, "This is who I am."

The final experience accounting for your adolescents' changes is *integration* or *consolidation*. Integration is solidifying or pulling together all the physical, intellectual, emotional, social, and

spiritual growth teenagers have experienced throughout childhood and adolescence. It ends up incorporating all of their
abilities and thoughts and feelings into a cohesive and settled self.
This is the process that will eventually enable them to have a
stable and enduring sense of "This is me." It enables them to
incorporate previously changeable emotions into a more balanced
emotional life and to solidify their values and vocational interests
and spiritual commitments.

An adolescent's personality consolidates naturally out of the
processes of differentiation, separation, and individuation. First
adolescents must find out who and what they are *not* (differentiation). Then they must become less dependent (separation). Next
they need to find out that they are unique individuals with their
own special gifts and interests and abilities (individuation). And
finally, they must pull all of this growth together into a relatively
stable and enduring personality, ready to take their place in the
community of adults (consolidation).

In practice, each step of differentiation, separation, and individuation is followed by a process of consolidation. For example, after
two-year-olds go through a chaotic period of stubborn negativism
in order to differentiate and separate from their parents, they
become a bit more settled and independent and mature. They
have consolidated the growth of the stubborn phase into a more
mature understanding of themselves so they don't have to keep
fighting and resisting as they used to. In a similar way, once junior
high age children pass through a phase of differentiating
negativism, they feel less childish and more mature. As a result,
they are typically able to be more assertive and confident without
being so negative. They have consolidated their previous growth
and integrated it into their maturing personalities.

In a similar way, once pre- and early adolescents become aware
of their biological distinctiveness and are comfortable with it, they
are prepared to integrate this new understanding of themselves
by beginning to date and to relate more closely to the opposite sex
in middle adolescence. Each new step toward maturity grows out
of the past developmental accomplishments that have become a

part of their personality through consolidation. Taken together, the four processes of differentiation, separation, individuation, and consolidation will account for most of the maturing your sons and daughters experience in adolescence.

Understanding: A Parent's Best Friend

If you are the typical parent of an adolescent, you will have a variety of feelings as your child passes through the teen years. Your effectiveness in parenting will depend as much on your sensitivity to your own feelings as to those of your sons or daughters. If you are irritated or upset by your fourteen-year-old son's need to argue and challenge you, for example, he may have a harder time separating from you. Or if you are uncomfortable with your daughter's physical development and sexual attractiveness, she will find it more difficult to feel good about her sexuality.

These feelings are entirely normal, but you need to be careful not to let them push you into unhelpful ways of interacting with your teenagers. You can handle your feelings and reactions in one of three ways. First, you can simply act on your anxieties and irritations and let your children suffer the consequences. You can decide, "That's just the way I am. They will have to get used to it." Two other approaches are much more helpful. You can use your feelings and reactions to understand yourself and you can use them to understand your adolescents.

Ivan used his emotional reaction to his son Morgan to understand himself better. When Morgan started challenging and arguing with his father, Ivan's first response was anger. He was furious that his son had the gall to challenge his beliefs, and he told him so. But Morgan wouldn't quit. Ivan kept getting more and more angry and finally came for counseling. After a few sessions, Ivan started to see his problem. His own father was a stern and proper man who never allowed Ivan and his sisters to question his judgment or authority. Even to ask why was taken as a sign of disrespect. Ivan rebelled for several years as an adolescent, but when he had a family he reared his children the only way he knew—just like his father.

When Ivan's son started questioning his authority, it triggered several reactions in Ivan. He resented being challenged. His father didn't have to listen and answer questions and Ivan wasn't about to either. But Morgan's questioning also set off another dynamic for Ivan. Having lacked the opportunity to feel good about his own ideas and test them out on others as a child, Ivan was now frankly afraid of being challenged. He wasn't comfortable sitting down with anyone and discussing pros and cons. The only way he felt secure was to reach a quick conclusion and fight for it tenaciously.

As Ivan realized why his son's efforts to become adult were so upsetting to him he felt less threatened and more comfortable letting his son grow up. Over a period of months, he even learned to set aside times to sit down with his son and allow him to talk about anything that was on his mind. By facing his own inse- curities and fears, Ivan was able to sidestep a potentially serious problem in his family and pass on a much better pattern of relating to his son.

The other positive way of handling your upsetting reactions is to use them as a kind of psychological Geiger counter to point toward the specific developmental struggles or conflicts your teenagers may be facing. Your being irritated by your teenagers' stubbornness and negativism, for example, may be a signal that they are trying to differentiate from you and learn to think for themselves. They are either in the pre- or early adolescent stage and trying to prove that they have a right to their opinions. If you are worried about the consequences of your teenagers' behavior, they may be in the practicing stage of early adolescence and trying out some potentially dangerous "adult" actions. Your anxiety may reflect your fear that, in practicing being adult, your children may injure themselves or be unaware of hurtful conse- quences.

If you feel frustrated because one moment your teenagers are stubbornly telling you to mind your own business and the next are crying for your help, that is a likely sign that they are struggling with the dependency-independency crisis of middle adolescence. And if you are feeling lonely or abandoned by their actions, your children may be in late adolescence and making some final moves away from you.

In each instance, your feelings can direct you to the issues or conflicts your teenagers are facing. Instead of denying your own emotions, or acting on them harmfully, you might use them to understand yourself or your adolescents and turn your feelings into one of your great parenting resources.

Marianne did this for her fifteen-year-old daughter Teri. Marianne told me, "I used to get so frustrated by her moodiness. Every day brought a new disaster and she thought the world was terrible. I kept telling her to grow up and stop feeling sorry for herself. Then I started wondering why her feelings were so upsetting to me, so I dragged out my diary from my sophomore year of high school. I was shocked. On nearly every page I had described some horrible situation or unhappy feeling. I started crying as I remembered those days. And all of a sudden I could be more sympathetic toward Teri. I realized I was uncomfortable with her painful feelings because they reminded me of my own. Once I saw that, and told Teri how I had felt when I was a sophomore, I didn't need to tell her she should shape up or change her feelings. I began to listen and sympathize with her emotions." Marianne's understanding brought Teri the support she needed to cope with her upsetting feelings and move more confidently toward adulthood.

Chapter Highlights

Parenting teenagers can be delightful, rewarding, difficult, or frustrating. Understanding a few basic principles of adolescent development can help maximize the positive side of parenting and minimize the negative.

- God designed the human personality to go through a series of developmental stages from complete dependency to mature independency and interdependency
- At each stage of development, children have one or more major needs or challenges they must master in order to move smoothly on to the next stage of development
- Every teenager passes through the stages of adolescence in his or her own unique way and at his or her own speed
- Most adolescents experience temporary periods of exaggerated childishness or immaturity alternating with more mature behavior
- The changes your adolescents are experiencing will open them up to the most significant growth of their lives since infancy
- Even your adolescents' problems can give you a second chance to help them grow toward maturity
- The more sensitive you are to your own emotions and your own adolescent struggles, the more helpful you can be to your teenagers

With these principles in mind, we now move on to the specific stages of adolescence. In the ten chapters of Part Two, two or more chapters will be spent on each stage of adolescence. We first discuss the major characteristics and needs and struggles that teenagers of that age face. Then we offer specific suggestions for helping your teenagers through that stage in a subsequent chapter or chapters.

NOTES
1. Illustrations in this chapter are from Dr. Lewis.
2. Luke 2:40.
3. Luke 2:41-43.
4. Luke 3:23.

PART II

THE BIRTH OF AN ADULT

Sooner or later, the child must either run the risk of neurosis or free himself from his parents and follow his own devices, his own tastes, his own inclinations. Few parents welcome this awakening of individuality in their children.
PAUL
TOURNIER

CHAPTER FOUR
PREADOLESCENCE: THE CALM BEFORE THE STORM

The preadolescent is like a maple tree in March. Like the tree's sugary sap flowing without visible outward effects, the preadolescent's hormonal system is signaling the body to begin final preparations for maturity. Around ten years of age for girls and a couple of years later for boys, a small relay center in the brain[1] sends a chemical message to the pituitary gland telling it to start preparing the body for the onset of puberty. Secretions from the pituitary gland flow through the bloodstream to the testes or to the ovaries, causing production of the hormones that will start accentuating maleness or femaleness in the next couple of years. During this time, the body is readying itself for the distinctive differences between maleness and femaleness, and the mind is getting ready to distinguish between childish and adult thinking.

The intellectual abilities of ten- to twelve-year-olds are rapidly expanding. Preadolescents begin to engage in abstract thinking and see broader relationships and issues. They begin to probe beneath the surface of what they are told or what they see. And they will soon be able to grasp the symbolic problems they will encounter in high school algebra and geometry. The same capacities that prepare your children for these tasks will also soon cause them to start questioning your authority and to be less than satisfied with pat answers, parental prohibitions, and conventional logic that places everything in neat black and white categories.

Nearly everything that happens during the preadolescent period of life can be understood more clearly when it is seen as part of the process of becoming physically and mentally different or distinct. In order to start cutting the cords of childhood dependency, your sons and daughters must first become aware that they have minds of their own that are distinct from yours and bodies that are different from the opposite sex. Although preadolescents don't move any great distance from you either emotionally or physically, they do undergo important physical and emotional changes that prepare them to start moving away from you during adolescence proper.

No Longer "the Smiths' Girl"!

The development of your preadolescents' intellectual abilities presents them with the first hurdle on their journey to adulthood. Faced with rapidly increasing intellectual abilities and an innate need to find out how to use them, adolescents start to ask themselves, Am I a person with a mind of my own or am I simply an extension of my family? During the first decade of their lives, much of your children's identity has been tied up in the family. Although they have had minds and wills of their own in many matters, they have still been fundamentally dependent upon you. To outsiders—and partly to themselves—they have been "the Smiths' girl," "the Joneses' boy," or "one of the family." And because they have been physically and economically dependent on you, your children have based a lot of their security and confidence in you. They have allowed you to make the big decisions of their lives and they usually didn't strongly differ with you on major issues. This "family identity" is entirely normal and necessary. Even Jesus was known as "the carpenter's son."[2] But in order to become adult, your children must exchange this family identity for an individual identity; preadolescence is the time your children will begin to make that shift.

Just as five- to ten-month-old infants become aware that they are *physically* separate (different) from their mothers, preadolescents awaken to the fact that they are *mentally* different from their parents. They increasingly want to make their own decisions on how to use their time, wear their clothes, and spend their money. They may start demanding the same privileges as older family members. Status in the family becomes vitally important, and many eleven- and twelve-year-olds enjoy lording it over younger siblings to demonstrate their newfound power.

Toward the end of preadolescence, your twelve- or thirteen-year-olds' need to start thinking for themselves will probably bring a climactic end to the relative calm of childhood and usher in the tensions of their teenage years. Their increased intellectual abilities will enable them to think for themselves and create strong resistances to being "treated like a child." They may start arguing incessantly or disagreeing with you at every turn to prove they can think for themselves. Like twelve-year-old Audrey who said to a store clerk before buying a skirt, "In case my mother likes it, can I bring it back?" your daughter will need to differ with her mother to prove she can think for herself.

Children wear what their mothers tell them, while adults make their own clothing choices. Children go to bed when their parents say, while adults go to bed when they feel like it. And children eat what is put before them, while adults select the foods they want. So to become adult, your children must stop wearing and eating what you want, thinking what you think, and liking what you like. Instead, they will start wearing what they want, sleeping when they want, and thinking what they want. As frustrating as this growing independence may be for you, it is an essential step for preadolescents.

Until your sons and daughters can disagree with you, they cannot feel adult or independent. Although you will need to help them find acceptable ways of expressing their own opinions, disagreeing with you is an entirely normal and necessary step on their pathway to maturity. It is their way of mastering the first developmental task of preadolescence, learning to distinguish themselves mentally from you.

Something's Happening to My Body!

As I was getting off an airplane recently,[3] a boy in the window seat across the aisle stood up without looking and bumped his head on the storage bin above. Turning to his father with a proud smile, he said, "I guess you can tell you're growing up when you hit your head on the ceiling of the airplane!" That comment was enough to tell me the boy was a preadolescent—and probably about a dozen years of age. Sure enough, when the boy looked the other way and I asked his father how old he was, the father told me "Twelve!"

By eleven or twelve, most girls experience a growth spurt in the long bones of their skeletal frame and shoot up above the heads of boys their age. A glance at your children's sixth-grade school picture will probably reveal several tall, even gangly, girls and some very short boys. It usually takes a year or two for boys to catch back up again. These rapid physical changes present the second developmental hurdle encountered by preadolescents. At the same time they are asking, Can I think for myself? they must also start asking questions such as, What's happening to my body? What does it mean to be a man or woman instead of a child? How does my body compare to my friends' and peers'? and, How should I feel about my masculinity or femininity?

Although seven- to ten-year-olds are aware of being male or female, their sexuality hasn't yet become the major focus of their identity. Girls aren't obsessed with being feminine and boys aren't trying too hard to be masculine. In fact, children of this age are known for grouping with their same-sex friends precisely because they are not yet prepared to relate in a heterosexual manner. Until ten or so, boys and girls don't look radically different and their physical skills are very similar. Girls may outperform boys of the same age in some athletic contests and it is not unusual for them to compete in sports together. Fifth-grade girls also aren't afraid of being tomboys and fifth-grade boys aren't interested in impressing fifth-grade girls. Consequently, questions about masculinity and femininity and sexuality are not big issues for young children. During preadolescence, however, this begins to change.

Much like five- to ten-month-old infants explore their fingers, face, and arms to find out bodily who they are, preadolescents start experiencing the differences between male and female bodies that will shape their developing sexual identities. As infants find out they are different from their mothers, preadolescent girls learn they are different from preadolescent boys. They start developing a roundness and softness that emphasizes their femininity and their distinctive differences from their male counterparts.

Girls Will Be Women

Sensitive is the best word to describe preadolescent girls. They press their hands against their breasts because of the increased sensitivity around the nipples. While bathing they may discover increased sensitivity in their clitoris and prolong the rubbing of their genitalia. Many twelve-year-old girls become extremely concerned about their breast development since this is one of the most obvious indicators of sexual maturity. Some are obsessed with wearing a bra (whether they need one or not) and others totally avoid the subject. When a university sophomore in one of my developmental psychology classes recalled how embarrassing it had been to be the only ten-year-old wearing a bra while her friends were still reading comic books, another reminded her there was one thing worse—"to still be reading comic books when all your friends are wearing bras!"

Whatever the developmental rate, just before the onset of puberty most girls start turning from their same-sex groupings and occasionally sloppy, childish ways to become more interested in their feminine appearance. Their emerging sexuality also explains an almost universal phenomenon of early adolescent girls—boy craziness.

Kelley and Judy, both eleven years old, are reacting to their preadolescent development in completely opposite ways. Kelley practically refuses to wear dresses. Her favorite attire is a pair of jeans and a sloppy sweatshirt topped off with a baseball cap. Her greatest love is a young horse given to her by her father. More than anything else, Kelley enjoys going to the stables and riding her horse or hanging around the boys at the barn. She isn't really interested in the boys as boyfriends, however. She just wants to be "one of the guys." Kelley isn't sure she is ready for the changes accompanying womanhood and wants to delay them a bit.

Judy revels in the fact that her hair is becoming more luxurious and that her figure is taking on a distinctly female form. She is delighted with the idea of becoming a woman. She pleads to wear high heels and get a bra before she really needs one, and a bikini is the only style she wants to be seen in on the beach. Although Judy *feels* ready to become a woman, she may be no more ready than Kelley. In trying to jump headlong into adolescence she may be reflecting a desire to grow up so fast that she denies the fact that she is still an eleven-year-old child.

Both reactions are common among ten- to twelve-year-old girls who are entering the never-never land between childhood and adulthood. As one mother described her ten-year-old daughter, "With her pierced ears, boots, and experimental hairstyles, Carla is caught somewhere between childhood and young womanhood. Her father built her a Barbie doll house bigger than she is and she nurtures her doll family while singing Madonna songs!" Carla's mixture of dolls and Madonna is a perfect picture of the in-between years of preadolescence.

Boys Will Be Men

A couple of years later than in girls, the typical boy's pituitary gland sends a message to his testes to increase the production of testosterone. This hormone is largely responsible for the growth and development of male sex characteristics. A slight enlargement of the testes similar to the budding of girls' breasts is usually accompanied by a change in the coloration of the scrotal sac. This is followed by increasing sensitivity and size fluctuation in the penis and frequently by unconscious rubbing in the scrotal area. This is the time some boys are teased by older friends for going around with their hands in their pockets!

Twelve- and thirteen-year-old boys may be embarrassed by an unwanted erection. Genital touching, which used to be limited to rubbing and touching, takes on a new dimension as boys begin to masturbate. Some engage in mutual genital exploration. This does not necessarily indicate a sexual problem. Preadolescent boys are becoming sexually aware but aren't yet ready to relate to the opposite sex. Their same-sex exploration protects preadolescent boys from the girls they don't yet know how to relate to, while giving some expression to their sexual curiosity. Boys of this age may discover that with stimulation their orgasmic reflex is triggered even though no ejaculation of semen occurs. This is called a dry orgasm in young males. Once the secretion of seminal fluid has begun, preadolescence has ended and puberty has been reached.

Some preadolescent boys are approached by older boys and encouraged to enter into homosexual activities. Although a homosexual preference can develop if this continues, it will not if the boy's childhood years have laid a good foundation for his masculinity. Parents should be concerned about these explorations since they may reflect some lack of knowledge or anxiety about sexuality, but there is no need to panic. If they identified solidly with their fathers during their first decade of life, a few frank discussions about sexuality and normal opportunities to relate to the opposite sex will soon stabilize a boy's masculinity and prevent this from being any more than a brief exploratory experience. A sensitive, nonintrusive relationship with his mother also enables a boy to break away from his dependency on mother and gradually move toward other females.

In chapter 18 we will look at several steps parents can take to help children develop a secure sexual identity and healthy sexual attitudes and values. For now we simply want to point out the arousal of interest in their bodies and sexuality that begins during preadolescence.

Boys don't experience other major outward physical changes at this time. Although they will eventually have their own growth spurt, they will have to wait awhile. For the time being, their changes are more in their glands[4] and personality than in physique. They are beginning to think differently about themselves but this won't become readily apparent to others until early adolescence.

Touchy! Touchy!

If you have become used to a relatively dependable and noncomplaining girl of eight or nine, you may be shocked by the strong emotions and tantrums and negativity that erupt around the age of eleven or twelve. Almost overnight your daughter can become hypersensitive about her height, weight, hair, clothes, or status of the family. She may decide she hates her body. And girls of this age can cry at the drop of a hat and accuse parents of yelling or being unreasonable when they are only being firm. All these changes can be summed up in one word: hypersensitivity.

Check a family photo from this period. You will probably find an awkward-looking girl feeling uncomfortable over having her picture taken. In university classes that I teach on human development, many girls say they disliked being female at this time of life. Few if any boys express a similar dissatisfaction with being male. Preadolescent girls also tend to blame their parents for their shortcomings. When my wife commented to our then twelve-year-old daughter that she had thighs like mine, my daughter glared at me and said, "You and your lousy old genes." Now that she is slim and shapely I get absolutely no genetic credit!

Some girls go through a period of unexplained depression about this time. Psychologists don't know for certain, but this may relate to their upcoming departure from their mothers. When asked to draw a picture of their family, many ten- to twelve-year-old girls draw a picture with their mother placed off to the side and themselves in close proximity to father. Preadolescent girls are also notorious for complaining that their parents (especially mothers) don't understand them. They also tend to reject her attempts to offer consolation. These reactions seem to signal the ten- to twelve-year-old girl's preparation to separate from her mother and find a feminine identity of her own. Since they are starting to lose their previous closeness with their mothers, they feel sad about it.

Other preadolescent girls become sloppy and careless about their room, clothing, or personal hygiene. Even girls that have formerly been neat, responsive, and successful in school may regress to less mature ways of coping. Since adults are expected to be neat, they seem to want one final fling at being a child. Coupled with negative peer pressure, this can produce some hectic times around the home.

Martha was an intelligent, responsive, and dependable ten-year-old prior to entering the fifth grade. Then her behavior radically changed. She became depressed, cried frequently, and began neglecting her school work. Her mother attributed it to her age and thought she would "just grow out of it." After several weeks, however, Martha's teacher suspected more and told her parents she thought Martha was being pressured to stop being such a high achiever. When Martha's mother shared her teacher's concern with Martha, Martha tearfully confirmed that some larger girls had threatened to cut her with a knife unless she stopped showing them up in class. Fearing reprisals, Martha had suffered alone until encouraged to talk. Once steps were taken to protect her, she returned to her former level of competence. Although Martha's experience was extreme, it is by no means an isolated occurrence. Many preadolescent girls have inexplicable periods of moodiness and immature behavior due to the rapid changes in their lives or negative peer influences.

The sensitivity of preadolescent girls and their inability to control their emotions often has a kind of childish or regressive flavor. Under pressure of the physical and emotional changes of approaching puberty, many ten- to twelve-year-olds revert back to more childish actions such as crying, yelling, or giving up in frustration. But hang on; this too will pass. The physical, emotional, and intellectual changes of pre- and early adolescence are simply too much to handle calmly. In order to cope, your daughters revert to the only way they know of handling stress—crying or getting angry and blaming someone else. They need a few years to accept the loss of their childhood, learn new ways of adapting, and get their feelings back under control.

Last Chance to Be a Child

Some twelve- and thirteen-year-old boys retreat into a temporary regressive stage a bit like hypersensitive girls. They may make mother their confidant or become more dependent on her the way they were as small boys. These regressive phases are usually followed within a year or so by renewed efforts to separate from mother and stand on their own two feet. Once this happens, boys begin resisting their dependency on their mother and start associating almost exclusively with male friends. They ardently reject anything feminine in order to break away from their mothers and identify more fully with males. Girl talk and play is considered "stupid," and "masculine" things such as sports are in.

Some parents worry that these boys will never develop an interest in the opposite sex—but relax. They will discover girls—sometimes quicker than you think. Before they can feel manly and have a mature relationship with a woman, they must first give up being mama's boy. By temporarily rejecting anything hinting of femininity, they are getting ready to take the next step toward developing their masculine identities.

Many boys this age try to loosen their family dependency by staying home rather than going on a family outing. Some prefer a friend's family to their own. Others utilize a lengthy period of hostility to help them reject their dependency on their mothers. Even previously dependable sons may frustrate parents with aggressive inactivity to prove their autonomous power to say no to their parents. They may "forget" to do their chores or always arrive late for parent-related activities like dinner. Although irritating, these too are normal symptoms of the twelve- to thirteen-year-old boy's need to distinguish himself from his parents and start outgrowing his dependency on them. Anger and negativism are ways of making leaving easier. It is difficult to leave someone you need and love; it is easier to leave someone you resent and have little need for.

Overall, boys seem to find it easier to break the bonds of dependency on their moms than do girls. Our society still tends to value obedient and mannerly, and even dependent girls. But who wants a mama's boy? Picking up on these cues, most boys gain encouragement to grow up and move away from their mothers from their earliest years.

Boys have an easier time breaking their dependency on their mothers for another reason. When boys begin to leave their mothers, they turn naturally to their fathers as models for adulthood. In father, they find an example to help them develop a masculine identity while still being a bit dependent. But where do girls turn for their models of maturity? The same adult they are trying to separate from (mother) is the very one they need to follow in order to become a mature woman. They have to get away from mother to become separate and independent, but they need her to know how to become a woman. This is one reason adolescent girls need older females—the mother of a friend, a teacher, or a church worker. Their need to separate from their mother also explains why many girls resent their mother's involvement in their lives at one moment and feel angry and abandoned the next. They vacillate between wanting to cut the cord of dependency on mom and wanting her care.

Conformity: Vice or Virtue?

Preadolescents who are too complacent and conforming may actually be in more trouble than those who are a little negative and assertive. They may be avoiding the task of growing up and finding their own identities. Although neither extreme is ideal, it is often better to resolve dependency through a temporary flurry of resistance, negativism, or rebellion than through blind conformity that perpetuates dependency and freezes growth.

Although the prodigal son in Jesus' parable has received a lot of bad press, the reaction of his older brother who stayed home suggests that the prodigal wasn't the only one with problems. When their father threw a party to welcome the lost son home, the older brother flared with resentment.

> He answered his father, "Look! All these years I've been slaving for you and never disobeyed your orders. Yet you never gave me even a young goat so I could celebrate with my friends. But when this son of yours who has squandered your property with prostitutes comes home, you kill the fattened calf for him!"[5]

The older brother's problem was not that he stayed home to run the family estate. During the time of Christ, as in many succeeding generations, it was the accepted custom for the older brother to stay at home and take over the responsibilities of running the family affairs. Younger sons were expected to leave and find other means of support. The older brother's problems were reflected in his strong resentment toward his younger brother and his father for throwing a welcome home party for the wayward younger son.

The older son had not established an identity secure enough to rejoice in his brother's return. In the parable, he was described by Jesus as someone who never questioned his parents' authority. We are given the impression that he was basing his identity on conformity, hoping he would eventually receive everything his father owned. But his hostility at his brother's return reveals the failure of his comforming solution. He hadn't grown inwardly strong enough to be grateful that his brother was finally getting his life together.

Like adolescents who think they are more adult than they are, the younger brother recklessly struck out on his own. But like an overly dependent adolescent, the older son was embittered when his painstaking obedience didn't pay off with parental favoritism.

Chapter Highlights

Preadolescence is the last stage of childhood and a time of transition into adolescence. During these years your children will be getting ready to move away from you by starting to think for themselves and by becoming aware of their physical distinctiveness from the opposite sex. In the process, they may go through some regressive periods when they exhibit some very childlike behavior and some periods of increasing negativity. By the time they finish their preadolescent years, your sons and daughters will need to have a positive attitude toward their changing bodies and an awareness of their ability to think for themselves—apart from you. Let's review the major features of these years.

AGES
- Approximately ten to twelve for girls
- Approximately twelve to fourteen for boys

MAJOR DEVELOPMENTAL TASKS
- To begin to see themselves as distinct from their parents and to increasingly think for themselves
- To become aware of their approaching sexual maturity and their physical distinctiveness from the opposite sex

TYPICAL CHARACTERISTICS
- Relative calm in early portion
- Increasing emotionality and sensitivity in later months of this stage

- Temporary regressive phases with increased childishness or depression
- Rapid physical growth in girls
- Significant growth in intellectual abilities
- Dawning awareness of sexual feelings and sexuality

DANGERS
- Emerging needs to be different from the parents can be squelched—leading to a lack of confidence and passivity or excessive negativism and rebellion
- Sexual developments and feelings can be seen as bad, sinful, or abnormal

With these challenges and characteristics in mind, let's look at ways you can help your preadolescents successfully clear their main developmental hurdles and prepare for early adolescence.

NOTES
1. The hypothalamus.
2. Matthew 13:55.
3. Although Dr. Lewis and Dr. Narramore have coauthored this book, all remaining chapters are written from the more personal and readable first person singular "I" instead of the awkward "one of the authors." Unless otherwise noted, all personal and clinical illustrations in a chapter are by the author first footnoted. This illustration is by Dr. Narramore. All other personal and clinical illustrations in this chapter are by Dr. Lewis.
4. The prostate gland and seminal vesicles that will later store seminal fluid are growing, for example, but this is not outwardly apparent.
5. Luke 15:29-30.

Train a child in the way he should go, and when he is old he will not turn from it.

PROVERBS 22:6

CHAPTER FIVE
PARENTING PREADOLESCENTS

If you have eleven- and twelve-year-olds, you probably have already observed their growing need to think for themselves and to cope with the rapid changes in their bodies. In girls, the physical changes are obvious. And by age twelve, both girls and boys are showing at least a few symptoms of their need to differ with parents in order to establish their identities. But how should parents respond to a daughter's increasing sensitivity? How should we handle our preadolescent's emerging negativism and argumentativeness? How can we help them come to grips with their budding sexual development? And how can we help them learn to think for themselves without their becoming obnoxious in the process? In this chapter we offer several suggestions for helping your sons and daughters safely clear the two major hurdles of preadolescence: learning to think for themselves and coming to grips with their budding sexual development.

Be Available

When our children were eleven and eight, our family took a six-month sabbatical leave to another state.[1] My wife and I were writing every day but our evenings and weekends were entirely free. Each night we had some family time together. We talked with the children about their day, shared some games, or planned some interesting activities. Many evenings we gathered in the living room and listened to my wife read *The Hobbit,* by J. R. R. Tolkien, and other children's books. Then we prayed about our day and for friends back home and other things. Although we have always been close, that period of concentrated family time was like a magnet pulling us together. It gave us a chance to communicate our love, listen to each other, and have a lot of fun together.

I am convinced that this six-month period of relationship building was one reason our children handled adolescence well. It enabled Kathy and me to solidify our friendships with Richard and Debbie so that they saw us as encouragers and friends instead of parents who only showed up when they needed discipline or correction. It also let us fill up their emotional gas tanks so that they had inner resources for the trip through adolescence that lay ahead.

When our sabbatical was over, we vowed that we were going to maintain our slower life-style and preserve our family times together—but it wasn't easy. From the moment we walked in the door at home, the phone started ringing and responsibilities quickly filled our calendar. Every week we had to struggle to make time for family fun together. And we periodically had to sit down and rearrange our priorities and eliminate a few otherwise very good activities that were becoming barriers to our times together.

I realize you probably don't have the luxury of a professor's sabbatical leave and your schedule may be hectic. But I cannot overemphasize the importance of building happy relations with your children in the impressionable years just prior to adolescence. Everything you want to do for your teenagers will depend on how loved and understood they feel by you. Preadolescence is your last chance to relate to your children as children and to strengthen childhood feelings of intimacy that will nourish them for life. Their formative years are passing quickly.

If you haven't already done it, take a few minutes to consider how momentous this time can be. God gave you children to love and prepare for adult life in less than twenty years, and the majority of that time is gone. Their diaper days are gone. Their preschool days are gone. And their elementary years are over. Before long your children will be making life-changing decisions and setting out on their own. Have you done all you can to get them ready? If not, it's not too late. You still have a few impressionable years when they are open to your input. But you had better hurry—this is almost your last chance. If you haven't learned to have fun with your children, start now. Or if your children see you as a "heavy" who shows up only to discipline or tell them no, now is the time for that to change. You will find this effort as enriching for you as it is for your children. This is the very best preparation you can give them for adolescence.

Encourage Independent Thinking

At the same time you want to build supportive relationships with your ten- to twelve-year-olds, you also need to help them start breaking some of the childhood bonds that have tied them to you. Probably the most important of these is their reliance on you to make decisions for them. If you haven't already done it, cultivate the habit of asking your preadolescents' opinions on big and small decisions in the family. Give them plenty of opportunities to express their own ideas and perspectives. And be careful not to put down your children's opinions or squelch their independent thinking. Appreciating their ideas and taking them seriously communicates respect and tells preadolescents you want them to use their own heads and not necessarily agree with you on everything.

Rich and Judy Kelley did this naturally with their children. From the time Kim and Kent were a few years old, they were brought into family discussions, such as where to go out to eat and what to do as a family. Rich and Judy asked for the children's input about vacations. They gave them an allowance and had them buy most of their own clothes from the time they were ten. And by that time they were asking Kim's and Kent's opinions when they bought new furniture or a car. They didn't give the children the final say but they took their opinions seriously. When Kim and Kent hit adolescence, they had a lot of healthy confidence in themselves. They felt free to speak up in class and talk with their friends as well as teachers and other adults because they had years of experience having their ideas respected.

Children whose parents make a lot of unilateral decisions or tend to be critical or controlling have a harder time developing self-confidence. They may feel unappreciated or unintelligent or doubt their ability to express themselves. Some of them become shy or afraid of making their own decisions and expressing their opinions. Others become unduly negative to try to prove to their parents that their ideas are important.

If you have a predisposition to make all the decisions for your family or minimize your children's ideas or contributions, now is the time to learn to listen and to let them know their opinions count. As Ivan did when he saw himself reacting angrily to his son, you may need to consider why it is difficult to value your sons' and daughters' opinions and encourage them to participate meaningfully in your family's decisions and discussions. Once you can do this you will make it a whole lot easier for your children to establish their own secure identities. You will also help them over the first big hurdle of preadolescence—learning to think for themselves and discovering that they can be different from you and other adults.

Dads Are Parents Too

Children of all ages need two parents, but at certain ages one parent often plays an especially important role. During the first couple of years of life, for example, mothers nearly always have the strongest influence on their children. Even if dad is actively involved in caring for the child, it is mother who first nourishes and holds her infant at her breast. She is the primary care-giver.

During the next couple of years, mother is still the most important person in the young child's life, but fathers play an increasingly important role. During that time, fathers help toddlers move a little away emotionally from their mothers. As loving, familiar parents, fathers can give young children someone to move toward as they try to break their strong dependencies on mother. Fathers also serve as a second source of love and as role models, protectors, and instructors for their children.

In the year or two just prior to puberty, fathers also play an especially important role. Much as they did when children were two to six years old, fathers serve as important people for preadolescents to relate to as they move away from their long-standing dependency upon mother. They serve as way stations, providing support without the childish trappings that surround mother. Somehow it is not quite as childish to be dependent on your father as it is on your mother.

As preadolescent girls become aware of their sexual distinctiveness and start moving away from mom, they need a sensitive, likable, and available father. If dad is tender and affectionate and able to be open about his own life and needs, his daughter learns there are sensitive males in the world. This lets her know she won't have to settle for a domineering, distant, fearful, or insensitive man. Instead, she can hold out hope for a man a little like dad.

Occasionally taking your daughter out for breakfast or dinner for a relaxed time of catching up on each other's activities is one practical way of helping her develop good feelings about herself and her abilities. Giving her plenty of gentle understanding and affection helps her learn that she can have close and meaningful friendships with men without any sexual activity or intent. And seeing your wisdom or competency can help her learn that people can be strong and wise at the same time they are sensitive and loving. Regular opportunities for more than a quick "Hi, Dad" "Bye, Dad," help strengthen your relationship with your daughters, keep communication lines open, and enable girls to move optimistically toward maturity.

Some husbands with marital conflicts use the occasion of their daughter's sexual maturing and natural movement away from their mothers to endear their daughters to themselves and pit daughter against mom. They subtly encourage their daughters' put-downs of their mother or are drawn to their daughters because of their poor marriages. This can distort a young girl's attitudes toward herself, her sexuality, and her future marriage. She wants her father's attention, but she can't handle the blame she feels for coming between her parents. Girls of this age need their father's loving recognition of their emerging maturity, but not as third parties in their parents' conflict.

Preadolescent boys need a model of what it is to be a man. Spending time with a sensitive father goes a long way toward building healthy attitudes toward themselves and the opposite sex. It helps them gain confidence that they can become competent adult males. And it teaches them to be open about their needs and feelings and to share both exciting and frustrating times. Without this supportive apprenticeship for manhood, adolescent males can feel overwhelmed at the prospect of becoming men. They may feel they can never be successful like their dads. Or they worry excessively about challenges their dad could help them through. Some hide their fears of being unmanly by identifying with macho men who view women as objects to rule or seduce instead of people to respect and love.

Few things can help a young boy eventually become a loving husband and father more than a loving, available relationship with his own father or father figure. Dads who can express affection and play and relax as well as be serious give aspiring young men excellent models as patterns for their developing identities. And dads who are available to talk with their growing sons about their sexuality lay a strong foundation for their future attitudes toward their sexuality. Solo mothers can support their sons immensely by helping them build close relationships with a male relative or friend or teacher.

In short, both preadolescent boys and girls need an affirming, loving relationship with their father or a father substitute to clear the second hurdle on the road to maturity—developing a positive attitude toward their emerging sexuality and their masculine or feminine identities.

Some adult sexual problems are rooted in confusion that originated during this preadolescent period of awakening sexuality and sexual differentiation. If a preadolescent boy is told by his parent that it is wrong or sinful to masturbate or have sexual feelings just as he is becoming aware of his sexuality, he may squelch his developing sexual identity or develop intense guilt. Sometimes a boy reacts to these frightening or guilt-inducing messages by avoiding closeness with females other than his mother and older women. Others repress and distort their normal maleness. Preadolescent girls can become puzzled about their sexuality if their mothers are uncomfortable talking about sex or the human body. And girls whose fathers respond to their dawning sexuality with subtle seductiveness or tense detachment can become seriously confused. Loving relationships with both parents and healthy attitudes toward sex by both parents give preadolescents the maximum help possible to grow out of their childhood sexuality toward a mature sexual identity and a positive attitude toward the opposite sex.

Be Knowledgeable About Sexuality

If preadolescents are going to feel good about their developing sexuality, they need parents who can talk freely and naturally about the biological changes of adolescence. You don't have to be an expert on physiology, but you do need to be knowledgeable about changes taking place in your adolescents' bodies and the feelings they are likely to experience about those changes. Unfortunately, many parents have forgotten what it was like to sense something happening in their bodies that they didn't understand. Mothers, do you remember, for example, feeling self-conscious, sensitive, or excited as your breasts began to bud and enlarge? Did you sense at this time that your own mother or father felt anxious about explaining these changes to you? Or did you ever feel your mother was uncomfortable with your newfound interest in your father and your simultaneous steps away from her?

And fathers, do you remember standing in front of the mirror wondering whether you were developing like an older friend? Or feeling guilty over your sexual explorations? If you have unresolved anxiety over your own preadolescent sexual development, talking it over with a friend or spouse or counselor can help you be more helpful to your children than your parents were to you. Adolescents will seek out information, and if you don't offer it, they will find other ways to satisfy their curiosity. Unfortunately, some of their sources will not have the best values and their secret searches are likely to be shadowed by guilt or shame.

Preadolescence is actually a great time for parents to talk with their children about their sexuality. In a casual way, mother, you can explain to your daughter the meaning of her increasing sensitivity. You can explain that egg-producing ovaries are stimulated by hormones coming from the pituitary gland so they can start producing female sex hormones (estrogen). You can tell her these hormones cause breasts and hips to begin growing and rounding out in a one- to two-year process. And you can let her know that by the time puberty brings her first menstrual period, she will probably show all the outward physical signs of being a woman. This takes much of the mystery and potential confusion out of her feelings about her sexual development and diminishes her fear and guilt about the changes she is experiencing.

Fathers need to do the same thing with their sons. If you feel anxious or don't know just how to begin a conversation, look for an opening and jump in. One father used his sense of humor to break his fear of talking with his son about sex. Don shared a couple of funny events he remembered from his own preadolescence. One was a wet dream about a baby elephant running around in a pink tutu. "I don't have a thing for elephants," Don said, "but for some reason that dream aroused my body and caused me to have a wet dream!" Once the ice was broken, Don was able to talk about nocturnal emissions as a sign that puberty was beginning.

Too many parents abdicate their roles as teachers and encouragers during this crucial phase of life. They defer to experts such as teachers or ministers or youth workers and expect their adolescents to learn about their sexuality from these "professionals." But while these people provide important models and can do a lot for your children, they cannot substitute for you. Parents who are available to their preadolescents and knowledgeable about the physical and sexual developments of puberty make it much easier for their sons and daughters to feel good about their developing masculinity or femininity.

Beware of Overstimulation

By preadolescence, children should have their own space and times for privacy. We should not barge into their rooms nor they into ours, and they should not come into the bathroom when we are using it or dressing. All that usually needs to be said is, "At your age we all need our privacy. Mom and dad won't come into your room without knocking and we would like you not to come into ours." If they walk in on you when you are naked, don't panic, run for shelter as if you have been caught, or anxiously tell them to stay out of your room. Simply turn your back and remind them not to come in while you are dressing and slip on your clothes or a towel. Your goal is to provide privacy and avoid overstimulation or confusion, not to create guilt or shame.

Parents also need to be careful not to hug a preadolescent seductively. Like all of us, ten- to twelve- or thirteen-year-olds need frequent expressions of physical affection. But hugs when you are partially clothed can stir a preadolescent's dawning sexual feelings and trigger anxiety and guilt. After thirty-year-old

Crystal was divorced, for example, she started inviting her twelve-year-old son, Keith, into her bed each morning. Hurt by her husband's abandonment, she sought solace from her son. She wore revealing nightgowns and would draw Keith close and cuddle with him much as she had with his father. This continued for two years until she remarried and Keith was relocated to his own room.

Keith felt abandoned and confused. One day when Crystal returned home from work, she found him in one of her slips with lipstick on his face and wearing some of her perfume. Since he had been banished from his mother's bed and replaced by a stepfather, Keith was trying to reconnect with her by dressing in her clothes and becoming like her. His times in bed with his mother had become his way of becoming close, and in his own confused way he was trying to reestablish contact.

Without realizing it, Crystal had begun to distort her son's sexual development. The combination of an absent father and a seductive mother who kept him too close encouraged Keith to try to become like his mother so he wouldn't lose her. Wearing her clothes was his way of saying, "I'm like you, Mother. I won't leave you like Dad did. Now you won't leave me either, will you?" By starting to take on a feminine identity, Keith could also avoid the fear that he would have to compete "man to man" for his mother's love with his new stepfather. Fortunately, Crystal took Keith to a counselor who worked with him alone, as well as with his mother and stepfather, to get to the roots of his pain and confusion over his feelings of abandonment, his mother's seductiveness, and his sexual identity.

Some boys with similar experiences become prematurely sexually active. Others become so frightened by their mother's seductiveness that they retreat from the prospect of becoming adult males and cling to a boyish or even homosexual identity. By avoiding any close heterosexual relationships, they try to push their incestuous experiences from awareness.

Some parents go to the opposite extreme of Crystal. They become almost paranoid about hugging their opposite-sex adolescents for fear of being sexually seductive. One university professor wouldn't hug his daughter for years for fear that it would lead to incest. Unfortunately, his anxious avoidance of all physical expressions of love was nearly as hurtful as seductiveness. His daughter grew up very uncomfortable with her sexuality and even in marriage thought sex was bad. Fathers who don't express affection for their daughters imply that love is absent or that all affection is sexual and physical closeness is dangerous. Our goal should be to express our love in the same ways we did during our children's younger lives. We simply want to do this when we are clothed appropriately and avoid being seductive or sensual. Parents also help their preadolescents by being open about their own love and physical affection for each other. This reassures adolescents that love and sex are great but tells them mom and dad are already taken. They will have to find someone for themselves.

Learn to Handle Hypersensitivity

Eleven-year-old Janet had an extra dose of preadolescent sensitivity. If her older sister got anything she didn't get, Janet pouted and cried, "Unfair!" When her mother asked her to do anything around the house, Janet indignantly claimed she had already done more than her share. When a boy showed the slightest interest in her, Janet was on cloud nine. And when the smallest thing went wrong, Janet hit the pits.

Unfortunately, Janet's mother wasn't much better. She was excited and energetic when her business went well, but hit the skids when things turned tough. She set rigid limits for her children one day and dropped them the next. And she reacted to Janet's pouting by throwing up her hands and moaning, "What do you want me to do?" In many ways she was as inconsistent and emotionally out of control as her daughter.

When your preadolescent is in the middle of an emotional outburst of crying or frustration, don't jump into the middle of it and tell her to stop or assure her that "everything will be fine."

When an eleven-year-old girl is upset, no amount of reassurance will convince her she should feel otherwise. Every upset seems like the end of the world to her. First, just listen. Allow her to express her anger, hurt, or depression. Let her know by your sensitive listening that you care. But whatever you do, do not tell her, "Mother understands!" That will probably make her scream. If she is going to become different from you, she may not want you to understand. Besides, telling her you understand makes her feel a bit like a baby whose mother kisses the hurt to make it better. The Bible offers some excellent advice for times like these. It says we should be "quick to listen, slow to speak and slow to become angry."[2] Unfortunately, we tend to be quick to speak, quick to anger, and slow to listen!

If you really want to understand your preadolescents at times like this, you will learn to listen quietly until they have spewed out their anger and tears. Then (and only then) you may be able to offer a few words of encouragement or hope. Sometimes a silent hug is all they need. And sometimes the best thing to say is, "I'm really sorry, honey. I know it's hard. If there's anything I can do, please let me know." Later you may be able to go out together for a drive or get your daughter involved in something that will take her mind off her hurt. And after a day or so, you may be able to talk it over with her. But don't push too quickly.

The emotions of late preadolescents and early adolescents are highly volatile and must be treated sensitively. Your sons and daughters need the space to be different from you and the right to be upset if they want to. Young children may be told, "Don't act that way!" (even though that's not the best way to talk to young children either). But tell that to your preadolescents and they will probably get more upset. They may just want to be left alone for awhile or allowed to wade through their negative emotions without your interruptions or advice. This is another sign that they are differentiating themselves from you and wanting to have their thoughts and emotions according to their schedules, not yours.

Another way of dealing with your older preadolescents' emotional upheaval is to not only listen to what they are saying, but for what they are feeling but leaving unsaid. Try to hear their underlying hurts or fears. You might say, "That must really be discouraging," "That must really make you angry," or "Are you feeling sad, honey?" Preadolescents crave sensitive parents who understand their upsets and confusion, not simply their surface problems.

Provide Stability and Structure

Older preadolescents are just beginning to break out of their relatively quiet and stable childhood years. Their bodies are changing. Their minds are changing. Their schools and friends are changing. And their emotions are changing. Nearly everything is in a state of flux. In short, they are entering the most unsettling and revolutionary years of their lives. In the middle of their shifting world, they need a stable anchor. Relatively organized and calm parents help calm and reassure their children. Parents whose own schedules are irregular or whose lives are filled with excessive pressure or confusion compound their teenagers' emotional imbalance and hypersensitivity.

I realize it may be difficult to structure your schedule and I realize you may not be cool and collected by nature. But the fact remains: *children in these formative years need relatively calm and organized parents and a family that provides stability and a model of balanced emotional expression and control.*

John and Carol worked at this as their children were approaching adolescence. Even though Carol took a job selling real estate to supplement their family income, she arranged her schedule so that she could be home when the children returned from school at 3:00, and she limited her evening work to a maximum of two nights weekly. The whole family managed to have breakfast together most mornings and they regularly had supper between 5:30 and 6:00. On the nights Carol worked, John was always home. By coordinating their schedules, John and Carol were able to offer their children both the security of a regular routine and an available, non-preoccupied parent every evening. This let the children know that John and Carol intended to be readily available for them during their crucial adolescent years.

Although your emotional stability and availability are more important than a rigid schedule, a reliable family routine goes a long way toward offering adolescents a trustworthy place of security and support. By middle adolescence, your sons and daughters may prefer to ignore your family routines for their own activities, but it helps them greatly to know just when and where you will be in case they need you!

On to Adolescence

Preadolescence is a time when parenting can have its finest hour. As your sons and daughters leave this preparation stage for adolescence, they should have made a good start toward becoming aware of their physical distinctiveness from the opposite sex and their intellectual distinctiveness from you. They will have experienced rapid growth in their intellectual abilities. This will enable them to stretch their horizons far beyond the family and classroom to the world at large. They will also be more psychologically self-conscious and susceptible to emotional turmoil than they were a year or two ago. Your role is to support the unfolding of your preadolescents' God-given processes by providing all the encouragement, understanding, and stability you can. You also need to be getting ready for the more dramatic emotional and relational changes that will soon be taking place in your adolescents' lives.

Once preadolescents have begun cutting the childhood cords that bound them mentally to you and sexually to their same-sex friends, they will never again have such a limited view of themselves and their world. Their "age of innocence" is past and they must reshape their identity in the broader world beyond this family. This is the challenge of adolescence proper. That task is usually met with mixed enthusiasm and anxiety by early adolescents and by anticipation, sadness, or fear by parents. We realize we are losing our children but look forward to what they will become during the crucial years of adolescence.

NOTES

1. Illustrations in this chapter are by Dr. Narramore.
2. James 1:19.

It was a very curious thing. When I was about thirteen, my father's intelligence started to drop. His mental abilities continued to decline until I reached twenty-one, when these abilities began miraculously to improve.

MARK TWAIN

CHAPTER SIX
EARLY ADOLESCENCE: THE PRACTICING YEARS

Early adolescence, roughly thirteen to fourteen years of age for girls and a bit later for most boys, can be called "the practicing years." Leaving the safety of childhood behind, early adolescents are like fledgling birds learning to fly.[1] Their wings are weak and their knowledge of life's wind currents is meager, but they are eager to practice upcoming adult roles. If things went well during preadolescence, your sons and daughters are starting to feel pretty good about having a mind of their own and a body that is different from the opposite sex. These attitudes will need further stabilizing and strengthening, but they are off to a good start. Having cleared these first two hurdles, they are ready for the biological and psychological changes that now propel them headlong into adolescence.

Nearly everything your thirteen- and

fourteen-year-olds do during the next couple of years will make more sense if you see them as part of a process of practicing or testing out adultlike attitudes and actions. The rapid development of your early adolescents' intellectual abilities encourages them to continue thinking for themselves and differentiating their thoughts from yours. Their need to outgrow long-standing dependency on you will push them increasingly toward their peers. Their maturing physical and mental abilities will challenge them to attempt things they wouldn't have dreamed of a couple of years before. And their developing sexuality will awaken desires for closer relationships with the other sex. Since each of these activities is unfamiliar, early adolescents must go through a practicing period before new attitudes and behaviors can be maturely integrated into their personalities.

During this practicing period, many of your early adolescents' steps toward maturity will be awkward and uncertain. Their rapid physical growth, for example, can make them look uncomfortable and uneasy. Their growing heterosexual interests can alarm and overwhelm them. Their growing need to think for themselves can make them incredibly argumentative and stubborn. And their search for new friendships may be shadowed by fears of not meeting peer group expectations.

The challenges of adolescence heighten the sensitivity that began in the last months of preadolescence, and some early adolescents find this is the most chaotic and confusing time of their life. They are trying out adult attitudes and actions but, like vastly oversized clothes, they find they don't quite fit. Seventh- and eighth-grade girls can be especially volatile and unpredictable. They may cry at the drop of a hat, feel easily misunderstood, and have trouble maintaining emotional control. Even your best efforts at offering consolation may be met with a curt "Just leave me alone!" or "I don't want to talk about it!"

As your sons and daughters enter this phase of their journey to adulthood, they will encounter four major developmental tasks or hurdles. They will need to (1) learn to separate from you without excessive anxiety, (2) compete and compare satisfactorily with their peers, (3) find new friendships and relationships, and (4) continue developing their sexual identities. Each of these tasks will require a lot of practice. They will also trigger silent questions such as, Is it safe to be away from my family? How do I compare with my peers? Where will I fit in? and, Will I be liked by the opposite sex? In this chapter we will look at these important tasks and the conflicting feelings they stir up in early adolescents.

Look, Ma! No Hands!

Early adolescents leap into life with excitement and expectations unmatched by their abilities. Having begun to establish their distinctiveness from you and the opposite sex in preadolescence, they are thrilled with the opportunity to begin new endeavors without your supervision. They meet new friends. They listen to new music. And they leave home for longer periods. Every new activity is approached with excitement and anticipation. A trip to the mall or a visit to the movies without you is a big adventure. Like birds leaving a cage and flying to each corner of their new-found world, they practice being separate from you and trying out more adult behaviors.

Early adolescents' explorations are so exciting that some of them almost lose their sense of reality. They start thinking they can do anything and are impervious to the hardships, disasters, or consequences they may encounter. A few successes can make early adolescents heady with self-confidence and resistant to any restraints. Petty theft, alcohol, drugs, and premature sexual involvement can all be undertaken without a full awareness of their dangers. The only other time of life when human beings are so ready to explore yet so unaware of how many things can go awry is early toddlerhood—from ten to sixteen months of age.

Remember how your toddlers excitedly ran away from you to explore the world as soon as they could walk? They practiced being separate and suddenly felt "big." But how dangerous that time could be! They tripped and fell, overextended themselves, and ingested substances that weren't intended for the stomach. Since you couldn't watch them every minute, you had to let them learn a few things the hard way. Only after they pulled an end table or a chair over on their heads did they learn to be more careful. A few years later, the same thing happened as they learned to ride a bike or skateboard or attempted some other dangerous activity. Just when they proudly exclaimed, "Look, Ma! No hands!" they hit a tree or a curb and came crashing to the ground.

Early adolescents have a similar approach to life. To use psychological jargon, they can be quite narcissistic. Exhilarated by their newly discovered freedom and "maturity," they can be totally absorbed in their own world and oblivious to the consequences of their actions. Early adolescents can also be extremely sensitive and selfish—especially over privacy and sharing clothes and other possessions. If an early adolescent girl's sister tries on her blouse or skirt without permission, she is ready to kill. The slightest hint that her privileges or possessions are being usurped causes fits of anger or tearful appeals for fairness.

During this period, some adolescents can almost seem to forget that their parents exist. They are on the go, spending time with their friends and exploring their world, almost oblivious to you—until you tell them no or until they need something from you. It is almost as if they think you exist only for them.

This phase of self-centeredness is one reason early adolescents take so little responsibility for their part in family conflicts. Twelve- and thirteen-year-olds are remarkably good at recognizing other people's problems but are nearly blind to their own. They are unable to step outside of themselves and look objectively at the impact of their attitudes and actions. They also have trouble admitting they caused a problem because their self-esteem is so fragile that accepting blame makes them feel like total failures.

This self-centered or narcissistic stage of life is triggered by your teenagers' normal developmental processes. Early adolescents are in an in-between period. They are starting to withdraw their attachment from you but they have not reached the point of having stable, meaningful relationships with peers. This creates a love gap. They unconsciously think, *I am lessening my dependent love on my parents but haven't found a replacement. That's lonely. If nobody else loves me, I'll have to take care of myself and force people to give me what I need.* This creates a temporary flurry of exaggerated self-love and of using mom and dad when they are needed but ignoring them at other times. Much like toddlers learning to say no before they are mature enough to share, early adolescents must learn to assert their opinions and hang onto their possessions before they are able to love and give maturely. And, like toddlers, they tend to be oblivious to their mothers and others until they need them. Seen in this light, your thirteen-year-olds' temporary phase of selfishness is actually a necessary stage in their developmental progress.

This phase of exaggerated self-importance can serve another useful purpose. It helps early adolescents start feeling more competent and adult. When your sons and daughters were young children, you were at least three times their size. To them, you looked like an omnipotent, omniscient eighteen-foot giant. You were so intelligent, powerful, and wise they thought you could do anything you wanted. By comparison, they were weak, inferior, and inadequate. Their exalted view of you was comforting during their childhood years since they could bask in your strength and wisdom. But it also reinforced their smallness and inferiority. You were big and wise; they were small and naive.

In order for teenagers to start thinking of themselves as competent adults, they have to make a major change in this picture of themselves and you. And what better way to wipe out years of belief in your parents' omnipotence than to entertain the fantasy that you are now the all-intelligent, all-powerful one? Your early adolescents' temporary grandiosity and narcissism is one way of dethroning you from your lofty and exaggerated position in order to start building a more adult and realistic image of themselves.

"No!" Means "I Want to Be Adult"

Like thirteen-year-old Lori in chapter 1, many early adolescents go through a period of arguing or sassing or disagreeing with everything their parents say. Like temporary self-centeredness, this stubborn, negative phase is another expected early adolescent reaction. In order to separate from you, teenagers have to prove they can do things their own way. Negativism is one way of doing that. It is also a way of expressing their general unhappiness with life or venting pent-up frustrations from their day at school. But be careful. If you don't understand what your teenagers are trying to accomplish with their negativism, you can get caught up in a vicious cycle that goes like this:

Adolescent attempts to assert his or her independence by becoming more negative or resistant to parental demands. (This is a normal way of asserting one's individuality.)

Parent fails to see the hidden normal goal behind the negativism and feels threatened or challenged. (This reaction is also normal since teenagers don't bother to tell their parents this is just a temporary phase to help them grow up.)

Parent, feeling threatened or concerned, reacts to adolescent's attempt to loosen cords of dependency with anxiety, anger, or increased efforts to control.

Adolescent interprets parent's reactions as saying it is wrong to try to grow up. He thinks they want him to remain a child.

Adolescent, feeling patronized and misunderstood or restricted, reacts with more negativism, gives up, or turns to peers for support in growing up. (These solutions shut the parents out, cut the adolescent off from his parents' support, and dig deep chasms between the parents and the adolescent.)

Parent, still not understanding what the teenager is trying to accomplish, keeps resisting adolescent's attempts to grow up, or withdraws and leaves the teenager on his own.

Adolescent, lacking the parent's support, flounders and tries to find his own way, or turns to escapes such as alcohol, drugs, or running away. More fortunate adolescents compen-

sate for the lack of parental understanding and encouragement by throwing themselves into studies, athletics, church
and service responsibilities, or other constructive extracurricular activities.

In different versions, this cycle is lived out in homes throughout
the Western world. First, teenagers develop some assertive or
upsetting behaviors. Next, the parents fail to understand the
meaning of the behavior. And finally, things deteriorate into
repeated conflict or the teenagers have to turn to their peers for
understanding and help in growing up.

A similar cycle can be triggered anytime a teenager feels misunderstood. For example, teenagers can become obnoxious or hard
to live with around the house in order to act out some of the
anxiety they wouldn't dare reveal in front of their friends. If they
throw tantrums, argue stubbornly, or break into tears at school,
their friends will drop them in a minute. So they wait to express
their upsetting emotions at home. Adolescent negativism can also
express a sense of being out of control that puberty brings for
many teens. The physical, social, and emotional changes set in
motion at puberty threaten to overwhelm and overpower adolescents, so they need a safe place to unwind and "let it all hang out."
Unfortunately, home is the place.

Whatever its cause, the only way to break this potentially destructive cycle is to understand why your adolescents are becoming so negative and to encourage their efforts to grow up and cope
with the struggles of adolescence. Once you can accept your
adolescents' negativism as an effort to grow up or a symptom of
other adolescent struggles, you can find ways of providing the
emotional support they need. This relieves your adolescents'
anger and enables them to grow up much more easily.

What Do I Do Now?

Self-preoccupation isn't the only characteristic shared by
toddlers and early adolescents. Remember how your practicing

toddlers periodically realized they were too far away from you and beat a quick retreat to the safety of your arms? Their fear of being alone chased them back to mom or dad for emotional reassurance or "refueling." They were like cars with small emotional fuel tanks. You filled them up with emotional resources, such as cuddly hugs and expressions of approval and delight. Then they drove away and explored some more. But before long they ran out of gas again and came back for another emotional refueling. As long as you were available when they came in for a fill-up, everything was fine. But if you were gone or unavailable, they became frightened. They probably cried, ran through the house looking for you, or insistently tried to get you to drop whatever you were doing. How would you feel if your car was on empty and you coasted into the only gas station for miles around only to find it was closed for the weekend or the station manager was unwilling to sell you gas because he was too busy?

The anxiety that drives practicing toddlers back to mother is called "separation anxiety" because it is caused by their separation from mother. Like toddlers, early adolescents also experience anxiety over separation. They wander away from you to practice being adult. They start making more decisions without asking you first. They spend more time alone or with their friends. And they try out new activities. But periodically they think, *What have I done? Here I am leaving the security of mom and dad. Why am I giving up the love and safety I have had all my life?*

One moment these questions are the farthest thing from your thirteen- or fourteen-year-olds' minds. They feel good about themselves and are engrossed in exploring their expanding world. Moments later they realize they have climbed pretty far out on a limb and their anxiety over being away from you drives them back in your direction. But since dependency is distasteful to these aspiring adults, they soon mount a renewed desire to move away. This is followed by another encounter with separation anxiety and the cycle repeats itself.

When your adolescents are in the middle of this separation cycle, their feelings can be like a roller coaster. Arguments flare as they try to prove they can think for themselves. Childlike obedience is out and limits are tested to prove their growing independence. But when your early adolescents realize they are isolated from your childhood care, they can again become exceedingly dependent and childlike.

Figure I shows an early adolescent's predictable struggle to separate from his parents. The cycle begins with the adolescents' disenchantment with the dependency of childhood. The need to outgrow that childishness pushes him to start moving away from mom and dad. But before long, separation from his parents makes him anxious and drives him back for more support. Then the cycle repeats again.

FIGURE 1

THE SEPARATION CYCLE

Disenchantment with dependency→	Separation and excitement	→	Anxiety over separation	→	Renewed dependency and search for refueling	→	Disenchantment with dependency	→	Renewed efforts to separate

Overcoming this cycle of separation anxiety and becoming comfortable at a greater emotional distance from mom and dad is one of the four major tasks facing your early adolescents.

Most thirteen- and fourteen-year-olds make good progress in accomplishing this task if they have plentiful opportunities to move away from their parents and try things on their own, interspersed with opportunities to come back and be dependent and receive emotional refueling. They may show some normal separation anxiety by being reluctant to try a new experience, especially in an unfamiliar place or with unfamiliar people. Or they may want to stay home from school occasionally, or become upset when they don't know where you are.

But if you are available and accepting of your early adolescents' occasional needs to be childish while still encouraging their steps toward maturity, you will provide the support they need to move on toward adulthood. Their childish and dependent times actually provide an impetus to move forward again. It is like being on empty, finding a good gas station and filling up, then hitting the road again. Each time they are refueled, they find they can go a little farther on a tank of gas.

Some early and middle adolescents are excessively anxious over separation from their parents. For some reason, they lack the inner resources needed to start growing away from you. Here are a few signs of excessive dependency in early or middle adolescence:

- Unwillingness to spend a night away from home
- Frequent or regular refusal to go to school
- Highly anxious when they are away from their homes or parents
- Lack of enjoyable peer relationships
- Fears that something bad is going to happen to their parents or families

Any of these reactions is an important danger signal that tells parents a teenager is experiencing more than the normal amount of separation anxiety. If these reactions persist, we recommend that you seek out a professional therapist to help you and your teenagers get to the roots of their fears so they can keep maturing on schedule. If they don't, they can carry these patterns of dependency and fear throughout adolescence and right into adulthood.

How Do I Measure Up?

One survey[2] of 8,000 pre- and early adolescents revealed their three greatest worries: grades, looks, and popularity. Far down the list were drugs, violence, and nuclear destruction. More than half of the young people polled said they worried about grades and looks and 48 percent said they worried about popularity. *Notice that the three main worries all reflect your adolescents' need to achieve or be comparable to their peers. This is the second major developmental challenge facing early adolescents.*

The radical changes in your early adolescents' minds and bodies force them to reevaluate their self-image. During childhood, attitudes toward themselves were based largely on their relationships with you. Your love and training laid the foundation for their self-esteem. But as adulthood approaches, your sons and daughters must increasingly test out their attitudes toward themselves in the world beyond the home. One of the major ways they do that is by comparing themselves to others.

Thirteen- and fourteen-year-old girls study every aspect of their bodies, even when the results dismay them. They stand in front of mirrors practicing varied hairstyles. They shave their legs and sample makeup. And when something looks good on a peer, they want one like it. Time and again they ask themselves, Do I measure up? As one mother put it, "If she doesn't have the right clothes you can forget all the rest. They all feel better about themselves if they have designer labels on their clothes."

Constant comparisons can trigger some of the most painful feelings of adolescence—inferiority and self-hatred. Every deviation from the norm is an opportunity for adolescents to judge themselves as inadequate. Teenagers who already are sensitive or have poor self-concepts are especially vulnerable. Every time they compare themselves unfavorably they become discouraged or depressed.

The most important physical deviations for early adolescent girls are height and weight and breast development. Early maturers may feel out of step with their peers or unprepared for the attention they receive from older males. Some feel ashamed. Others become disgusted with young men because of the embarrassing attention they express. And girls who haven't received the attention they need from their fathers may welcome this new interest with undue eagerness long before they are emotionally mature enough to handle it. As soon as they date, they start getting deeply involved physically or emotionally in a vain effort to fill the void caused by an absent father.

The feelings early developers experience are nothing compared to the anxiety of girls who remain flat-chested and childish looking much longer than their peers. One study of upper- and middle-class Caucasian girls found that they tended to see their breasts as their most important sexual organ.[3] The size of a girl's breasts is as important to her as the size of the penis is to boys. The first bra is a badge of distinction saying, "Now I am mature." Peers can be unmercifully cruel to those with different bodily proportions because of their anxiety about their own bodies. Jokes about breasts looking like "two fried eggs" or "two pancakes" cut to the quick as the late-maturing girl applies these comments to herself.

Early adolescent boys are as sensitive as girls to the way they compare with their peers. They just don't talk about it as much. Some spend hours lifting weights or working out to develop admired physical attributes. Others spend equal amounts of time on sports or their clothes or other status symbols. And still others get caught up in hostile joking or put-downs of their peers in order to prove they are tough and fit in with an "in" group.

In our culture, late-maturing boys pay the greatest psychological price for being less than average. Physical prowess on the athletic field and masculine builds are stressed so heavily that boys who lack these attributes feel out of sync. Some withdraw into themselves, become depressed, or try to compensate in another area of competence such as studies, art, or extracurricular activities. Others may turn to rebellion, stealing, vandalizing, or using drugs and alcohol to prove they are "mature" even if their bodies don't show it.

Students who have a hard time with grades also have to struggle with self-acceptance. They look around at friends or siblings who sail through their course work and they feel dumb or slow by comparison. Whatever the deviation from the norm, however, early adolescents who do not quite live up to their peers tend to feel anxious, inferior, or inadequate. Coping with these feelings is one of the major tasks of early adolescence.

Who's Next?

Several years ago, *National Geographic Magazine* produced a television special about Jane Goodall's work with chimpanzees. In one scene, a female chimpanzee that had become separated from her regular social group was trying to find another group. Her initial attempts to enter a new group of chimpanzees were rebuffed as she was driven away by angry females.

The loneliness of that estranged chimp was painful to watch. Her lowered head and drooping shoulders bodily communicated her depression. But with each passing day some of the females ventured a bit closer to her. As they approached, she pathetically held out her right hand with the index finger extended. At first the females ignored her, but finally one of them reached out and touched her finger. From that point on, she was allowed to follow and eventually join in their activities. When she was finally accepted as a full-fledged member of the group, her posture and demeanor changed immediately. She lifted her head, drew up her shoulders, and began chattering with enthusiasm.

If you could watch a new girl try to find a social circle in an eighth- or ninth-grade class you might see some remarkable parallels. As your thirteen- and fourteen-year-olds begin to step away emotionally from you, they too experience a loss of intimacy and their previous closeness. To fill this void, they turn increasingly to their peers. This shifting of relationships explains why peer pressure can be so overwhelming. As your teenagers move away from you, they instinctively fill the emotional void with other relationships. Much as they used to turn to you, they now turn to their peers.

Developing good relationships with their peers is the third developmental hurdle facing early adolescents. This development is a two-edged sword. It presents your teenagers with fantastic new friendships and experiences. Teenagers can become each other's counselors and advisers. I have seen many adolescents support their hurting peers, encourage them to break off destructive dating relationships, stop using alcohol or drugs, and even help them get along better with their parents. Teenagers will listen to advice from friends which they would never tolerate from parents. On the other hand, the heightened importance of your early adolescents' friends can create new stresses and concerns.

Unless your adolescents have learned to think for themselves and feel good about your values, they may suppress your standards and ideals to gain acceptance into a certain clique. They may be pushed prematurely into dating and sexual intimacy. Or they may experiment with drugs and alcohol and join in delinquent behavior to fit into a group.

By early adolescence, your sons' and daughters' choices of friends will have a different flavor than when they were a few years younger. Preadolescents tend to select same-sex friends. They spend a lot of time exploring or sharing secrets, and the status of friends is largely unimportant. Although early adolescents are still looking for someone to share with, they start looking for friends among the opposite sex. They also start selecting friends of both sexes with qualities they idealize or admire. In the same way that they used to bask in your desirable parental attributes, early adolescents are now likely to seek out peers with the qualities they would like to have for themselves. These peer selections are another part of the normal narcissism of early adolescence. Not yet feeling strong and complete, thirteen- and fourteen-year-olds seek out friends partly so they can share in their desirable attributes.

If you have ever criticized your early adolescents' friends, you will remember how strongly they reacted. They probably became quite angry and defensive and accused you of being insensitive, prejudiced, unfair, or out of touch. They reacted almost as though you had attacked them personally. And in a way, you had, because they had chosen that friend in order to feel better about themselves and now you are disparaging that person.

Fourteen-year-old Shannon expressed the importance of her best friend this way:

ANOTHER ME

An outward looking mirror of myself,
and I, of you.
My shadow, my other half, my secrets holder, my

trouble bearer
and I, yours.
So alike that I often wonder—
  if we hadn't lived at the same time,
  at the same place,
  and fate had not liked our meeting,
Wouldn't we feel that something—
  a piece of ourselves—
  was missing?
Or perhaps that we, in turn,
  should be a part of someone else?
I am a puzzle with one missing piece;
  you are that piece.
Sometimes I wish I were you
  and you, me.
Because we are so different
  we have so much to share—
But because we are so alike
  we understand each other so well.

Shannon wanted her friend to be her "secrets holder" as young children do, but she also wanted her friend to be her "trouble bearer" and her "missing piece." Early and middle adolescents who have not developed a relatively strong inner sense of selfhood have especially strong needs for friends to fill this role. They seek out intense friendships, spend hours together, or select one "best friend." But if that friend doesn't constantly reassure them she is their "best friend," they become extremely jealous, hurt, and angry. Unfortunately, their excessive demands usually have the opposite of the desired effect. They drive potential friends away.

Developing Sexual Identity

A special part of developing new friendships and competing with one's peers is developing one's sexual identity. Thirteen-year-old Sherry's parents described her as a relatively quiet and compliant girl until shortly after her thirteenth birthday. At that time Sherry suddenly became boy crazy and overly concerned with her appearance. She started borrowing or exchanging clothes with a friend and tried to develop a trendy look. She borrowed her mother's makeup kit and began experimenting with eye shadow, lipstick, pancake makeup, and mascara. Then she tried different hairstyles and became angry or depressed when she couldn't produce the look she wanted.

Sherry's father was bothered by her efforts to look adult and told her she "looked like a little tramp with all that goo." One day he forbade her to use makeup and told her not to wear clothing he considered suggestive. Sherry defied him by putting on makeup at school and was grounded for it. The next day, Sherry ran away to a friend's house where she spent the night, saying she had her parents' permission. From that point on, Sherry's anger and rebellion only worsened.

When I met Sherry, she complained that she was being punished for doing the very things her mother did. "My mother is nice looking, but she has to work at it," she said. "She uses makeup and has her hair fixed and chooses dresses to get attention. So why can't I?" As for liking boys, Sherry wondered aloud if her parents would be happier if she were lesbian. Anger was welling up inside and she threatened to run away for good unless she was allowed to grow up.

Sherry's explosion grew out of her frustrated inability to master the fourth developmental task facing early adolescents—feeling good about her developing sexuality. Sherry had begun her menstrual cycle and was trying to become attractive and feminine like her mother. Wearing makeup and changing her hair and clothing style were her ways of practicing being a glamorous woman. It was fun to see how she looked in different clothes and styles. Unfortunately, Sherry's parents didn't think she needed any practice. Instead of encouraging her attempts to develop her femininity by complimenting her and helping her dress more maturely, they squelched Sherry's needs. This made her feel even more childish, stirred up intense anger, and programmed her family for constant conflict.

Like Sherry, most early adolescent girls have strong feelings about their developing sexuality and their physical attractiveness. Although most girls in our society are more aware of the basic facts of menstruation and sexuality than their mothers were at the same age, early adolescent girls still feel some anxiety and ambivalence about the onset of their period and sexual maturing. On one hand they feel a healthy pride in their development. On the other, they worry about how normal they are, how they compare with their peers, and how successful they will be at becoming mature women.

A few girls are so embarrassed over their physical development that they regress into the role of a little girl to avoid facing their dawning sexuality. Others deny their femininity by increasing their tomboy activities or turning their attention toward favorite pets who provide acceptance and solace until they develop the inner strength to live with their approaching adulthood. But however they cope, all early adolescent girls must somehow start to come to grips with their developing sexuality.

Budding Masculinity

Almost two years after girls begin menstruating, their male counterparts experience the onset of puberty. Although they may already have experienced dry orgasms in experimental touching, that seldom prepares boys for the first experience of awakening to find the bed wet with semen. Since many boys feel guilty or associate nocturnal emissions with the shame of wetting the bed, they hide the evidence but wonder if something is wrong with them. Rarely do they have the courage to talk openly to their parents, and most depend on older peers or books to enlighten them.

Fourteen- and fifteen-year-old boys generally experience an increase in erotic dreams and greater sensitivity in the penis. They have erections at embarrassing moments and sometimes it seems this part of their body is no longer under control. Their increased sensitivity ushers in fantasies about girls, and masturbation becomes an almost universal experience for adolescent boys. For both boys and girls, masturbation is a normal response to sexual development. It is a way of experimenting with bodily changes, enjoying the pleasurable feelings of sexuality, and relieving sexual and other tensions. It is one way teenagers learn to integrate sexuality into their total personalities.

In contrast to younger boys who stick together around school or athletic events, early adolescent males start spending more time with girls—or at least thinking about them. Their conversations with male friends often turn to girls or sex, and most begin dating in this period or soon after. Daydreaming and talking about girls is a way of practicing and getting ready to relate to the opposite sex in reality. Although these fantasies and sexual conversations and curiosities worry some parents, they are completely normal. If you have taken a natural, open attitude toward sexuality in your home, your adolescents won't engage in degrading discussions but they still will have some curiosity. It is natural to wonder about your sexual adequacy and the opposite sex as your sexuality is developing. And it is better to be practicing in fantasy than in reality.

Actually, most of us practice everything in our minds before we try it out in reality. We imagine a new job, or picture ourselves being successful in a school play or athletic contest. Unless it becomes escapism or a compelling preoccupation, fantasy is a positive way of anticipating the future and getting used to unknown territory. It usually means, however, that we aren't quite ready to embark on the new activity in reality. Have you, for example, ever overheard a group of high school freshman boys analyzing the girls walking by? Their hormones are opening their eyes to the opposite sex, but most of them have done very little dating yet. They may act knowledgeable and brag, "That's the one for me. She's a fox!" But they are more talk than action. By talking and fantasizing about girls they are preparing to move toward the opposite sex. But they aren't quite ready to take the plunge into serious heterosexual relationships.

Once teenagers start dating, they practice their sexuality in new ways. Asking for a date, spending unsupervised time with the opposite sex, and learning to communicate seriously are all adult activities. So are physical expressions of feelings such as hand holding, hugging, and kissing. The arrival of these behaviors poses one of the biggest questions facing the parents of early adolescents—when to let their children date.

If adolescents aren't allowed to practice increasingly mature ways of relating to the opposite sex, their normal development may be hampered and serious conflicts may ensue. But if adolescents date too early or aren't prepared for the levels of involvement they may face in dating, they can stumble into premature physical or emotional intimacy and make serious mistakes. Early adolescents don't realize the sexual hurt and turmoil they can encounter in premature emotional entanglements. Many actually don't realize that having sexual intercourse only once may result in a pregnancy. Their early adolescent naivete allows them to rush headlong into adultlike activities without imagining the potential consequences.

Although more and more teenagers are coming to believe there is nothing wrong with premarital sex, early and middle adolescents are simply not emotionally ready for sexual intimacy. The biblical teaching that sexual intercourse is designed for marriage[4] is reinforced by an understanding of the normal developmental processes of adolescence. Teenagers must first separate emotionally from their parents. Then they must grow out of their exploratory narcissistic phase. Then they must consolidate their own identities and learn to relate maturely to others. Since this process of leaving their parents and developing an adult identity comes only with time, you shouldn't be afraid to establish limits on your early adolescents' dating or postpone dating until they are well into middle adolescence. Young teenagers need to know you want them to reach out to the opposite sex, and they need increasing opportunities to do this. But not until young adulthood are they emotionally ready for marriage and total sexual intimacy.

In chapter 18 we will return to this topic and look at ways to help adolescents cope with their sexualilty and feel good about their masculinity and femininity, without jumping prematurely into intimate physical relationships. For now we simply want to call your attention to your early adolescents' increasing interest in the opposite sex and their growing concern over their masculinity or femininity.

Chapter Highlights

Early adolescence marks the beginning of your sons' and daughters' aggressive movements away from you and their earliest practicing of adult behaviors. In order to move steadily toward adulthood, early adolescents need to develop enough confidence to start separating from you without excessive anxiety. They must learn to make new friends outside the family. They must learn to compete and to compare themselves favorably to their peers. And they must develop more mature attitudes toward their sexuality. Through all of this, they will also be practicing more adult behaviors and testing out their maturing abilities. Let's review the major features of these early adolescent years.

AGES
- Thirteen to fourteen for girls
- Fourteen to fifteen for boys

DEVELOPMENTAL TASKS
- Begin separating from parents and family
- Learn to make their own friends outside the family circle
- Feel good about their dawning sexuality
- Feel comparable to their peers

CHARACTERISTICS
- Testing parental limits
- Increased desire for independence, often accompanied by demanding attitudes and irritability at home

- Excitement and elated mood over new experiences and opportunities
- Marked increase in importance of peer values in relation to parental values
- Developing interest in heterosexual relationships and being attractive to the opposite sex
- Attempting (practicing) adult behavior and experimentation
- Occasional angry outbursts over the need to be separate and adult
- An appearance of unconcern for parents punctuated by occasional signs of separation anxiety

DANGERS
- Excessive neediness or separation anxiety may block normal movements away from dependency on their parents
- Freedom without sufficient caution may result in dangerous activities and premature experimenting with adult activities
- Excessive parental control may undercut self-confidence or create anger and rebellion
- A lack of validation of increasing maturity may undermine self-esteem
- Insufficient validation of developing sexuality may cause repression of God-given sexual feelings or lead to premature efforts to validate their sexuality with their peers
- Feelings of guilt or confusion over sexuality may develop
- Unsupervised or unguided peer relationships may lead to impulsive, harmful actions or premature experimenting with adult activities

If your thirteen- and fourteen-year-olds are showing several characteristics of early adolescence, they are probably right on track developmentally. The tasks they face, however, usually trigger some upsetting emotions and a difficult time of life. In chapter 7, we will look at ways of helping your sons and daughters clear the developmental hurdles of early adolescence and cope with these conflicting emotions as smoothly as possible.

NOTES

1. Illustrations in this chapter are by Dr. Lewis.
2. "Why Kids Worry," *U.S.A. Today,* October 18, 1985.
3. B. Rosenbaum, (1979). "The Changing Body Image of the Adolescent Girl" in Max Sugar, ed., *Female Adolescent Development* (New York: Brunner/Mazel).
4. See, for example, Genesis 2:24-25; 1 Corinthians 7:2-5; Proverbs 5:18-19.

He that is slow to anger has great understanding.

CHAPTER SEVEN
PARENTING EARLY ADOLESCENTS

Flying coast to coast on a business trip, I sat just in front of a teenage girl and her parents.[1] She appeared to be about fourteen and was at odds with her mother and dad from the moment they boarded the plane. The first argument was over the window seat. She won. The next was sparked by her request to stumble over her parents and go to the rest room before the plane was off the ground. She lost. Every topic of conversation set her at odds with at least one parent. After half an hour of squabbling they tacitly struck a truce and the parents began reading as the girl stared out the window.

Halfway through the flight, apparently distressed by all their fighting, the girl turned toward her mother and asked, "When I turn sixteen can I move out?" With an air of indifference the mother answered, "If you want to." Her father, who had been absorbed in a magazine, looked up and angrily asked, "What did you say?" "Ask Mother!" the girl shot back. "I was talking to her!" "I asked you!" her father retorted. "Now tell me what you said!" A bit subdued, the girl replied, "I just asked Mother if I could move out when I'm sixteen." "Of course you can't!" her father spat. "And I never want to hear you say those words again until you are eighteen!" Then they all lapsed into a sullen silence.

This family is a classic example of an early or middle adolescent's separation struggles aggravating long-standing patterns of poor communication. This girl was fed up with the tense atmosphere in her family and looking forward to the time when she could break away from her parents, establish her separate identity, and escape the conflicts of her home. But neither parent was helping. Her mother's uncaring permission to move out at sixteen would set her prematurely free. Her father's angry dismissal of her question ignored both her acute unhappiness and her growing need to separate emotionally. His unwillingness to discuss her feelings made a bad situation worse. By ordering her not even to "say those words again" until she was eighteen, he was denying her the right to think for herself and programming her for sure rebellion.

Neither parent knew how to face their family's problems realistically. The father thought the problems would go away if nobody talked about them, and the mother apparently thought the only solution was for the girl to leave. Nobody knew how to communicate like mature adults, and neither parent was helping the girl feel good about growing up. All the parents could do was try to turn her into a silently obedient child until she reached eighteen, when they would turn her loose. But like most adolescents, she wasn't about to be silenced until then!

Unless this girl and her parents come to some better understanding, they are headed for years of conflict and heartache. The daughter simply must have more understanding and encouragement than she is receiving now, and her parents need at least as much help understanding their own pain. None of them are prepared for the journey the daughter will be taking in the coming years.

Learn to Listen

Above all else, the girl behind me on the plane needed her parents' sympathetic ear. Her question to her mother actually meant: If you don't understand me and if we can't love and support each other, wouldn't it be better for me to leave and try to make it on my own? Unfortunately, her blunt way of framing the question and her angry tone of voice disguised her pain and made it difficult for her parents to understand. When teenagers talk this way, we have to decode their hidden messages if we are going to get the conversation back on a constructive track.

If this girl's mother had responded to her question about moving out with, "Why do you ask, Susan?" she might have gotten a clearer picture of her daughter's pain. Or the mother could have replied, "It feels bad when we fight over everything, doesn't it?" or "We've all been uptight lately and need to find a better way to get along. Let's find a time to talk when we get home." Any of these responses would have told the girl that her mother wanted to understand. If those attempts at more effective communication failed, her parents could have told her frankly, "For some reason, we are all fighting too much. When we get home we are going to find a counselor to help us get along better."

Fourteen-year-old Amy's mother was able to be much more helpful than the parents on the airplane. Marianne and Amy were starting to get into one argument after another. Amy got upset every time her mother asked her to do anything around the house and Marianne was beginning to nag incessantly over her daughter's undone chores and "forgotten" responsibilities. Marianne also found herself resenting her daughter's bad attitude. After one especially rancorous hassle, Marianne spent a morning by herself thinking and praying over her relationship with her daughter. She loved Amy and knew she was basically a "good kid." But she also realized she and Amy were about to enter into a cycle of fighting that could undermine their relationship and cause some deep and potentially serious hurts.

After talking her plans over with a friend, Marianne told Amy she didn't feel good about their fighting and would like to find better ways of getting along. She said she would like to start by taking Amy out to breakfast and listening to the things that Amy wished were different around the house. She promised not to say one word of criticism and not to offer any advice. She just wanted to hear what Amy had to say.

Amy wasn't excited by her mother's offer but agreed to go along. At first she was tentative and didn't say much. Then she started sharing things that bothered her. Her sister's using her clothes, her parents' fighting, her mother's nagging, and her father's criticisms of her friends were at the top of her list. It took an hour to express all of her frustrations, but when she finished she hugged her mother and said, "Thanks for being interested and for not telling me what to do. I know that must be hard." Then she added, "Mom, I know I'm hard to live with sometimes and I want to do better. I just get so upset I don't know what else to do."

That conversation marked a turning point in Amy's relationship with her mother. Once Amy knew her mom wanted to understand her needs and feelings she found it easier to be direct when she was upset. Since their breakfast talk went well, Amy and her mother decided to set up future breakfasts out to talk and find better ways to resolve their conflicts. During their third breakfast they decided to make some rules to help them be more sensitive to each other. They came up with these four and posted them on the refrigerator door:

1. We will warn each other when we have had a hard day or are especially upset.
2. We will tell each other how we feel when things go wrong but we won't blame each other for our upset feelings.
3. We will call a truce if we start to fight and wait for a better time to talk it over.

4. We will go out together once each week and set aside part of that time to talk over any problems; then we will put problems aside and have some fun together.

Marianne's and Amy's rules weren't profound but they did hit on some important principles of communication. Over a period of months, Amy and her mother grew a lot closer; at the same time Amy also started feeling more adult. Since her mother and she had worked together to improve their relationship, Amy felt more confident about her ability to communicate and solve problems. This gave her increased confidence at school and with her friends and a greater sense of inner peace. Marianne's sensitive listening also helped Amy continue the process of differentiating her own ideas from her parents' and of practicing being adult.

Marianne was helping Amy accomplish these two important developmental tasks by living out two biblical proverbs: "A soothing tongue is a tree of life"[2] and "The purposes of a man's heart are deep waters, but a man of understanding draws them out."[3] Marianne soothed her daughter with sensitive words and sympathetic listening and drew out the things that were upsetting her.

If you start to fall into a cycle like Marianne and Amy, you might try some similar ways of breaking out. Sometimes you can begin by doing fun things together. An athletic event, a concert, a visit to a local attraction, or a shopping trip that doesn't involve any tense communication can help break the ice. After a few good times, you can work on listening carefully to your son's or daughter's thoughts and feelings without offering any advice. Sometimes it helps to set a definite time to get out of the house and go to a quiet, neutral place to talk. Wherever and whenever you talk, be sure you shift into a listening mode instead of a reactive one. Leave out all critical or judgmental remarks. Ask your son or daughter to tell you when they feel understood by you and when they feel you haven't heard. Talk about the issues that cause conflicts in your relationship and ask what would make life better.

Although your early adolescents will sometimes tell you they don't want to talk, they usually do. They may just need a little time to quiet down or sort things out for themselves before they want to share their thoughts with you. Or it may take a while before they learn that you are really there to understand, not to offer advice or criticism. Once over that hurdle, you are on your way. Your problems won't vanish, but both you and your adolescent can learn to sense conflicts coming and find ways to avoid them or work them out before things fall apart.

If you have trouble understanding your teenagers or if you tend to react instead of listen, you may need someone to talk to about your own reactions. We parents have our own needs and it is hard to listen to a moody or argumentative teenager when we ourselves are irritated or upset. After a sensitive friend or counselor helps us get a handle on our own needs and feelings, we find it much easier to understand our adolescents. Marianne did that when she talked to a friend about her frustrations before she talked to Amy. By sharing her frustrations with her friend, she was able to put her feelings and reactions into perspective and get ready to listen better to her daughter.

As you are making time for some uninterrupted discussions, don't overlook the importance of regular, daily interaction. The contacts of a high school daughter with her mother after school are no less important than those of the elementary age girl. But while we can sit a ten-year-old down and question her about her day, we may have to catch our adolescents on the run and be careful not to ask too many prying questions. As thirteen-year-old Caroline told her dad when he asked one question after another, "Look, Dad, my friends don't talk to their parents and I'm not talking to you. Forget the twenty questions!"

Caroline didn't want to cut off all communication. And she certainly wanted her parents' supportive love. But she couldn't handle her father's "twenty questions" and was asking him to find another way of being friends. Her sensitive father was able to do just that. He found that by talking a little about his own day, attending some high-school functions, and showing a casual (but not too great) interest in her friends, he kept their communication lines relatively open.

Enjoy Their Efforts at Becoming Adult

Since early adolescents are just beginning to practice adult behaviors, they need a lot of encouragement and support. Every time you allow your early adolescents to do something more adult, you are helping them grow up and separate from their childhood dependency on you. Every time you affirm their success in meeting life's demands, you support their movement to maturity. And every time they sense your happiness over their new experiences you help them develop a happier and more optimistic attitude toward life.

Simple things like letting early adolescents stay up later, letting them go places with their friends, or giving them more substantial chores around the house all tell your sons and daughters you realize they are becoming more adult. So does asking for their input on buying a new car or furniture for the home. Redoing an adolescent's room is another simple but practical way of validating their increasing maturity. Wallpaper that replaces the flower or doll patterns your daughter had as a little girl can symbolize her increased maturity. So can a new mirror or study desk or bedspread. Although these changes may not seem major to you, they can serve as minipassage rites for early adolescents. They show you are siding with their desires to grow up instead of trying to keep them like a child.

Supporting your early adolescents' participation in school and extracurricular activities also validates their growing maturity. Every event that expands their social circles, teaches new skills, or gives opportunities to try out some leadership responsibilities helps affirm your teenagers' movement toward independence. Your interest tells them their activities are important, and your support helps them gain confidence to keep on growing toward adulthood. Even if sports or band concerts or music groups or the rally squad are not highly interesting to you, you need to support their interest by sharing such activities with your adolescents. The more you take pleasure in your teenagers' activities, the better they will feel about themselves.

Even when your teenagers' enthusiasm seems excessive, or

when their expectations are unrealistic, don't throw cold water on them. That is like telling an excited toddler, "Don't run around the house so happily. That is immature and stupid." Instead, tell early adolescents, "That's exciting," or "That must be a big job." If they are overly idealistic, they will find out soon enough. What they need from you is the knowledge that you want them to tackle the world.

If you need to raise questions or voice reservations about a venture, share in their excitement and enthusiasm first. Then, very tentatively, wonder aloud if they *might* be biting off a little more than they can chew. If they don't agree, drop it and encourage them as much as you possibly can. If they eventually decide they attempted too much, don't tell them, "I told you so." Tell them something like, "It's hard to judge ahead of time how much you can do," or "That was really tough, wasn't it?" You might also refer to a time when you overshot your limits. Your self-revelation helps them sustain their optimism while gradually facing life a little more realistically.

Teenagers whose parents have difficulty enjoying their activities can grow up feeling isolated and unable to relax and enjoy life. Some successful physicians and attorneys I have counseled, for example, were unable to feel good about their successes. Upon hearing that they passed their bar exams or received their state licenses, these mature men and women could only say, "That's nice," and then get on with their next job. They were unable to enjoy the thrill or fulfillment of finally completing years of study and letting their achievements soak in. As these adults traced back their inability to enjoy their successes, they invariably recalled their parents' failure to get excited about their achievements or share in the fun of their activities. These high achievers felt their accomplishments were insufficient to satisfy their parents or merit enjoyment. Some developed workaholic life-styles that focused on winning or achieving but never on enjoying life.

Sharing your adolescents' excitement about life helps them integrate a joyful, positive attitude about both work and play. It also helps them over two of the major developmental hurdles of early adolescence: gaining confidence that they can function and compete successfully in the adult world, and finding out they feel fine while operating a few steps away from mom and dad.

If you are comfortable with your own desires to have fun or to experiment or to be admired and show off your abilities, you will find it easier to accept and enjoy your teenagers' excitement and their occasional grandiosity. If not, loosen up. Your teenagers need to see that you enjoy life and want them to do the same. Too much work and all seriousness around the house take a lot of joy out of adolescence and leave teenagers feeling empty, shallow, or depleted. Sharing spontaneously in some of their happy, carefree moments not only lightens the mood around your home, it affirms their emerging self and offers your approval.

Affirm Their Developing Sexuality

When thirteen-year-old Sherry[4] ran away from home after her dad forbade her to wear makeup and accused her of "looking like a tramp," she was reacting to her parents' attempt to squelch her dawning femininity. Sherry's parents could have avoided this estrangement if they had recognized her God-given need to accept her budding sexuality and start practicing being a woman. Sherry's father could have complimented her on her looks and, if her clothes were too extreme, asked her to modify them just a bit. Sherry's mom could have allowed her to use a little makeup while seeking other ways of encouraging her growing sense of adultness. She could offer to take Sherry shopping for some new clothes. And they could have used this opportunity to discuss her increasing maturity.

By supporting Sherry's initial efforts to become more adultly feminine, her parents could have built bridges that would have carried them through Sherry's adolescence. Unfortunately, their inability to affirm her approaching maturity drove a wedge between them that blocked the very thing they wanted to accomplish—helping her grow up smoothly. Think how different Sherry would feel if her father admired her new dress or whistled approvingly when she came into the living room in her first formal dress instead of saying it was too tight or too low cut.

If you run into this situation, dad, whistle first or find some other way of letting her know she looks attractive. Then, after complimenting your daughter on her maturing looks, if you feel you must say something, casually wonder aloud if it *might* be a *little* too tight. If it is already too late to change anything, or if your wife bought the dress with your daughter, keep quiet. You will only hurt your daughter's feelings and make things worse. Talk to your wife later and find a supportive way of solving the problem or learn to live with it. You don't have to say something to your daughter every time you feel a little nervous.

The difficulty Sherry's parents had in affirming her growth toward feminine maturity undoubtedly had something to do with their feelings about their own sexuality. Like most of us, Sherry's parents probably had their greatest problems with their daughter in areas where they had their own hang-ups. The accusation that Sherry looked like a tramp revealed her father's deep fear or guilt over his sexuality. He must have struggled greatly with his own sexual desires as an adolescent (or an adult). For him, if his daughter looked feminine and attractive, she was like a prostitute. Although his sad accusation tells us more about the father than Sherry, it will undoubtedly make it difficult for Sherry to develop good attitudes about her sexuality and create difficulties in her relating intimately and healthily with the man she eventually marries.

As your children enter early adolescence, remember that stylish, "in," or even slightly sexually provocative dressing is a way many teenagers practice their maturing sexual roles. Although you should help your adolescents dress appropriately, keep in mind that they need to be free to make a fashion statement that they are becoming men and women. Don't be quick to conclude that a short skirt, a tight blouse, or displayed muscles or chest hair are sure signs that your teenagers are about to give themselves over to unrestrained hedonism and sexuality. Your teenagers may need some guidance or limits on their clothes, but exercise your responsibility with a sensitivity to their needs to demonstrate their maturing sexual roles as well as their needs for appropriate dress.

Be Real!

Do you find it easy to occasionally share your own adolescent experiences or struggles with your teenagers? If so, that's great. Giving teenagers an honest glimpse of your own adolescence is one of the very best ways of helping them cope with the struggles they will have as teens. It encourages them to share with you more freely and lets them know that they can trust you because you can empathize with their situation. A teenage girl whose mother has confided some of her own adolescent struggles will take comfort that at least one troubled adolescent became a successful adult. If mom could do it there is hope for her. Adolescents who know their parents did some fun or crazy things as teenagers also feel better about their impulses and wishes to do some "weird" things.

When my daughter Debbie was feeling bad for getting a traffic ticket for going ten miles an hour over the speed limit, I told her about the time I got a ticket—for doing ninety—when I was her age. Debbie was shocked that her mature, conservative father had done such a stupid thing and she immediately felt better about her own problem. Some parents are reluctant to discuss experiences like this with their children because they are afraid they will set a bad example. Actually, sharing your problems usually sets a better example. It says, "We all do some foolish things, but let's learn from them and be more careful next time." Teenagers respond much better to parents who talk like this than parents who "maturely" warn their teenagers to drive safely or behave in certain ways while acting like they never had a problem in that area.

Parents who are hesitant to share their own adolescent struggles dig a chasm between themselves and their teenagers. If your teenagers are worried about acne, for example, don't assume a parental manner and admonish them to "Wash your face or they will never get better!" or tell them, "You ought to expect acne with all the sweets you eat!" Instead, say, "Zits are really a hassle, aren't they? When I was a sophomore I tried every doctor in town to try to get rid of mine."

Talking about your awkward experiences with acne, dating, friends, or grades can lessen your sons' and daughters' anxiety over their own struggles. Our goal isn't to brag about our exploits or belabor our adolescent struggles. It is simply to let our teenagers know their conflicts are normal and that mom and dad survived some similar experiences. This erects a bridge of understanding that helps your teenagers cross more confidently into adulthood.

Know Their Friends

When Keith and Carol's children were approaching adolescence they wanted to be sure they had some influence over the friends their children would run around with. They realized Ryan and Diane would be making new friends and they wanted that influence to be as positive as possible. Although Ryan and Diane often had friends over as children, Keith and Carol made a point of letting them know they were happy to have them continue inviting friends over during their junior high and high school days. They told the youth director at their church they would open their house and swimming pool for the youth group. And they encouraged their teenagers to occasionally invite a friend over to dinner with the family.

When their church established small fellowship groups, Keith and Carol purposely joined a group of three other couples whose teenagers seemed to have their act together. Although the couples were not Keith and Carol's best friends, Ryan and Diane liked their children, and Keith and Carol were committed to help them develop healthy friendships. Once a month these four families met together for a potluck dinner, games, fellowship, and a time of prayer and sharing. In between they occasionally had a fun night

THE BIRTH OF AN ADULT

or took a weekend camping or ski trip together. Over the next few years, those teenagers became some of Ryan and Diane's very best friends. They went to concerts and ball games together. They drove each other around based on the availability of cars and drivers licenses. And they had some serious times talking about their own needs and praying for each other. In short, they played important roles in each other's lives during their adolescent years.

Keith and Carol helped their teenagers over the third hurdle of middle adolescence, developing peer relationships, by selecting a fellowship group that met Ryan and Diane's needs as well as their own. Since the fellowship group included both teenage boys and girls, Ryan and Diane also had opportunities to develop meaningful friendships with members of the other sex and continue developing their masculine and feminine identities. Proverbs says, "He who walks with the wise grows wise, but a companion of fools suffers harm."[5] Ryan and Diane's friends made them wiser and made Keith and Carol's parenting much easier.

If you are worried about the potentially negative influence of your teenagers' peers, don't sit idly by and let it happen. You can't dictate who your teenagers' friends will be, but you can be aware of their friends and exert a lot of positive influence. Since early adolescents are beginning to practice being adult, they can easily get caught up in some potentially hazardous relationships and activities. It is your responsibility to minimize these risks, and one of the best ways is to be aware of your early adolescents' friends.

You can increase the probability that they will select friends with good attitudes and values by making your home available as an informal gathering place. You might also develop friendships with adults whose teenagers are the same age as your own. Some parents change churches or enroll their children in a different school in order to create better social and spiritual opportunities for their adolescents. Others get involved in school or church activities so they can be more aware of their adolescents' peer culture. One way or another, maintain a healthy interest in your early adolescents' friends and their activities without becoming intrusive or overly involved.

Set Realistic Limits

Children are something like kites. At first you have to both hold them close and put in a lot of effort to get them off the ground. But as they grow up you gradually give them more and more string until they are a waving distance from you. Learning to let out the slack is one of the basic tasks of parents of early adolescents. The trick is learning how much slack to let out at any particular time. We must give them increasing freedom to fly away, but we shouldn't let go completely until they safely learn to fly by themselves.

If you are going to err with thirteen- and fourteen-year-olds, it is better to be a bit overly careful than to abandon them to their own undirected choices. Proverbs 14:12 says, "There is a way that seems right to a man, but in the end it leads to death." This is certainly true of early adolescents.

Thirteen-year-olds are not ready to spend unlimited time with whomever they choose or go wherever they please. You need to see that they get home at a reasonable hour. You need to be aware of their friends and set realistic limits on where they go and what they do. You need to see that they don't enter into intimate relationships with the opposite sex. You may need to see that dating is postponed for a couple of years if your teenagers seem to lack inner strength to avoid deep entanglements. By the time your sons and daughters turn fifteen or sixteen, you will have less direct influence over their choice of activities and friends, but in early adolescence you should still exercise appropriate controls.

Early adolescents need later curfews, greater latitude in selecting friends, and a larger say in their activities than in childhood. But that doesn't mean we should remove all limits and set them free. Letting children begin solo dating at twelve or thirteen, for example, is usually unwise. Early adolescents are not ready for intimate relationships and unsupervised dating times with the opposite sex. Research indicates that girls who begin dating at a young age and date frequently are more likely to have premarital intercourse.[6] Their ability to set limits and control their strong emotions lags behind their passions and desires. In fact, approximately 80 percent of teenagers who start dating at twelve engage in premarital intercourse before they finish high school, while only 20 percent of teenagers who delay dating until sixteen engage in intercourse before they graduate.

On the other hand, early adolescents do need opportunities to have a boy or girl "friend" or to "go around" together at church or school. And middle adolescents need to tackle tasks such as driving, dating, and working. Unnecessary delays in letting adolescents tackle these activities generate harmful parent-teen battles and undercut your children's ability to take responsibility for their lives. To make teenagers wait until they turn seventeen or eighteen to date, for example, is probably being insensitive to their increasing maturity. It makes them think there is something wrong with their interest in the opposite sex or creates understandable resentment.

When our children reached early adolescence, we sat down over dinner and had a talk about when they might start dating. At fourteen, studious Richard couldn't have cared less. When we asked him when he thought he wanted to start dating, he quickly replied, "After I get my doctorate!" But like many pre- and early adolescent girls, twelve-year-old Debbie said, "How about now?" After talking it over we decided sixteen would be appropriate. We told Richard and Debbie we wanted them to spend time with their opposite sex friends at group activities and school and that we might make an exception for special occasions. But overall, we felt they didn't need to go on solo dates until they were about sixteen. That was fine with Richard, and although Debbie thought she might want to date earlier, she didn't fight it. By setting a realistic age we gave her something to look forward to and assured her we wanted her to grow up, but at a safe rate. In the meantime we tried to produce an environment that made it easy for our children to gradually break away from us and move toward new friends.

One day right after Debbie turned fifteen she came home from school and, with a sigh of relief, announced, "I'm sure glad you told me I couldn't date till I'm sixteen." Somewhat surprised, I asked, "Why is that?" She answered, "Peter asked me out and I really didn't want to go so I just told him, 'My dad won't let me date!' " Our limits had given Debbie the security she needed. She didn't want to hurt Peter's feelings but she didn't know how to tell him no. Although she was glad to be asked, our limits gave her the freedom to say no and took some pressure off of her.

Two weeks before Debbie turned sixteen she excitedly came home and announced, "Next week I'm going out with John!" "Oh, Debbie," I responded with mock seriousness, "you know we decided you wouldn't date until you're sixteen." "I know," Debbie confidently replied, "but I knew you'd let me go!" And of course we did. The idea wasn't that sixteen was a magic or legalistic age. It was a guideline, and Debbie knew we wouldn't want her to pass up this opportunity for a date.

You may decide to let your adolescents date at fifteen, or even fourteen. But whatever the age, keep two facts in mind: early adolescents need to feel your support of their desires to grow up and they need to be protected from getting into situations they aren't prepared to handle.

Early adolescents will usually accept a reasonable delay in taking on adult responsibilities if they have something definite to look forward to and the knowledge that you do want them to grow up. Complete freedom to choose their clothes, date, drive a car, take a job, and go wherever they want with whomever they please are on the horizon, but they aren't here yet. Early adolescents need to know that we see those freedoms coming and will help them move toward them step by step as they are ready.

Encourage Responsible Choices

In order to become emotionally independent, teenagers must learn to make decisions and live responsibly with the conse-quences. Just before our children entered junior high school, we went on an allowance system that provided them money to buy their clothes and take care of most of their other needs and activities. We agreed to pay for all of their school expenses and take care of family and church-related activities, and they were responsible for everything else. We figured out how much they needed over a year's time, divided it by twelve months, and threw in a few dollars for "mad money." Then we carefully explained that they would have to portion out their money if they wanted to save enough for the end of the month.

Richard took to this like a banker. He had always been tight with his money and quickly found every sale and discount store at the mall. He bought glue for the holes in his tennis shoes and put his shoe money into a savings account.

Debbie was just the opposite, an impulse buyer. The day we gave Debbie her first allowance she went immediately to the mall and found a cute, cuddly stuffed animal. It cost seven dollars more than her entire allowance. Thinking quickly, she made a deal with her brother. "Richard, you still haven't given me a birthday present. Why don't you just give me five dollars?" Richard forked over the five dollars, although he personally thought it was "stupid to spend money on a dumb animal." Still two dollars short, she asked, "Richard, could you loan me two dollars?" "If you pay me interest," he replied, and the deal was settled. Not three hours after receiving her first allowance, Debbie had spent it all and was in debt to her brother.

My wife and I sat back and waited for our daughter to learn her first lesson in financial responsibility. But a few days later, just when she was realizing she couldn't afford some things she really needed, Debbie received a birthday check from her grandmother. That carried her over until the next payday. But the next month she wasn't so lucky. When she ran short again she had to pass up some things she needed. The lesson hit home and she soon learned to spread out her resources more responsibly. Now she is an excellent shopper who rarely pays full price for anything. In fact, a couple of years after her stuffed animal episode, Debbie walked into the living room modeling an entire new outfit. When I commented on how nice it looked, she proudly asked, "How much do you think I paid?" After I guessed forty dollars, then thirty, then twenty, she said, "Nope. I got it all at a garage sale for fourteen dollars!" I couldn't help but remember her first allowance and her twenty-seven-dollar stuffed animal. She had come a long way!

An allowance or after-school job that provides a few dollars for spending money is a great way of learning responsibility. Handling their own money gives teenagers practice in living with the consequences of their decisions. They need freedom to make some mistakes and learn from their own decisions—whether good or bad.

Early adolescents also need increasing latitude in selecting their own clothes and styles of dress. By the time they reach junior high, your children should have the major say in what they wear. That doesn't mean you abdicate parental responsibility and let them wear outlandish styles. But it does mean they should be free to choose their clothes within broad limits. By early adolescence your role shifts from choosing your children's clothes the way you did when they were younger to setting an example of appropriate dress, advising, serving as a sounding board, and moderating your teenagers' tendencies to slavish conformity or outlandish dress. Here, as in so many other areas, we need to find a balance. Criticizing early adolescents for wanting to dress like their peers tells them we don't understand their needs, and it causes needless conflict. But doling out money for adolescents to fill their closets with designer clothes or outlandish styles is equally unwise.

This same principle applies in other areas. Twelve- and thirteen-year-olds need increasing freedom to make decisions—including some poor ones. But if we don't set some parameters we are equally unhelpful. During early adolescence, we should discuss decisions with them and set some limits, while still giving increased freedom. By late adolescence, they should be making most of their own decisions.

Be Sensitive to Sensitive Areas

Sharon, now a mother in her thirties, wrote me[7] about her experience of being too tall as a teenager:

As far back as the third grade I knew I was a misfit. I suffered intense shame over my height and searched for tall friends so I would not stand out. It really became painful a few years later when most of my girlfriends began to date. No one ever asked me out. Boys didn't want to be seen with me since I was taller than they were. High heels were out of the question and I was often teased. I tried to be good-natured but inside I was dying. Clothes and colors were also a problem. I could never wear green for that invariably brought forth comments about the "Jolly Green Giant." I learned how to slump to take a couple of inches off my height, but that ruined my posture.

Finally, around the age of sixteen, something changed. My friends were beginning to shoot up and that helped, but it was more than that. Suddenly I just didn't care anymore. Where I had avoided high heels before, I bought the sharpest spikes I could find. I even gave up the "two color" outfits that I had used to cut up my body into parts and began wearing chic solid color dresses and pantsuits. I was finally able to say "hang it" and be myself. It was a long time in coming, and I still have some inner scars from those terrible years, but I finally learned to like myself the way I am.

Sharon's feelings are common for teenagers who are struggling with the developmental task of comparing favorably with their peers. Any deviation from the norm can be acutely painful, but physical differences are especially disturbing. Teenagers can be incredibly insensitive and hurtful to their peers because of their own insecurity about their looks and size. Joking about others is their way of saying, "I'm normal. They are different."

You can help self-conscious adolescents by listening to their worries about their inadequacies or their differences. Don't quickly reassure them as soon as they express dissatisfaction with their abilities or looks. Draw them out and let them tell you how they feel. Tell them, "That must be hard, honey," or ask them how they feel. Then you might ask them if any of their friends have noticed or made comments. Sometimes this question will trigger several stories of how their peers tease them or make hurtful comments.

Once your teenagers tell you what they are experiencing, you are on your way. The biggest part of the solution is knowing someone understands. When you reach that point, you might ask how they are trying to handle the situation, or you might share a similar struggle you or a friend encountered. Throughout it all, however, remember that what your son or daughter needs most is not an answer but a sympathetic, listening ear. Once your teenagers know you understand, you can let them know that although it is painful now, these differences are usually gone in a few years and people will eventually be much more interested in who they are and what they do than how they look. You might even pull out one of your old pictures that is sure to provoke a laugh!

Help your teenagers realize that the important thing is how they *feel* about themselves. When Sharon began to accept herself, she stopped feeling weird and cared less about what other people thought. And when she stopped acting as though she were abnormal, other people stopped thinking of her as so different.

If we have taught our children from early years that they are created and loved by God, they will find it easier to cope with their differences. Our children need to know that our perspective and God's perspective is that they are valuable, gifted, significant, and lovable people just the way they are. Although it is inevitable that we must compete in our society, the most important thing is knowing who we are and developing and using our own gifts, not fulfilling everyone's expectations —or even our own.

Paul's analogy that the church is like a physical body with each part having its role to play[8] can be a reassuring perspective. Teenagers need to know that God doesn't want us all to be alike. The knowledge that conformity and competition are not in God's plan is also helpful. The apostle Paul, for example, wrote, "Let everyone be sure that he is doing his very best, for then he will have the personal satisfaction of work well done, and won't need to compare himself with someone else."[9] Although simply reading a verse or two of Scripture won't make your adolescents' emotional pain disappear, the knowledge that their parents and God understand their situation and value them just the way they are helps ease the hurt and lets them feel better about their uniqueness.

You can also help a teenager like Sharon by sharing practical ways of handling the hurts that come from insensitive people. You might share how they can take someone aside and say, "I know you may not realize it, but I feel very bad when you joke about my size." If that doesn't work, you can help them develop "comeback" lines when others tease them. By helping them communicate their feelings directly, or stand up to degrading challenges, you give a way to manage current struggles as well as helping develop confidence in their ability to solve problems and build honest relationships in the future. This helps with two of the developmental tasks of early adolescence: learning to compete and compare favorably with their peers and developing new relationships.

Watch Your Worry

Throughout this chapter we have tried to show how you can help your teenagers practice their upcoming adult roles. Two things may stand in the way: (1) your fear that they aren't ready to make good decisions and (2) your tendency to hang on too long. Let's face it, the changes your teenagers are experiencing can be frightening. They are learning to disagree and argue with you. They are practicing adultlike behaviors. They are starting to listen to their friends as much or more than to you. They are getting interested in the opposite sex. And they don't think through all of the consequences of their actions. Any one of these developments has the potential of making parents nervous—let alone the whole batch. In fact, this may be the most anxiety-producing part of parenting.

Didn't it bother you at least a little when your adolescent started acting negative or began to argue with you? Don't you worry a little when your teenagers are out with their friends at a new activity? Aren't you a little concerned when they start to date? And don't you wish they had better judgment? If you add in some memories of your dangerous adolescent explorations and the fear of losing control over your children, it is no wonder most parents are anxious about their adolescents. It is more abnormal *not* to worry at least a little. But be careful. If you let your worry get the best of you, it will make it a lot harder for your teenagers to separate from you. They will sense you are hanging on too tightly and start fighting more to get away.

Remind yourself that disagreements over clothes, hairstyles, curfews, and friends are not important primarily because of the rightness or wrongness of the issue. Instead, they are important because they represent your teenagers' efforts to emancipate themselves and assert their own opinions. Also, remind yourself that your teenagers are not trying to be obnoxious and upset or hurt you. Their goal is to put childhood behind them and learn to think for themselves and become independent, not make you miserable.

When thirteen-year-old Sherry's father accused her of "looking like a tramp," he let his anxieties get out of hand. That made it impossible for him to understand either his daughter or himself. It would have been so much better if he could have talked his feelings over with his wife or a friend or counselor. He could have said, "I get so mad when I see my daughter dress that way." Then he could have explored his angry feelings and the fears or guilt that lurked behind them. Once he understood his own emotions, he might have found it easier to understand Sherry's feelings and her need to move toward maturity.

If you find yourself upset with your teenagers' efforts to separate from you or if your teenagers accuse you of being rigid or babying them, talk your feelings over with a friend or spouse or counselor. They can help you sort out which of your concerns are legitimate and which reflect your own anxieties.

A Second Look

Your availability to understand and validate your adolescents' efforts at becoming adult will be important throughout their teenage years. It plays an especially important role, however, in helping early adolescents cope with their special developmental tasks of early adolescence. Early adolescents need your sensitive availability as they begin to move away from you and practice being more adult. They need your help in establishing new relationships, learning to compete with their peers, and testing out their feelings about their sexuality and their abilities to relate to the opposite sex. If they know you support their efforts at growing up, they feel freer to keep moving on toward greater independence and maturity. If things go well in early adolescence, your sons and daughters will get their feet wet with the waters of adulthood. By the time they reach fourteen or fifteen years of age, they will have:

- begun making new friends
- started practicing more masculine or feminine roles
- become increasingly ready to accept new challenges and compete with their peers
- established growing confidence in their ability to function outside the home and live at an emotional step away from you.

These abilities will still be a little fragile but they will have practiced them enough to be ready for middle adolescence — the next stage in their teenage years.

NOTES

1. Personal and clinical illustrations in this chapter are by Dr. Narramore unless otherwise indicated.
2. Proverbs 15:4a, NASB.
3. Proverbs 20:5.
4. Chapter 6.
5. Proverbs 13:20.
6. P. H. Dryer. "Sexuality during adolescence" in B. B. Wolman, ed. *Handbook of Developmental Psychology* (Englewood Cliffs, N.J.: Prentice Hall, 1982), 559-601.
7. Dr. Lewis.
8. Romans 12:3-8.
9. Galatians 6:4, *The Living Bible.*

*Middle
adolescents
are caught
between
their
conflicting
desire to
maturely
encounter
the adult
world and
their desire
to be taken
care of and
remain
dependent
on their
moms and
dads.*

THE AUTHORS

CHAPTER EIGHT MIDDLE ADOLESCENCE: ENCOUNTERING THE REAL WORLD

I will never forget the look on our sixteen-year-old Todd's face soon after he bought his first car, a ten-year-old, two-door Ford.[1] Behaving like a responsible adult, he had taken his car to our local Shell station to be serviced, parked it, and walked home. But when he came in the door we had to inform him that the car had apparently slipped out of gear and smashed into another car. How helpless and defeated Todd felt! He was devastated. "Here, Dad," he said morosely, handing me the keys. "You'd better take these. I can't seem to do anything right."

Todd's crisis is typical of middle adolescents. Between fourteen and sixteen or seventeen, your teenagers will move farther away from you emotionally and start cutting their cords of dependency more aggressively. They will begin to challenge you and other authorities. And they will take more responsibility for their own needs, decisions, and activities. Cars and telephones become bridges to the world outside the family. Dating, working part-time, and thinking about college and the future all make their appearance in the transition years of middle adolescence. Each of these activities helps your teenagers become more independent. They can also drastically increase the possibilities for failures and disappointments.

As your middle adolescents move toward adulthood, they will face at least five new developmental tasks or challenges.

- They have to find ways to reconcile their increasing freedom and independence and feelings of maturity with their longstanding desires to be taken care of by you
- They have to start growing out of their naive and somewhat self-centered view of life in order to face some of the difficult realities of the world
- They must integrate their maturing sexual desires and identities and learn to relate to the opposite sex in a more adult manner
- They must make some revisions in the way they perceive themselves and others
- They need to undergo some changes in their emotional lives that will enable them to handle their feelings more maturely and feel more solid and settled inwardly

In this chapter, we will describe the first three of these developmental steps. We will begin with the need your teenagers have to start resolving their conflict between dependency and independency.

Help! Life's Tougher Than I Thought

If early adolescents rush naively into new experiences thinking the world is their oyster, middle adolescents soon learn that someone is stepping on their oyster! As with Todd, their naive early adolescent excitement is shattered as they suddenly realize they are not the unlimited, powerful adults they imagined themselves to be. This triggers an extremely vulnerable period. One minute middle adolescents are feeling ready to face the challenges of adulthood. Minutes later, they bump into a problem and feel as helpless as a little child. Each failure challenges their optimism about life and makes them want to run back to the safety and security of mom and dad.

Remember what your children were like when they were sixteen- to twenty-four-month-old toddlers? They were learning to separate from you and alternated between wanting to do things for themselves and wanting you to do things for them. They started playing alone for longer periods of time and didn't cry or panic as quickly if you temporarily left their presence. Yet they periodically hustled back to you to show you what they had discovered or get a little support and love. Because they were becoming increasingly independent but still needed to return regularly for some emotional refueling and sharing of their explorations and accomplishments, Dr. Mahler labeled this the rapprochement (or reapproaching) period.

At a much more advanced level, middle adolescents go through a similar reapproaching phase. This is why you will probably hear an inflected "Mom?" the instant your middle adolescents come in the door from school. They want to know you are available in case they need you. Then, sons tend to head for the refrigerator or get on with their own activities, while daughters may seek you out and tell you a little about their day.

When middle adolescents check in for encouragement and support, they will probably be looking for one of three things. First, they may simply want emotional refueling. They love you and don't want to be shut off from your love and care. Second, they may want to share their excitement over an accomplishment or interesting incident in their lives. Like toddlers looking for a gleam in your eye as they show you their newest finding or accomplishment, middle adolescents want you to share in the excitement of their discoveries. Third, they may be looking for encouragement or help when they feel overwhelmed or in danger of failing.

Although your middle adolescent's periodic returns for emotional support may not look very different from your early adolescent's, they serve a different psychological purpose. Twelve- and thirteen-year-olds move away from you to start breaking the bonds of emotional dependency. They return when they are feeling lonely or frightened. The anxiety that pulls them back is triggered by their separation from your loving presence. Middle adolescents experience some separation anxiety, but they are more likely to be upset by the threatening prospects of coping with adult responsibilities. It is usually an encounter with an overwhelming task or a celebration of a success in coping with their world that brings a middle adolescent back to you, not so much their fears of being separated from your love.

Middle adolescents are like people caught on the ledge of a burning building. They know they can't go back to their former security, but in some ways the hot ledge feels safer than taking the plunge toward a safety net below. Between the safety of the net and the danger of staying put is one brief, frightening interlude. For your middle adolescent, the burning ledge is the increasingly unacceptable—yet sometimes appealing—dependency of earlier childhood. The net below is the visible yet untested net of their personal inner resources. Psychologists call this the rapprochement dilemma.

In order to jump off the ledge of dependency, your middle adolescents must edge away from you to test their own resources. They must prove to themselves that they don't have to give in to their childish wishes for you to protect or take over for them. But if they move away too quickly or too far, or if you aren't available when they come back for reassurance, they feel abandoned and cut off from the support they need.

As middle adolescents struggle with their conflicting desires between dependence and independence, some become vulnerable to feelings of depression. The optimism and enthusiasm of early adolescence are likely to be replaced with feelings of discouragement or failure. Finding out the world can be tough, losing their childhood innocence, breaking away from their previous closeness with you, and comparing themselves to their peers can create a lot of sadness. Some middle adolescents give in to their feelings of discouragement or helplessness by choosing to remain dependent. They elect the safety of childhood over the problems of adulthood. Others deny their wish to remain dependent on you by becoming demanding and bossy with their friends or siblings. They turn others into the needy ones and they become the strong ones.

The swaggering, tough-looking adolescent with a cigarette hanging between his lips is a classic example of someone trying to hide his underlying dependency or fears of adulthood by looking overly self-assured. Other middle adolescents mask their fears of failure or their wishes to be taken care of by throwing themselves into a frenzy of activity. As long as they are active, they don't have to think about their loss of your support or the possibility of encountering failure. Still others frantically seek to fill the void created by losing the security blanket of your love by trading it for a security blanket of their peers.

Anger often peaks at this age as teenagers struggle with their conflicting desires to be independent but also to be taken care of. When their desires to be independent predominate, they can deny all of their weaknesses and dependencies and be stubbornly independent. Yet because their adult feelings aren't yet sufficiently settled, many blame their parents or find other scapegoats for their upsetting emotions. In the process, they can suddenly turn parents into enemies blocking their path to maturity instead of friends wanting to help them on their way. During this phase, they are likely to see you as either all good or all bad. Few middle adolescents are able to realize that their parents are normal humans with their share of both strengths and weaknesses. Under the pressures and frustrations of this difficult time of life they either love you or hate you!

All of these coping styles can be used a little by normal middle adolescents. Somehow they have to cope with their mixed feelings about becoming adult. Middle adolescents who don't resolve this dilemma are likely to keep living it throughout their lives. They may attach themselves to a mate or friend who will take care of them or fight their battles for them much as you did when they were younger. Or they may remain emotionally distant from others in order to avoid being absorbed into childish dependency, which would mean losing their sense of autonomy and freedom. Adolescents who sacrifice independence for the safety of childhood ties will stunt their growth and never become mature and independent. But teenagers who reject emotional closeness in order to demonstrate their independence may cut themselves off from close and loving relationships as adults.

The healthiest adolescents are those who learn to tackle difficult problems alone when necessary but are capable of asking for help and being mutually interdependent. They don't fear being engulfed or controlled when they admit their needs but they aren't afraid to work alone either. In chapter 10, we will discuss ways of helping your teenagers find that balance.

Facing Reality

Driving home from work one Tuesday evening, I tuned in to a documentary on unwed mothers. The reporter was interviewing a fourteen-year-old girl who had just given birth to a baby boy. The girl talked freely about getting pregnant, giving birth, dropping out of school, and becoming a mother. Near the close of the interview, the reporter asked, "Are you going to start using birth control now?" Quite nonchalantly, the girl spontaneously answered, "No." Taken aback, the usually unflappable reporter blurted out, "Why not? You might get pregnant again." "I know that happens sometimes," the girl replied, "but I don't worry about it. Besides, it's just like having a baby brother!"

A few days later I was walking through our local shopping mall and heard loud rock music blaring above the usual din of noise. Looking toward the sound, I faced a fifteen- or sixteen-year-old adolescent carrying his portable stereo and wearing a T-shirt boldly proclaiming, "If it's too loud, you're too old!"

These teenagers were showing exaggerated, but not uncommon, tendencies associated with the second developmental hurdle facing middle adolescents: The need to learn to face reality. They were highly lacking in both self-awareness and sensitivity to other people. The unwed mother's total unconcern about becoming pregnant seems almost incomprehensible to responsible adults. And the young man's insensitivity is an irritating phenomenon. But many early and middle adolescents are nearly as cavalier and out of touch with reality. Whether in premarital sex, reckless driving, or going to a party where drugs and alcohol are available, many early and middle adolescents do not yet have the ability to assess a situation for danger, judge reality accurately, and respond accordingly. They are still living under the narcissistic illusion that nothing bad can happen to them or that some providential parent will magically rescue or protect them.

Many young adolescents, for example, say they did not know that they could become pregnant by having intercourse "just once." Others bitterly say, "I knew it happened to other people but I didn't think it could happen to me." The fact that car accidents are the number-one killer of adolescents reflects this inability to assess potential dangers realistically. Middle adolescents assume it always happens to the "other guy."

Much of the advice of the book of Proverbs is intended to help budding adults learn a more realistic and responsible view of life. Proverbs 1:4, for example, says that the book was written "for giving prudence to the simple [naive], knowledge and discretion to the young."[2] Then the book goes on to encourage youth to listen to their parents' instruction,[3] to avoid negative peer influences,[4] and to learn discernment.[5] The entire book can be seen as wise counsel for adolescents approaching adulthood. Given the naivete of early adolescents, that counsel is especially timely for middle adolescents emerging from that self-centered stage.

Over the years of middle adolescence you should see a gradual shift from self-centeredness and naivete toward an increased sensitivity to others and to the realities of the world. Although that process is usually not completed until late adolescence or young adulthood, middle adolescents start moving in that direction. These changes occur partly because middle adolescents have more raw intellectual ability and life experience than they did a few years earlier. Many middle adolescents, for example, have seen a friend or acquaintance injured or even killed while drinking and driving. Others know peers whose lives have been damaged by drugs or who have become pregnant outside of marriage. These can be somber lessons for near adults.

Middle adolescents also become more realistic because of some internal changes. As they grow emotionally less dependent on you, they are forced to pay increasing attention to the world around them. Since you are no longer around to warn and protect them, middle adolescents must take on these life-preserving responsibilities for themselves. If they don't watch out for themselves, no one will. Taken together, the combination of your middle adolescents' intellectual development, widening life experiences, and increasing independence from you should help them become more alert to the consequences of their behavior and take a more accurate and realistic approach to life.

Maturing Sexuality

At the same time middle adolescents are struggling to find a new balance between dependency and independency and face the realities of the adult world, they encounter a third important developmental hurdle—integrating their maturing sexuality into their personalities. During preadolescence, your sons and daughters became more aware of their physical distinctiveness from the opposite sex. In early adolescence, they practiced relating to members of that sex by fantasizing about someone they had a crush on or by "going around" with someone—often for only a few weeks. As middle adolescents, your sons' and daughters' increasing maturity and the upsurge in both their biological sexuality and their interest in the opposite sex prepare them for the next step in their heterosexual development.

The heterosexual hurdle of middle adolescence actually presents your sons and daughters with a threefold task. *First,* they must learn to relate more frequently and seriously with the opposite sex. Most middle adolescents begin to date sometime in this period of life and their attitude toward themselves and the opposite sex undergoes important shifts. They are a little more confident about their masculinity or femininity than they were a couple of years earlier and they are a little less threatened by the opposite sex. Their maturing heterosexual relationships will probably be accompanied by less self-centeredness and an increased ability to give to others. You may notice a significant decrease in self-preoccupation and an increase in preoccupation with a boy or girlfriend.

Second in your middle adolescents' heterosexual development is their need to learn to feel more masculine and feminine in their relationships with you. Instead of seeing you and your mate as the only adult males or females in the family, middle adolescents need to start seeing themselves as being adultly masculine or feminine like you. For fifteen years, "eighteen-foot giant" mothers have seemed so big and mature that their daughters doubted they could ever be their equal. And "eighteen-foot giant" fathers have seemed so adult that their sons wondered if they could ever compare.

Since teenagers won't wake up one morning and suddenly feel like competent adults, they must find ways to gradually feel more adult in comparison to their "giants." Have you noticed, for example, how many middle adolescents pass through a stage of conflict and irritation with their same-sex parent? Everything that parent does is suddenly "stupid," "wrong," or "awful." Middle adolescent girls can be especially obnoxious to their mothers. And middle adolescent boys may be constantly complaining or fighting with their fathers. Although not all adolescents go through this angry, critical phase, some dissatisfaction or competition with the same-sex parent is normal and even necessary.

In order to throw off their childish perceptions of themselves, your middle adolescents must decide, "I no longer want to bask in mom's or dad's maturity. Now I want to be as big and strong and as adult as they are." Since middle adolescents haven't traveled this road before, they don't know how to gradually develop their feelings of competency while easing you off your parental pedestal. Instead, they unconsciously decide that the best way to build themselves up is to chop you down to size!

By criticizing and complaining and putting her mother down, a teenage daughter can feel more adult and feminine by comparison. And by chopping down his dad, a middle adolescent son can feel more manly and adult. Seen in this light, your middle adolescents' angry attacks and criticisms of their same-sex parent are sometimes their way of saying, "I am becoming an adult," "I know as much as you," "I can do some things better (more adultlike) than you," or "I can be a better man (or woman) than you." Your middle adolescents' anger at their same-sex parent also makes it easier for them to separate from you and give up their feelings of dependency. It is easier to move away from someone you resent and find fault with than someone you idealize and need.

If this faultfinding and anger is difficult for you to understand, think how your teenagers handle competition on the soccer or football field or in other contests. Do they appreciate contestants on the opposing team and calmly pursue their goal in love? Probably not. If they are normal, they get anxious and excited before the competition, fight for all they are worth during the game, and then gloat over how good they are if they win, or yell and scream how awful the other team or the referee was if they lose. A win helps them feel adult. A loss makes them feel like childish inferiors.

In the race to become adult males or females, you are your same-sex adolescent's first competitor. Your sons and daughters will feel like winners if they start seeing themselves as being as masculine or feminine as you. Criticizing and fighting and chopping you down to size are some of the ways they try to beat you at the game of life. Only as they chalk up some wins over mom or dad can they reshape their self-image from that of children to adult men or women.

The *third* part of your middle adolescents' sexual development
is learning to control their sexual desires and feelings. The upsurge in sexual energy and awareness that began at puberty nears
its peak in middle adolescence. Fifteen- and sixteen-year-olds are
biologically mature enough to engage in sexual intercourse and
produce children. They are socially mature enough to relate more
seriously to the opposite sex. And they are incredibly curious
about human sexuality. When all of these are added together, it is
little wonder that most middle adolescents have to struggle with
their sexual drives and feelings.

Like the rapprochement dilemma and the need to increasingly
confront reality, your teenagers' sexual feelings and their movement toward the other sex can create tremendous emotional
upheavals. On the one hand they are being propelled toward
heterosexuality by God-given processes of biological and
psychological development. On the other hand, they lack confidence in their ability to relate to the opposite sex and they wonder
how to handle their feelings and desires. This creates nagging
questions: Am I attractive? Are my sexual feelings normal? Am I a
competent male or female? Is it sinful to masturbate? and, How
far should I go on a date?

To cope with these questions, adolescents turn to one of several
strategies. Some try to ignore their anxiety over their sexuality by
rushing headlong into dating and sexual activity. Even as thirteen-
or fourteen-year-olds, they want to date regularly and seriously.
They are excessively boy or girl crazy and prone to becoming
overly involved physically. Other middle adolescents try to deny
their sexual feelings by neglecting their hygiene or dress or diet.
By overeating or dressing in ways unconsciously calculated to
make them unattractive to the opposite sex, they avoid facing their
sexual feelings. If the opposite sex is not interested in them, they
have nothing to fear from their sexual urges.

Other adolescents bathe or wash obsessively to convince themselves of their "cleanliness." Still other adolescents try ascetic
self-denial to block pleasurable but frightening sexual feelings
from awareness. They build a rigidly disciplined or intellectual

life-style or develop compulsive interests in religious or philosophical topics to avoid their frightening physical and sexual
desires.

Sixteen-year-old Bill threw himself into his studies and church
activities. He made himself an hour-by-hour schedule beginning
at 6:00 A.M. each day and carefully filled in every slot until 11:00 at
night. He was a voracious reader and spent a lot of time reading
books on self-sacrifice and discipline. Although there were several
girls in his circle of friends at church, Bill never dated. He spent
most of his social time in discussions about public problems,
philosophical issues, or theological questions. Sometimes he
commented on how "frivolous" or "superficial" dating and other
social activities were.

Although some of Bill's perceptions and commitments were
good—and even admirable—he went too far. His excessive emphasis on the intellectual and spiritual side of life was a way of
avoiding his social and sexual and spontaneous side. Even the
Bible indicates we can be too religious: "Do not be overrighteous,
neither be overwise—why destroy yourself?"[6] Righteousness and
wisdom are great virtues, but denying an entire part of your
personality with a one-sided emphasis on another isn't spirituality.
It is a way of avoiding frightening or guilt-inducing thoughts or
feelings.

If you think back to your own adolescence, you will probably see
a little of yourself in one or more of these strategies for coping
with sexuality. Normal adolescents may resort to a little of any or
all of them. Major problems only come when teenagers try either
to deny totally their sexuality or to give free reign to it. Since
middle adolescents are not ready for the intimacies of sexuality,
premature sexual activities create a tangle of guilt, confusion, and
hurt. But since it is time to start relating more deeply to the
opposite sex, a denial of sexuality isn't helpful either. The ideal is
for middle adolescents to be aware of their maturing sexuality, to
feel good about it, and to gradually develop meaningful relationships with the other sex. In chapter 18, we will discuss specific
ways of helping your adolescents find this balance.

Three Down, Two to Go

This completes our introduction to the first three developmental hurdles facing middle adolescents. Between the years of fourteen and sixteen or seventeen, your sons and daughters need to (1) reconcile their increasing independence with their conflicting desires to be taken care of and to remain dependent, (2) start growing out of their naive and overly idealistic view of life so that they can face reality more clearly, and (3) solidify their sexual identities and come to grips with their sexual desires. In chapters 10 and 11 we will look at ways you can help your middle adolescents with these tasks. Before we do that, however, we want to look at two other important developmental tasks of middle adolescence. They are the topics of chapter 9.

NOTES

1. Personal and clinical illustrations in this chapter are by Dr. Lewis.
2. Proverbs 1:4.
3. Proverbs 1:8.
4. Proverbs 2:1-9.
5. Proverbs 1:10-19.
6. Ecclesiastes 7:16.

CHAPTER NINE
MIDDLE ADOLESCENCE: CHANGING ATTITUDES AND FEELINGS

Soon after he began his sophomore year of high school, Keith,[1] a bright and inquisitive middle adolescent, started pestering his teachers. He asked question after question, such as, "Why do we have to learn algebra if we're not going to be mathematicians?" and "What use is this in real life?" When his teachers' explanations failed to satisfy him, Keith decided that education was a "vicious cycle" in which teachers taught useless facts so students could teach the same useless information to the next generation.

Like Keith, many fourteen- to seventeen-year-olds begin challenging their teachers, parents, pastors, and other authorities. It is as if their brains opened up and a scanner signaled, "Look how childish you have been till now. All your life, your parents and teachers have told you what to do and how to think. Do you really believe everything they taught you? Do you want to remain a child or do you want to grow up and become like your parents and make your own decisions?" *This questioning of authority grows out of the fourth major developmental task facing middle adolescents. They need to make major changes in their understanding of themselves and others. They must stop seeing themselves as smaller, less powerful, and less intelligent than adults. They must develop the confidence that they can think for themselves and do much of what you and other adults used to do for them.*

Every stage of life brings a maturing understanding of ourselves and others, but teenagers need to take some quantum leaps ahead in their self-perceptions. Preadolescents, for example, have to recognize their increasing intelligence in order to start distinguishing themselves mentally from their parents. Early adolescents have to see themselves as less needy and dependent in order to start separating from parents and practicing adult behaviors. Middle adolescents must start seeing themselves as more adult sexually in order to start taking a more serious interest in the opposite sex.

Each of these developments requires a reworking of your teenagers' childhood self-images as well as their images of you and other adults. Teenagers must increasingly see themselves as being as intelligent or potentially competent and wise as adults.

Although your teenagers need to modify their self-concepts throughout the entire span of adolescence, we have chosen to stress those changes in detail in this chapter because many of them occur during the middle adolescent years. These changes have the potential to radically reorient your adolescents' lives and in many ways are the most important happenings of all their teenage years. They impact your teenagers' self-concepts, their attitudes toward authority, their values and commitments and consciences, and their ability to take responsibility for their own lives.

The Birth of Self-Esteem

Before we can understand the radical changes that must take place in our teenagers' attitudes toward themselves and others, we need to take a brief look back at the way children's attitudes toward themselves and others are formed. At birth, your infants' personalities have fantastic potential and a rough outline of their distinctive physical, mental, and emotional features. But it takes years for their unique self-concept to take shape. From early infancy, every experience influences your children's attitudes toward themselves and others. Positive and loving experiences lay a foundation for good feelings about themselves, and negative and destructive experiences undermine their confidence in their abilities. Two aspects of this development are especially important. The first is a process psychologists call internalization.

Internalization is the process of taking into one's own personality the attitudes and values and characteristics of key people in one's life—especially one's parents. Each encounter with another person leaves an impressionable child with an imprint of how he saw himself and others in that situation. If a toddler's glee over being able to run across the room by himself is matched by the excited approval of his mother, he stores in his mind a picture showing him ably exploring his world with the approval of his mother. Repeated experiences like this build self-confidence and help him feel good about his ability to cope with life. They also link a happy emotion to their memory of mom's approval.

Years later, that ex-toddler can approach new tasks with confidence because he has a picture of himself as competent to try new things, a picture of an approving parent, and an enjoyable emotion about his ability to function independently. His mother's approving smile has been incorporated into his personality where it keeps offering encouragement for years to come. Loving, peaceful, and happy experiences in early life are like money in the bank. Children who build up a good account of emotional currency will be able to draw on their account throughout their lives. By mirroring your children's joy and happiness and encouraging them to try new tasks, you have built up their self-esteem and helped them create a healthy emotional bank account.

If a toddler's explorations are frequently met by an anxious or disapproving parent, he represses his excited feelings and incorporates mental pictures of himself as bad for wanting to explore and of a disapproving parent. Years later, when faced with similar opportunities to explore his world, that teenager or young adult may be hesitant to try, because that would conjure up his inner disapproving memories and emotions. His youthful feelings of pleasure and excitement have been buried beneath his parents' disapproval and he tends to feel depleted or void of enjoyable emotions. When he goes to his emotional bank he finds his account of enjoyable experiences is overdrawn.

Negative early interactions can even inhibit a child's ability to learn. When parents fail to reflect their children's joy in exploring and learning, some children lose interest in all new experiences and knowledge. They become depressed, turn to other pursuits, or plod through their studies with little enthusiasm because they lack encouraging, enjoyable memories and motivations.

Over the years of childhood, your sons' and daughters' internalized pictures of their interactions with you and other significant people gradually shape their attitudes toward themselves and others. Just as your children pick up some of your physical mannerisms and habits and patterns of speech, they also incorporate your attitudes and values and emotional reactions. At first, your children's memories of you are very concrete pictures. As a young child reaches for a forbidden cookie jar, for example, he may actually visualize you walking into the kitchen and catching him.

Over a period of years this concrete "inner parent," which is simply an internalized version of you, gradually matures into a more general set of values and standards and ideals and attitudes. Even when you aren't present, these inner attitudes keep reminding them that they are loved and cared for and that they should abide by certain values. When your adolescents do well at school, or finish a chore around the house, these memories and attitudes offer approval much as you used to when they were younger. And when they forget to mow the yard or do a chore, their inner mental images remind or scold them much as you did in the past. Taken together, these memories make up a good deal of your children's personalities. They form the foundation of your children's self-concepts as well as their attitudes and values.

Consider the development of their consciences, for example. Because your sons and daughters have taken in many of your attitudes and values and feelings, their consciences will reflect a lot of you. Some of their standards and ideals will probably be like yours or your spouse's, and some of their ways of motivating themselves to live up to their ideals will probably bear a strong resemblance to your methods of motivating them or your ways of motivating yourself. In fact, have you noticed that sometimes your own conscience still sounds a little like your own mother's or father's? If you listen to yourself the next time you succeed or fail, you may notice that your inner exclamations of delight or despair or criticism, and even your tone of voice, sound remarkably like your mother or father did years ago. That's because you spontaneously took in many of their emotional reactions and ways of correcting you when you misbehaved.

Your teenagers' impressions of others develop in much the same way as their attitudes toward themselves. If the bulk of their interactions with important people in their lives were happy, they tend to have positive expectations of other people they meet. But if many of their childhood relationships were touched by anger, depression, anxiety, or lack of involvement, they develop an expectation that most other people will be the same. As your children move into high school and start developing friendships beyond the family, their perceptions of others will be especially important. Teenagers who tend to see others as likable and friendly will find it easier to make friends and get along well. But adolescents who expect their peers to be angry or rejecting or preoccupied or controlling will have a harder time building meaningful relationships.

Living in a World of Giants

At the same time your sons' and daughters' self-concepts are being shaped by their experiences with you and others, they are also impacted by another process that begins largely in their own minds. Although we can't know infants' specific thoughts, we do know that even before they are able to speak, they have a wide range of desires and wishes and primitive thoughts or perceptions. Infants feel hungry, for example, and want to be fed. They also feel angry if their needs aren't met.

Since infants and toddlers haven't matured enough to perceive reality accurately, they engage in a very primitive form of thinking. As best as we can understand, they seem to do a lot of magical thinking. If they want their mother's breast or a bottle or a toy, for example, they have a mental image of that object. Then when mother supplies the breast or bottle, they seem to think their wishes have magically made that happen. Each time their desires result in their wishes being fulfilled, their belief that they have power to bring about whatever they desire is reinforced.

Around a year of age, children gradually begin to find out that their wishes aren't as magical and powerful as they first seemed. They hear mom and dad say no and find out they can't always have their way. But even then, some of their magical thinking persists. Older children often daydream that they are as strong and knowledgeable as their parents. They imagine that they can settle scores with the neighborhood bully. Or they identify with television cartoon heroes who have extraordinary strength or cunning. In these experiences they picture themselves with fantastic magical attributes that they wish to have but don't possess.

These imaginations impact your children's developing self-concepts as much as their actual relationships with you. Their fantasies combine with the reality of their own achievements and the internalized pictures of themselves, received from you, to shape their image of themselves. Instead of seeing themselves as they really are or as you saw them, they see themselves as a mixture of those two pictures and their own childhood fantasies.

But the story doesn't end there.

As we saw in chapter 6, parents look like omnipotent, omniscient, eighteen-foot giants to their children. Consequently, when your children developed their self-concepts they didn't picture themselves as three or four or five feet tall children with parents who were five foot nine. Instead, they saw themselves as tiny little shrimp living in a world of eighteen-foot giants. No matter how well they did in comparison to other children, they still saw themselves as extremely small or powerless in relationship to you. Imagine how you would perceive yourself if you lived with two eighteen-foot giants that weighed five or six hundred pounds. Even if your giants were warm and loving, you would still feel inferior or small.

This combination of developments means that the self-images your children bring to adolescence are not based solely on objective perceptions of themselves and others. Instead, they are built up from the mix of their actual abilities, the way other people have treated them, their childlike fantasies, and their perceptions of themselves in relationship to the eighteen-foot giants that live around them. In some ways, your children may have some very realistic images of themselves; in some ways they will overestimate themselves; and in some ways they will underestimate themselves.

This somewhat unrealistic self-concept is the reason teenagers have to undergo some major changes in their attitudes toward themselves and others. *In order to learn to see themselves and others realistically, your sons and daughters will gradually have to bring all of these perceptions into a more objective balance. Finding that balance is the fourth developmental hurdle facing middle adolescents.* It requires growing out of both their overexaggeration of themselves and their underevaluation of themselves.

Settling Emotions

This brings us to the fifth developmental task of middle adolescence. At the same time fourteen- to seventeen-year-olds are developing more objective attitudes toward themselves and others, they also need to experience changes in their emotional lives. Fourteen-year-old Katie, for example, seems to be living on an emotional roller coaster. When everything is peaceful and going her way, Katie is a delight to be around. She is happy and spontaneous and full of life. But the minute she runs into trouble or has a misunderstanding with a friend, Katie loses it. She is also hypersensitive around her mother and constantly complaining about her younger sisters.

"She's in my room!" Katie protests, or "Mom, she looked at me that way again!" Sometimes she comes excitedly home from school to share about her day, and sometimes she comes home in a depressed funk or bitter anger announcing, "I hate him," "She hates me," or "We hate each other." Like Katie, many middle adolescents go through a period of strong emotionality. Their glandular changes, the necessity of coping with major physical and social developments, and their upsurge of interest in the opposite sex combine to shake their emotional equilibrium. Feelings become increasingly difficult to manage and even small changes in routines or imagined slights and rejections cause major upsets. They can be easily frightened and confused by their emotions.

This increased emotionality means that you will need to help your sons and daughters learn to handle their emotions. Specifically, most teenagers need to experience growth in four areas of their emotional lives.

First, they need to become more comfortable with their feelings—both positive and negative. They need to become less troubled by strong feelings of love and joy as well as intense feelings of fear, discouragement, and anger.

Second, they need to learn that strong and even conflicting emotions (like love and anger) can exist together without causing damage. They need to find out they can truly love someone and still be angry at them. Early adolescents, for example, may angrily announce, "I hate him. I never want to see him again." Older adolescents are more able to admit, "I love him and I hate him" or

"He makes me so mad. I wish I didn't like him."

Third, teenagers need to develop clear boundaries between their own thoughts and feelings and the thoughts and feelings of others. Early adolescents often confuse their own thoughts and emotions with the emotions and thoughts of others. When they are angry with a friend they may think, "She hates me," instead of, "I hate her." During middle and late adolescence, your teenagers need to grow out of this confusion.

Fourth, teenagers need to learn how to communicate both their positive and negative feelings appropriately. They need to move beyond temper tantrums, fits of anger, and depressed withdrawal so they can communicate their fears and angers and joys more directly and maturely.

This maturing of your adolescents' emotional lives can be seen as a series of developmental trends that began in infancy. Infants and children have very distinctive ways of handling their emotions. In early life, their feelings are intense and uncontrolled. They can also be exceedingly upsetting. Infants whose anger is unattended, for example, may become enraged and afraid they will destroy or hurt the very people and things they need. Infants and toddlers whose cries go unattended may cry themselves into an uncontrollable panic or, if neglected long enough, into a despairing, listless depression.

Because infants' and toddlers' feelings can be overwhelming, mothers and other caregivers have to function as their emotional control system. When your own infants cried, you probably determined what was wrong and tried to help. If they were anxious, you picked them up and gently quieted them. If they were angry or distressed, you let them express those feelings without retaliating or abandoning them. Your gentle talk told your children, "I know you are frightened or angry or upset, but I am not. I will help you until we can calm those feelings." Over a period of years, your children internalized your soothing talk and gentle explanations until they learned to quiet and control themselves a lot like you used to.

The emotional lives of infants have another distinctive feature.

Infants can hardly tell the difference between their own feelings and someone else's—especially their mothers.' When infants feel fine, they assume their mother and the whole world feels fine. When they are upset or angry, they assume their mother and the whole world feels the same. This is a precursor of the older child who angrily blurts out, "You hate me!" when momentarily hating you.

A little of this confusion is normal, but as children mature they need to gain a clearer understanding of the difference between their feelings and the feelings of others. People who regularly attribute their own feelings to others are bound for untold interpersonal conflicts. Instead of recognizing and acknowledging their uncomfortable feelings, they accuse teachers or friends or fellow workers of all kinds of negative motives or emotions.

We can summarize the changes your sons and daughters need to make in their emotional lives during childhood and adolescence like this. They need to progress:

FROM:	TO:
intense emotional reactions without any balancing intellectual understanding	emotional reactions balanced by intellectual understanding and broader perceptions of life
impulsive and immediate emotional reactions	more thoughtful, yet still rich and spontaneous, emotional expressions
being at the mercy of their environment	being sensitive to but not overly dependent on the environment
confusing their feelings with the feelings of others	distinguishing between their feelings and the feelings of others
a tendency to be overwhelmed by upsetting emotions	being comfortable with strong emotions

As your adolescents experience this maturing process, their inner lives become progressively stronger and more settled. Instead of vacillating rapidly between highs of ecstasy and lows of depression, they will become more balanced in most of their emotional experiences. They will learn to experience a range of feelings and to tolerate conflicting emotions because they realize

that in time their positive emotions can prevail over even turbulent
or depressing or angry ones.

Remaking the Inner Parent

This completes our survey of the five developmental challenges facing teenagers between the years of fourteen and sixteen
or seventeen. Middle adolescents need to:

- find ways of reconciling their increasing independency with
  their longstanding desires to be dependent on others
- start growing out of their naive and self-centered view of life in
  order to view the world more realistically
- integrate their maturing sexual desires and identities into their
  personalities
- make major changes in the way they think of themselves and
  others
- develop a more balanced and mature emotional life.

These developmental tasks can be understood as ways your
teenagers leave behind their dependency on both their real
parents and their inner psychological parents. For all of their lives
your teenagers have seen you as their authority figures, their
physical and emotional providers, their rescuers, and their moral
and spiritual models. They have also seen you as their major
source of love, the regulators of their self-esteem, and the control-
lers of their emotions and impulsivity. Either through your actual
presence or your inner psychological presence, you have taken
these responsibilities for your children.

Now, as adolescents, they must move away from both their
physical and psychological dependency on you. They will never
leave behind their nurturing, guiding, and security-providing
memories of you, but they must rework them in order to see
themselves as able to do many of the things you used to do for
them. Instead of relying wholly on their memories of your values
to guide their choices, for example, they must learn to judge

situations for themselves. Instead of naively assuming all of your spiritual and political decisions are inspired, they need to rethink them for themselves. And instead of feeling good about themselves because you approve of them, they must learn to feel good about themselves because they believe they are doing what is right for them. Your years of love and your values and perspectives have provided the framework and foundation for their attitudes, values, and decisions; but they must rework them if they are going to become their own.

Thirty-eight-year-old Ruth came for counseling for persistent doubts about her adequacy as a wife and mother. She worried incessantly that she was harming her children or failing them. She felt she was a poor cook and housewife. She felt she should enjoy entertaining company for her husband. And she felt she was never good enough. When her husband pointed out her many strengths, Ruth appreciated it momentarily but didn't really believe him.

As therapy progressed, it turned out that Ruth's mother had been a "supermom." She was a leader at her church and involved in PTA. She was a perfect housewife, an outstanding cook, a great hostess, and a sacrificial mother. Unfortunately, Ruth wasn't like her mother in any of these ways. She was an adequate cook but not "outstanding." She liked eating out more than cooking at home. And frankly, her three children often got on her nerves. When she compared her performance with her mental image of her "supermother," she fell painfully short.

During therapy Ruth realized how dependent she still was on her memories of her mother. Even though her mother had already passed away, Ruth didn't feel free to set her own standards for cleanliness, cooking, entertaining, or parenting. Her mother's super standards were etched so firmly in her mind that Ruth wasn't emotionally free to set her own. Anytime she deviated from her mother's expectations she condemned herself and felt inferior and inadequate. One day in desperation she cried out, "I still feel like a child. Even though I'm thirty-eight years old, I'm still trying to please my mother."

Thirty-five-year-old John had the opposite reaction to his memories of his parents. His domineering father taught him a detailed set of legalistic "No-no's." Instead of trying to live up to his father's standards, John left the church at eighteen and made a career of rebelling against his father's values. He drank heavily, left his wife and children, and generally opposed everything his father stood for. Rebellion was John's way of trying to throw off his father's rigid standards and free himself from slavery to a memory of a parent he could never please. Unfortunately, his new life-style wasn't free at all. John was actually as driven to rebel against his inner parent as Ruth was to please hers. His efforts to do the opposite of everything his father wanted reflected the same bondage to the memory of his dad that he felt to his actual father twenty years earlier. If he had truly developed his own values, he would not have been so driven and bound to his self-destructive behavior.

Ruth's and John's struggles to separate from their inner parents were not unusual. As an adult, Ruth kept trying belatedly to win her mother's approval and John kept trying to force his father to accept him as he was by refusing to live up to his standards. All of us have at least a few of these struggles. If our parents wanted us to be doctors or missionaries or educators, it can be difficult to settle for something else. Whether our parents were conservative or liberal, politically and religiously, it can be very difficult to consider anything different. And if our parents were critical or aloof or demanding, it is often hard for us to outgrow these lifelong patterns of reacting.

Children and adolescents who feel that they can never please their parents, or teenagers whose parents make them feel guilty for thinking their own thoughts or doing things their own ways, have special difficulties growing away from their "inner parents." They may struggle for years to throw off their inner doubts and fears and criticisms. Your teenagers will find it easier to become less dependent on their inner memories of you if they know you love them just the way they are. That way they can walk away from childhood with a picture of an approving parent who has confidence in their abilities to make good decisions to enjoy and to cope responsibly with life. This inner parent frees teenagers to become what God intended them to be.

Most teenagers do not jettison their parents' values or reject all of their ways of looking at life as they go through the process of reshaping their understanding of themselves and others. Instead, they go through a stage in which they test out their ability to take care of themselves, make their own decisions, and select their personal standards in order to prove they no longer need to be dependent on you. Once they have done this, they are free to adopt many of your values and to build on your example and love, while mixing in new role models, to mold their own unique identities. The end result of this process is that they should no longer feel the need to be taken care of by you or to be like you in order to feel good about themselves. They should be able to take care of themselves, select their own values, and feel good about developing and using their own unique gifts and talents. In short, they will have become like you in the sense that they can run their lives as relatively mature adults, but not like you in a carbon-copy way.

What's Normal?

On several occasions, we have discussed the increased independence, competitiveness, and negativism you can expect to see at different stages of adolescence. By now you may be asking, How much of this is normal? Most parents don't mind a little negativism, and most parents want their teenagers to become more independent. But where do we draw the line between normal efforts at being independent and just plain obnoxious or even pathological hostility?

Every child is different, but we have a few guidelines. Normal early and middle adolescents will probably show one or more of the following characteristics:

- increased assertiveness
- more direct expression of their own opinions about clothes,

entertainment, politics, family activities, etc.
- "forgetting" to do their chores or family responsibilities
- complaining about chores and family activities
- "goofing off" or "being silly"—especially around their friends
- making a few decisions you disagree with
- keeping some secrets from you
- occasional stubbornness
- periods of a critical or condemning attitude toward parents or other authorities.

Although these reactions can be irritating or upsetting, a little of any or all of them are well within the normal range.

By contrast, a relatively small portion of adolescents display one or more of the following characteristics:

- chronic irritability and negativism
- rebellion or defiance
- a "don't care" attitude toward parents and all authorities
- an inability to work cooperatively, even with their peers
- frequent depressing or raging outbursts
- prolonged angry withdrawal.

These reactions are generally beyond the normal range. They are usually caused by teenagers' longstanding negative feelings about themselves, a lack of understanding and communication in the family, a lack of inner emotional stability and strength, or the feeling that their parents somehow don't trust them to grow up. If your adolescents are consistently displaying these attitudes or behavior, we recommend you seek out professional help. They may just reflect a passing phase, but a professional can help you determine that and get to the root of the problem if there is one.

Middle Adolescent Highlights

As your middle adolescents move toward maturity, they will be making major changes in their perceptions of themselves and others and in their emotional lives. They will almost certainly question you and other adults as never before. They may also go through periods of intense emotions. At times they will be loving and excited and at times they will be angry or discouraged. At times they will need you and at times they will be stubbornly independent.

Overall, however, you should see your sons and daughters gradually becoming clearer about who they are and what they want and how they feel. They will start accepting more and more adult responsibilities. They will start facing life a little more realistically. And they will become increasingly settled emotionally. All of these changes will reflect their decreasing emotional dependence on you and their increasing maturity and confidence in their own resources. Here is a summary of the distinctive features of middle adolescence.

AGES
- Fourteen to seventeen for girls
- Fifteen to eighteen for boys

DEVELOPMENTAL TASKS
- Reconcile their needs to be increasingly independent with their desires to be taken care of
- Start growing out of the naive optimism and narcissism of early adolescence
- Become more comfortable with their sexual feelings and in their relationships with the opposite sex
- Reshape their mental images of themselves as children into more adult self-images and understandings
- Become more comfortable with their emotions and learn to handle them more maturely

CHARACTERISTICS
- Optimism and enthusiasm of early adolescence are replaced with increased realism and, sometimes, a period of depression

- Increase in adult responsibilities such as work and driving
- Anxiety over coping with adult responsibilities
- Vacillation between going ahead with adult activities and shying away from them
- Periodical returns to mom and dad for propping up, encouragement, and validation of their successes
- Self-esteem is not firmly established and is highly vulnerable
- Independent thinking increases

DANGERS
- New challenges or failures may overwhelm middle adolescents and make them doubt their ability to live life without parental help
- Parental unavailability may cause a shadowing, dependent style of coping
- Premature separation from your support may lead to an inability to become emotionally close or to pseudoindependence
- Sexual intimacy can lead to deep hurts or premature efforts to establish intimate relationships before the capacity for mature love and independent selfhood is developed
- If the loneliness that accompanies separating from parents and the discouragement that comes with perceived failure are combined with significant family problems, some middle adolescents become very depressed or turn to drugs, suicide, or other forms of escapism

With these developmental characteristics and challenges in mind, we will devote the next two chapters to the subject of parenting middle adolescents. Although the ways you relate to your middle adolescents will help them clear each of the five major developmental hurdles, chapter 10 will give special attention to ways you can help your teenagers with their rapprochement struggle between dependency and independency. Chapter 11 will deal especially with ways of helping your adolescents develop more realistic images of themselves and ways of handling their emotions. We will defer a detailed discussion of adolescent sexuality until chapter 18.

NOTES

1. Personal and clinical illustrations in this chapter are by Dr. Narramore.

CHAPTER TEN
PARENTING MIDDLE ADOLESCENTS: BEING THERE AND BEING LEFT

When Todd's Ford slipped out of gear and rolled into another car at the service station,[1] I tried to strike a balance between taking over his problem like the parent of a young child and abandoning Todd completely to his own resources. I knew Todd was feeling like a failure, so I assured him that these things happen to everyone. I also told him about an accident I had years ago. I helped him think through the situation and went back to the station with him for support. Then I stood back and I let Todd ask the manager if he should contact his insurance agent or if the station's insurance handled the damage. Fortunately, the manager didn't make things difficult for Todd and the crisis quickly dissolved. Within a couple of days Todd's car was fixed and he was ready to go again—a bit wiser and more experienced and better prepared to cope with the knocks of life.

Help Them—But Not Too Much

Todd's experience illustrates the first of five important principles for parenting middle adolescents that we will consider in this chapter. *Parents need to be available to help their teenagers when needed, without robbing them of opportunities to meet new challenges for themselves.* By trying to strike that balance with Todd, I helped him confront several middle adolescent developmental hurdles: facing up to reality, changing his inner picture of himself (in the direction of being more adultly responsible), and resolving the rapprochement conflict between dependency and independency.

By telling Todd about my own accident and going with him to the station, I helped him feel more comfortable with his feelings of failure and let him know he could face them without being overwhelmed. I essentially told him, "It's OK to feel bad when you hit a difficult time. Everybody does, and sometimes we feel like giving up. But when you hit a rough spot, admit how you feel, talk it over, give yourself a little time, and then get the courage to go back and try again."

Combined with letting him confront the service station owner, this approach helped Todd struggle with the rapprochement crisis of middle adolescence—his conflict between wanting to be independent and wanting to be taken care of. I didn't let him quit, but I also didn't roughly send him out with the admonition, "Solve your own problem." This helped him avoid the two extreme solutions to the rapprochement crisis of middle adolescence—remaining dependent in the face of difficult responsibilities or acting prematurely tough or independent in order to deny his feelings of need and helplessness. It also helped Todd change his inner pictures of himself and me. No longer was he the small, helpless child who could expect dad to step in and rescue him or solve his problems. I would be available for consultation and support, but I would not do it for him. Instead of being taken care of *by me,* Todd was now expected to be *like me* and work out his own problems with appropriate assistance.

Parents of middle adolescents need to find a similar balance between supporting teenagers and allowing them to confront their own problems. If your middle adolescent daughter has a conflict with her teacher, don't jump in immediately and try to solve it for her. Help her think through what she can do. Ask leading questions. Suggest that she talk directly to her teacher to try to clear up the misunderstanding. Encourage her to talk to her school counselor or principal or other appropriate person. And if it is something she needs to learn to live with, sympathize with her but tell her we sometimes have to get along with other people's hang-ups. Unless her teacher is doing something unethical or seriously injurious, don't phone or visit the teacher or principal. Doing so would tend to infantilize your adolescent—not to mention the possibility of threatening and angering the teacher.

Even when the situation seems to call for your intervention, ask your adolescent's permission first. She may prefer to avoid the embarrassment of creating a stir. Whatever you decide, keep this principle in mind: *middle adolescents need your sensitivity and encouragement but they also need to learn to work out their own problems.* Parents who prematurely rescue their teenagers rob them of opportunities to develop their own strengths and program them to get stuck at the early adolescent stage in life where they believe someone will always magically rescue them. On the other hand, parents who prematurely leave their teenagers to their own resources set them up for depression, anxiety, or pseudotoughness that masks their true feelings.

The Bible gives excellent insights into finding this balance. The apostle Paul wrote that we are to "Carry each other's burdens, and in this way you will fulfill the law of Christ."[2] Then, three verses later, he makes the apparently contradictory statement, "For each one should carry his own load."[3] What did Paul mean? And why did he give us apparently conflicting advice?

The solution is in understanding the Greek words Paul used. In verse 2, Paul used the Greek word *baras.* In verse 5, he used the word *phortion. Baras* refers to a heavy or oppressive object, whereas *phortion* refers to a normal load or object. In verse 2, Paul was saying we are to help others bear their "burdens"—their heavy or oppressive problems. But in verse 5, he says each person is to bear his own "load" or portion. Teenagers need your help in times of crisis or urgency but they don't need you to carry their own normal portion of responsibilities. Balancing your support with opportunities for them to handle their own responsibilities provides the best environment for confident growth toward maturity.

Be Present But Invisible

When our daughter,[4] Debbie, was fifteen she tried out for the high school cheerleading squad. It was an exciting and anxious time. She practiced hard before the tryouts and hoped for this new opportunity to know more kids and have a Christian influence in her large public high school. Since several girls tried out for each slot, the competition was fierce. Selection day came and Debbie was chosen. Thrilled, she and the other girls immediately started preparing routines for football season. Several times they came to our house to practice, but one thing quickly became apparent. They did not want us watching. They were laughing and joking while trying new routines, and they didn't want any mothers or fathers observing their floundering efforts.

When the first football game rolled around, my wife and mother-in-law excitedly anticipated going to watch the cheerleaders. When Debbie heard Kathy's and Mildred's excitement, she made it very clear that she did not want them at her first game. She was nervous about her performance and didn't want them watching every move she made or "oohing and aahing" over how great she was. Like normal mothers, Kathy and her mom initially felt hurt. But sensing Debbie's discomfort, they skipped the game. At the next game, they sat unobtrusively at the back of the bleachers and quietly watched the girls. When I arrived at the game, I discreetly walked around the cheerleaders at a safe distance and smiled knowingly to Debbie without arousing any of her friends' attention. Then I went to the other side of the field to talk to the fathers of some of the players. From these rather distant vantage points, we watched the girls perform.

My daughter's aversion to public attention from her family reflected her struggle with the rapprochement crisis of middle adolescence. She wanted our interest and attention, but she also needed enough space to feel adult. When her mother and grandmother got excited about watching her perform, she started feeling childish. This leads to a second principle for parenting middle adolescents: *be present but invisible.*

Like Debbie, all middle adolescents want you to watch their athletic or musical performances and be proud of them. But also like Debbie, they don't want to be singled out from their friends by hovering parents. During school plays or church Christmas programs, children's parents sit near the front and cheer their children on. Parents of adults sit farther back and watch respectfully and quietly. Performing adolescents desire to be treated like adults.

If your middle adolescent has ever turned to you and said, "Mom, will you please stay home?" or "Dad, don't make such a big deal out of it," you have seen your teenagers attempt to find this balance in their closeness to you. These statements are your teenagers' ways of telling you, "I need a little more space"; "Don't get quite so close"; "Don't treat me like a child"; or "Don't call attention to my inexperience at adult activities." Some middle adolescents will even tell you, "It's OK to come as long as you sit in the back and don't say anything." Many middle adolescents feel these things but don't know how to tell you.

If you are like most parents, these requests can feel like rejection. You think, *Wait a minute. You are my child! What right do you have to push me out of your life after all I've done for you?* But they are not *your* children in the sense that you possess them. God placed them in your home for love and protection and training until they are ready to assume responsibility for their own lives. You don't "own" them and they are trying to make that clear to you. If you are feeling a little rejected and shut out, that is a good sign your teenager is trying to cut cords of dependency on you.

Instead of giving in to your hurt feelings and making your teen feel guilty for wanting to be more independent, give her the space she needs. If your feelings bother you a lot, talk to your spouse or a friend for consolation and perspective. Don't let your feelings of rejection place stumbling blocks in your adolescent's path toward maturity.

Stay Available

At the same time middle adolescents want parents in the background, they want them readily available. This is a third principle for parenting middle adolescents. Even young adults home from college confess to a brief disappointment if they return to an empty house. They can handle your absence, of course, and we don't recommend you sit around waiting for your late adolescents to come home. But middle adolescents need you available if possible. They need your affirmation of their successes and want you to share in their excitement and accomplishments. In contrast to young children, however, middle adolescents usually prefer to share in the safety of your home, and they often want to initiate conversation about how hard things were or how well they did before you give your opinion!

Fifteen-year-old Bobbie's mother, Delores, didn't realize how much love and support her daughter still needed. Delores worked in a demanding accounting job to support herself and her daughters and needed Bobbie's help around the house. But Bobbie was not cooperating. When things reached the breaking point, Delores came to a psychological clinic requesting help in dealing with Bobbie's attitude. Delores told her therapist how at the end of a stressful day at the office she wanted to put on some comfortable clothes, fix a little something to eat, and watch television. All she asked was a little cooperation from her daughters. Her older daughter was no problem. She was conforming, obedient, and a good student—clearly a source of pride and a comfort to her mother.

Bobbie was a different matter. She complained about their

home, the food, her clothes, and anything else that was handy. When she got frustrated she slammed doors and went into a childlike tantrum. Delores' therapist made a tentative observation. "Sometimes a child who reacts this way is feeling emotionally abandoned. Even though their parents love them, they inwardly feel uncared for. Do you think Bobbie might have any feelings like that?" "I don't know," Delores replied coolly, "she has lost her father and I am too tired to do much with her after a day at work. But she certainly knows I love her."

The next week, Delores brought her daughter to the therapist. After chatting about a few things and putting Bobbie at ease the counselor asked Bobbie what made her so angry at home. Much to the surprise of her counselor, Bobbie quickly answered, "My mother's smoking." "What about your mother's smoking makes you so angry?" the counselor asked. "Because she is going to get cancer and die, that's what," Bobbie answered sullenly. When Bobbie's counselor asked her what made her so upset with her sister, she replied, "She is going to leave too. She is going to college in September." Bobbie's counselor knew then that her tentative interpretation had been correct. Bobbie had already lost her father and now she expected to lose her mother to cancer and sister to college. At the time she needed a support base to reach out to the adult world, she thought she was about to be abandoned.

Bobbie was experiencing what some psychologists call abandonment rage. Since she didn't feel loved and didn't know how to express her loneliness directly to her mother, she became obnoxious. Although Bobbie's mother loved her, she was too busy and too tired for Bobbie to get the message.

Some adolescents who don't experience enough parental support develop a "shadowing," dependent, or depressive life-style. They withdraw from most social activities with their age mates so they can stick as close as possible to a parent or another adult. Others who feel emotionally abandoned turn to sexual promiscuity or drugs or alcohol for consolation. Their premature disconnection from parental nourishment leaves them with an unquenchable hunger for love, which they try to satisfy through sexual encounters or with depression, which they try to escape through drugs or alcohol.

Even when you love your children dearly, it is possible to slip into a pattern similar to that of Bobbie's mother. It is easy to get so busy that we overlook our children's needs. Since we love our teenagers, we assume our love is deeply embedded in their minds and fail to regularly communicate it. Teenagers are not so different from spouses in that regard. We all need to be reminded that we are loved and we all need our loved ones available to express their caring. Other parents assume that because their teenagers are so busy with their own activities and friends, they don't need their parents anymore. But even though middle adolescents are finding new sources of support, there is no one like mom and dad, even though many teenagers won't come right out and say it.

Especially during the early years of middle adolescence, teenagers need someone home when they return from school. One study of middle adolescent "latchkey children" found they were more depressed, engaged in more solitary drinking of alcohol, and were sexually active at an earlier age than teenagers who had a parent at home when they returned.

If one parent cannot be at home when your teenagers return from school or work, take steps to be as accessible as possible. Be sure they have your work phone number. Have them call you briefly when they get home, or call them. Arrange for a grandparent to be at home when they arrive, or find some other way to help them connect after a long day at school. Your availability reaffirms your love for your children and lets them know you are not emotionally abandoning them to their own devices as middle adolescents.

Support Adult Responsibilities

For weeks, fifteen-year-old Beth's excitement had been building. She was soon to get her driver's license. Every time the family went out together Beth wanted to drive so she could practice. She just *had* to take her driving test the very day she turned sixteen, so her mother, Barbara, took her to the Department of Motor Vehicles. Beth passed her test and, of course, had to drive her mother home. Then she went off by herself to visit a friend.

For several weeks, Beth almost disappeared. Every time her parents turned around she was driving to the store, a friend's house, or a church or school activity. It didn't matter where, she just wanted to drive. Driving was Beth's way of exercising some newfound "adultness" and putting a little space between herself and mom and dad. She was on the go so much that Barbara and her husband began to wonder if they would ever see her again. They thought about restricting her activities so that she would spend more time at home, but wisely decided to let her try her wheels, hoping this was just a phase. They didn't let her have the car every time she wanted it but did try to accommodate her when that was possible.

Sure enough, the newness wore off after a few weeks and Beth started asking for the car only when she needed it. By allowing her a lot of freedom, Barbara and her husband enabled their daughter to test out some adult responsibilities. This helped her take one more step out of her conflict between dependency and independency and furthered her revision of her image of herself from that of a child to an adult. No longer did she have to be driven places. Now she could transport others. Beth's parents were practicing a fourth principle for parenting middle adolescents: *encourage and allow teenagers to take on increasingly adult responsibilities.*

Taking a part-time job is one good way for middle adolescents to take responsibility and keep learning about the realities of life. Although not every middle adolescent should take a job, work can be a maturing experience. It gives adolescents a chance to try out some adult skills and prove they can take care of at least some of their material needs. The Bible says, "It is good for a man to bear the yoke when he is young."[5]

If you have overheard a couple of middle adolescents talk about looking for a job or their first few days at work, you understand what I mean. They share horror stories over being interviewed, describe the manager of the store or a customer in vivid detail, relay a funny story or two, and tell how great or hard or horrid their job is. But running throughout the entire conversation is a sense of pride that they are making it on their own. They are no longer totally dependent on their parents' money and they are griping about their jobs or their low pay—just like their parents.

Although part-time jobs can be excellent growing experiences, many teenagers have plenty of homework and school or church activities to keep them busy. If your adolescents are learning responsibility in these ways, they may not need a job to help them grow up. It isn't helpful to pressure teenagers to take a job just because you think "every sixteen-year-old should have the experience."

If you believe your adolescents aren't responsible enough to take a job or already have too much to do, don't raise those questions the moment they tell you they might be interested in getting a job. Listen to their excitement and enthusiasm first. Affirm the value of work and the possibility of a job. Then, very sensitively, voice your concern that they not take on more activities than they can handle. Be sure you don't squelch their interest in a challenge since this may be their first serious attempt to be adult. It should be a joyful, anticipated time.

If after listening you are convinced your teenagers might be biting off more than they can chew, you might compromise by telling them a job is fine as long as they keep up their grades or do their household chores or other responsibilities. But it is usually better to let middle adolescents take a job if they want it. If it turns out to be too much of a burden, they will find out soon enough. Then they can cut back or quit and learn from their experience. That way they will profit from *their* experience, not *yours*.

If your middle adolescent daughter isn't involved in extracurricular activities and is "goofing off" or not taking her studies seriously, a part-time job may be an important step in growing up. In that case, feel free to initiate the idea of a job. Look for a good time to ask her if she has thought about an after-school or summer job. If she quickly rejects the idea, pursue her gently and tell her you have thought about it and believe it might be helpful to her and the family. Ask her to think it over and see that she takes a serious look at the way she spends her time. You might also tell her it is time she start paying for more of her own clothes or helping cover the cost of car insurance as well as getting experience in the workaday world. Middle and late adolescents should not have large amounts of time on their hands or have their parents provide all of their financial needs.

Activities such as taking a part-time job, driving a car, and serving in responsible positions at school and church help teenagers master several middle adolescent developmental tasks. They help them learn that they can cope in the adult world without caving in to their wishes to be dependent. They help reshape their attitudes toward themselves and others so that they can see themselves as more competent and adult. They help them handle the new feelings that are triggered by unfamiliar responsibilities, and they offer tangible proofs that they are no longer dependent children. They are becoming like you instead of being cared for by you.

Give a Gentle Nudge

A public broadcasting station recently featured a nature film that held a fifth principle for parenting middle adolescents. It showed a mother starling teaching her young to fly. The mother perched on a branch with a worm in her mouth and teasingly dangled it toward her brood in the nest nearby. Then she slowly began fluttering her wings to model the mechanics of flight. Soon one of the young birds began to flutter its wings and made its first attempt. The distance was short and the effort awkward, but the first little starling landed safely and received his reward. One by one the other starlings learned to fly.

Teenagers need the same kind of encouragement to try new tasks. They need some motivation (the worm), a good example (the mother demonstrating how wings work), and the recognition that mom or dad will help but won't do the job for them (the worm held at a far enough distance to force them to fly). Like young starlings, some adolescents are hesitant to leave the nest. Their built-in urge to become independent seems to have been repressed. Whether it is because parents have been overprotective or the children lack confidence in themselves, these teens need an extra nudge to keep them moving toward independence. It is as though they are riding a teeter-totter between childhood dependency and adult independence. If they don't get a little encouragement, or if they aren't forced to take a chance now and then, they will fall back to the dependent side.

Sam helped Evan over this developmental hurdle by applying a fifth principle for parenting middle adolescents: *give them a gentle nudge.* When Evan asked his dad to buy him a used car, Sam agreed to make the down payment and pay half of the monthly payment if Evan would handle the rest of the payment and all of the insurance and other costs. Evan had hoped for more, especially since his best friend's father had just bought him a car. But when his dad held firm, Evan found himself a job and soon was able to afford the car.

A gentle nudge can take the form of encouraging your son or daughter to get a job, repair his or her own car, or try out for a part in a play. You might decide not to increase their allowance so they will have to finance their growing social life with some gainful employment. You might suggest they open their own checking account and balance their monthly bank statement. Or you may require your fifteen-year-old to do his share of household or garden tasks. Cooking lessons from mom or dad can help teenagers feel better about their ability to function as adults. Even having your teenagers set up their own doctor's appointments encourages them to take more responsibility for themselves. Anything that requires them to do for themselves what you used to do, without their feeling abandoned, leads toward healthy independence.

Some middle adolescents are especially fearful and have a

serious problem with introversion and withdrawal. They tend to isolate themselves from their peers, stick around their homes, and don't develop normal social interactions. If your teenager is like this, try to discern why he is afraid to leave the nest. Does he have a serious lack of confidence? Has he been overprotected or received subtle messages that you don't want him to leave? Is he overwhelmed by the prospect of failing in the world? Is he afraid to leave because he doubts you will be available when he needs to return? Teenagers like this may be suffering from hidden anxiety or depression and need more than just a little encouragement. If your teenager fits this description, we encourage you to seek out a professional therapist to get to the root of these deeper problems.

Chapter Highlights

In this chapter we have looked at ways of helping your sons and daughters meet some of the developmental challenges of middle adolescence. We have focused especially on ways of helping middle adolescents reconcile their conflicting wishes to be taken care of and to become more independent. We have looked at ways of helping them learn to face reality. And we have begun to consider ways of helping them change their inner images of themselves.

The most important concepts of this chapter can be summed up in one principle: *parents of middle adolescents need to find a balance between loving availability and respectful distance.* Your middle adolescents need you available for laughing and relaxing. They need you available for serious talks. They need you available to share in their victories and successes. And they need your consolation when things get tough. But at the same time, they also need the freedom to move further from you toward their own adulthood. They need you available so they can leave you.

Most of the suggestions of this chapter are designed to help you ease your teenagers out of the excited, exploratory days of early adolescence into the tougher times of middle adolescence. By being sensitive to their struggles with the realities of adult life you can help your teenagers maintain much of the optimism of their youth and avoid caving in to the discouragement or depression that overwhelms many middle adolescents. Healthy middle adolescents find ways to feel supported and encouraged by you while steadily becoming more confident and independent. Here are a few things you can do to help:

- help them—but not too much
- be present but invisible
- stay available
- support adult responsibilities
- give a gentle nudge.

NOTES
1. Illustrations are by Dr. Lewis unless otherwise indicated.
2. Galatians 6:2.
3. Galatians 6:5.
4. Dr. Narramore.
5. Lamentations 3:27.

CHAPTER ELEVEN PARENTING MIDDLE ADOLESCENTS: PUTTING AWAY CHILDISH WAYS

Thirty-two-year-old Brian[1] sought psychotherapy because he suffered severe anxiety attacks whenever he met with his boss in the corporate board room. Since Brian was a successful and confident person in most ways, he was mystified by these sudden attacks. He only had them in the board room and only in the presence of his boss. During therapy Brian recalled a time when he was five years old. Like many boys this age, he tried on his father's suit coat, and with the sleeves dangling to the floor, came proudly strolling down the hall. Instead of being greeted by an admiring father saying, "My, you look great in daddy's suit," he heard his father arrogantly pronounce, "You may wear my coat, but you will never fill my shoes." The sensitive boy was crushed. At the moment he was aspiring to be a man like his dad, his father chopped him down.

During Brian's childhood and adolescence, his father continued his competitive, derisive ways. When he played basketball with Brian, he always had to win. Then he gloated about his "moves" and told his son, "You'll never beat your old man." Time after time, Brian's father told him in so many words, "You'll never be a man like me." Years later, Brian was unconsciously transferring his fear of his menacing father to his supervisor. He still felt unsure of his ability to compete with an aggressive male. When Brian's father squelched his son's efforts to feel manly, he programmed Brian to have a troubled time clearing the fourth developmental hurdle[2] of middle adolescence: learning to feel like a competent adult. In this chapter we will discuss ways of helping middle adolescents successfully clear that hurdle and the hurdle of developing a more mature emotional life. We will begin with ways of helping teenagers grow out of their childish self-concepts and learn to think more adultly about themselves.

Putting Away Childish Thoughts

Think of the radical changes in attitude toward themselves and their parents that children must experience in the second decade of life. As a ten-year-old girl approaches puberty, her self-image and image of her parents probably look something like this:

View of Parents	View of Self
Larger than life and powerful (18′ giants)	Small and relatively powerless (she can hardly imagine being like her parents)
Intelligent and able to understand almost anything	Less intelligent and unable to understand many things
Independent and capable of functioning in the world beyond the home	Dependent and incapable of functioning in the world beyond the home (but with some fantasies of being as competent as an 18′ giant)
Able to protect and take care of others	Needing to be protected and cared for by others
Authorities on moral and spiritual issues	Dependent on moral and spiritual authorities for her values and beliefs

Now consider what that same girl's perceptions of herself and her parents should be by young adulthood.

View of Parents	View of Self
Normal people with some special gifts but with very human strengths and weaknesses	Normal adult with some special gifts but with very human strengths and and weaknesses
Intelligent and knowledgeable about things but not all-knowing or all-wise	Intelligent and able to learn about most things but needing a lot more knowledge and experience
Capable of functioning in the real world, but they do have limitations	Capable of functioning in the real world but aware of some limitations and need for greater training or experience
Possess some good values and spiritual commitments but are not infallible	Responsible for choosing her own spiritual commitments and values
Capable of meeting many or most of their own needs while still being healthily interdependent with others	Capable of meeting many or most of her own needs but still being healthily interdependent with others

Making the transition from these nine- or ten-year-old perceptions of themselves and others to adult perceptions is one of the most important tasks facing middle adolescents. Several suggestions from chapter 10 can help you help your teenagers make this shift. Giving them increased responsibilities, for example, helps them feel more capable and adult. Being available but nonintrusive helps them develop increasing confidence and lets them know they can count on you when they really need you. And giving them a gentle nudge lets them know that you expect them to take increasing responsibility for their lives as they grow older. But there is more that you can do.

Getting Off the Pedestal

Like Brian, your teenagers need to compete successfully with their "giant" parents to close the gap between their childhood perceptions of themselves and their exaggerated eighteen-foot views of you. If Brian's dad had felt more secure, he could have affirmed his son's desires to feel manly. He could have occasionally let him win at basketball. And he might have talked about his own feelings of inferiority or excessive competitiveness as an adolescent.

Accepting your teenagers' competitiveness and desire to be adult like you is one of the best ways of helping them change their image of themselves. Young children feel powerful and secure because they view their parents as competent and powerful. Young adults must relinquish this borrowed power and replace it with a sense of their own competence and mastery. In the process, they have to dethrone us from our idealized position. *When your teenagers challenge you, remember they are trying to grow up.* Instead of fighting or overreacting, remind yourself that it is natural for middle adolescent boys to criticize their fathers and for girls to compete against their mothers.

Don't be afraid to set limits or say no when necessary, and do help your teenagers find acceptable ways of expressing their negativism. But don't put them down or imply that they are bad for wanting to compete or be like you. That just reinforces their feelings of childishness and makes them more resentful. Affirm their growing abilities and strengths and wisdom. Value their ideas. Let them win occasionally. And let them know you want them to become competent and adult. Become a supportive partner in their growth toward maturity—not a threatening competitor.

Being honest about your limitations is another way to help your sons and daughters feel more adult. The apostle James encourages us: "Confess your sins [faults] to each other and pray for each other so that you may be healed."[3] When you talk about your weaknesses or failures, you let your teenagers know that you are not an omnipotent eighteen-foot giant and that you have problems too.

When my teenagers were feeling afraid to go to the bank and open a checking account, I shared how even as a young married adult I sometimes felt anxious when I first met a teller at a bank or some other person in an "official position." Then I went with them to offer moral support. A few years later when they felt overwhelmed by the confusing instructions on their income tax forms, I let them know I still didn't understand some of the directions. Then I helped them a little but made sure they figured out all they could without my help. Knowing that I had been a little intimidated at the bank and by the IRS helped them feel OK about their own fear and confusion. They realized "giants" don't just automatically know everything.

You can do the same thing for your teenagers by telling them about a time you messed up something on your job or felt nervous or discouraged. Being honest about your own needs and problems helps teenagers realize that adults struggle. This helps them to feel less intimidated by their approaching adulthood. It also has a benefit for you. If you help your teenagers gradually slide you off of your parental pedestal, they won't have to work so hard to suddenly knock you off!

Accentuate the Positive

Fifteen-year-old Donna's father was teaching her to drive in their stick shift car. He backed the car out of the garage, moved over to the passenger side, and gave Donna instructions. Donna listened carefully and tried to follow her dad's advice. But like many new drivers, she gave the car so little gas it died.

"Give it a little more gas next time," her dad advised. Donna did, and the car jerked forward much too quickly. "Slow down!" her dad yelled. "You'll kill us both!" After a couple more false starts, Donna was on her way. As she turned onto the street her father anxiously reminded her, "Be sure to look both ways." "I already did," Donna replied, starting to get annoyed. A minute later her dad anxiously told her, "Watch out for the traffic in the other lane." Right after that he again cautioned her, "Slow down, don't you know the speed limit here?" By that time Donna was near tears. "I'm doing my best," she shot back. "Just leave me alone." When her dad warned her once more, Donna angrily pulled the car off the road, got out, and told her dad, "If I can't do it well enough for you, you drive!"

Donna's dilemma reflects a common characteristic of adolescents: *they are extremely sensitive to criticism.* Since middle adolescents are just testing out their ability to be adult, even slight suggestions that they have performed inadequately can spark intense feelings of failure or resentment. Parental anxiety about their performance totally drives them up a tree. Remember what it was like when you were a teenager trying to master the steering, accelerating, braking, and signaling on a new and unfamiliar car? Now add an eighteen-foot giant hovering anxiously over you watching every move. Periodically, the giant yells, "Watch out!" "Be careful!" or "Slow down!" How does that make you feel? If you are like most people it frightens, discourages, or angers you. Learning to drive is hard enough with the help of a calm instructor, but a nervous "giant" makes any adolescent feel like giving up or angrily shooting back, "Leave me alone. I can see it!" or "If you don't like it, drive yourself!"

Since few parents can sit calmly while their fifteen- or sixteen-year-olds are lurching the family car down the street, it is best for the more even-tempered parent to handle the instruction. Better yet, invest a few dollars in a driving school and remove yourselves entirely from this difficult situation. Driving instructors are paid to be calm while people are doing things that could easily get them killed!

This same thing is true of your teenagers' feelings about their grades or friends or clothes or jobs around the house. They are extremely sensitive to criticism in these areas. Parental criticism and worry undermine confidence. In their place, teenagers need encouragement and praise. Calm reassurance and abundant praise give teenagers confidence to keep on going. Comments like, "That's good," "You're doing great," and "You'll get it," all bolster your teenagers' confidence that they can learn to function as adults. The apostle Paul told the Christians at Thessalonica to "encourage one another and build each other up."[4] Middle adolescents need regular doses of parental affirmation and building up.

This doesn't mean that you ignore your adolescents' failures or allow them to neglect their chores or responsibilities around the house. Middle adolescents still need some limits and need to be held responsible. But they need to be helped in adult ways. If your teenagers "forget" to do their chores or are unhelpful or un-cooperative around the house, take positive action. Sit down and tell them you need to find a way to help them keep up their share of the work. Assure them you know they have a lot to do but that you need to work out a solution. Ask if they haven't been feeling well or if there are other reasons their jobs aren't getting done. If they have been feeling bad, or have a good excuse, listen to their feelings or frustrations. Then gently but firmly let them know you understand and help them find some way to get their chores done or improve their attitudes or behaviors.

If your teenagers are failing to do their chores, you might discuss some specific consequences that will be carried out if they con-tinue to "forget." If it is your son's responsibility to wash the car each week, for example, you might let him know that if he doesn't wash the car by a certain time on Friday, he can't use the car that weekend. If it is your teenager's responsibility to feed the dog, you may decide to give the dog away if he doesn't. Or if it is your dog, you may decide that if your son forgets to feed the dog, you won't fix his meals that day. You have a lot of options, but the important point is teenagers need encouragement and specific consequences to remind them to carry out their responsibilities, not criticism and nagging.

If your teenagers have a bad attitude, you can help them find direct and nondestructive ways of expressing their hurts or needs. Instead of attacking others or retreating into sullen silence you might suggest that they come directly to you and say, "Mom (or Dad), I'm really hurt (or angry, or upset, or discouraged)." "When you put down my friends, I feel horrible." Tell them you want them to let you know how they are feeling, but that it is easier to under-stand when they tell you directly instead of lashing out, yelling, "I hate you!" or withdrawing to their room. If they can learn to express their feelings in direct yet nonaccusing ways, everyone will feel a whole lot better. You can help by listening sensitively and sympathetically and modeling that same kind of direct but sensitive communication of our feelings.

Step by Step

Not long ago I[5] was asked to speak at a Lions Club luncheon. About thirty men gathered for the meeting and I gave a brief talk on being a father. At one point, I asked the men how many had ever taken their sons or daughters to visit their work. Not one man raised his hand. This is an increasingly common reality among urban families. Living miles from their parents' work, many children never see their mom or dad in action at their jobs. But how can we expect children to start picturing themselves as potentially successful employees unless they have some firsthand experience with role models? A job or professional career can seem like a giant task for teenagers who have never seen that they are made up of a series of ordinary human activities within the capacity of everyone.

It is great if young children have a chance to visit their parents at work. But by middle adolescence your sons and daughters should definitely have this opportunity. They need as clear a picture of your job as possible. Seeing you in action helps demystify the world of work and makes you look a little less "gigantic." If your children can carry some materials for you, read a report you wrote, or help you with part of your job, that is even better. It gives them firsthand experience that tells them they can do some of the things you do.

From the time our own children were four or five, I[6] took them with me on a couple of speaking engagements each year. Richard and Debbie would sit in the auditorium with a book or drawing pad to keep them busy while they listened with one ear to my lectures. They watched the people, memorized my jokes, and listened intently to any stories I told about our family. When

Debbie was five she came up to me during a break in one of my Saturday seminars. "Daddy," she asked with a cute but forceful look, "aren't you going to tell them about the time I ate the soap?" She knew she was making a contribution to my job by giving me some illustrations and she didn't want to be neglected.

When Richard and Debbie got a little older, I would introduce them to the audience and ask them a few questions in front of the people. Then one day when Richard was ten or eleven, I bravely asked him if he would like to talk to the people. We were in a large convention center with about 1,500 people for an all-day seminar. Richard replied, "Sure, but what would I say?" I told him I would have the people ask a few questions he could answer. We sat on the front of the speaker's platform with a microphone and I told the audience they could ask Richard anything they wish about our family or himself. My only instruction to him was, "Don't lie." For fifteen minutes these total strangers asked Richard all sorts of questions about our family, his sister, and his friends.

The first question was, "How do you get along with your sister?" Others asked about how we disciplined our children and if we practiced what we preached. Richard enjoyed it and so did the people. It injected a dose of practical reality into the seminar and, fortunately, added to my credibility. But more importantly, for Richard, it said, "You can do some of the things your father does." By the time he and Debbie were middle adolescents, they hosted an entire hour of one of my seminars on parent-teen relationships. It is no accident that they now have confidence to speak and discuss issues with all sorts of people. Their experiences helped them see that they did not have to remain dependent children. They could change their images of themselves. No longer was I the only one able to lecture and help people with their families. They were budding adults who knew that some adult activities were not beyond their reach.

This same principle applies to all sorts of adult activities. Learning how to cook, trim the yard, plant a garden, paint the house, sew some clothes, or fix the car all help teenagers feel more adult and less like needy children. Even though it is sometimes easier to do these things yourself, your adolescents need the chance to learn. They also need some step-by-step instructions or examples. Instead of simply instructing your teenagers to paint the garage, arrange a bouquet of flowers, or fix dinner, do that job with them a time or two. Go through each step the first time with them assisting. The second time, have them do more of the work but with a little help from you. By the third time they will probably be ready to handle it by themselves. This improves their confidence and lets them see how they can learn to handle adult responsibilities.

Although everything in this book is designed to help adolescents develop a more realistic appraisal of themselves and others, let's summarize several specific ways you can help your teenagers develop more adult self-images:

- give them increased responsibilities
- be available and supportive but not intrusive
- allow them to learn from the consequences of their actions
- give them a nudge out of the family nest
- let them see how human and fallible you are
- encourage and affirm their growth and progress
- keep criticism to a minimum
- be a model of a competent adult
- help them learn to perform adult responsibilities step by step.

Your teenagers' self-concepts will change slowly, but you can help them outgrow their childhood perceptions of themselves and learn to feel like competent, budding adults by your sensitivity, encouragement, and support.

Maturing Emotions

In chapter 9, we saw that middle adolescents need to become more comfortable with their emotions, find out that strong and conflicting feelings (such as love and hate) can coexist, develop clear boundaries between their own emotions and the emotions of others, and learn how to communicate their feelings appropriately. Since it takes a while to adapt to the physical, social, and psychological changes of adolescence, these changes won't happen overnight. Sometimes your sons' and daughters' feelings will burn like red hot coals. They will fling them around the room, toss them at you or someone else, or run into their rooms to try to cool them down. Depression, fear, love, anger, and even excitement can all alarm and confuse your adolescents.

Some maturing of your sons' and daughters' emotions will happen naturally. As your teenagers get used to their changing minds and bodies, they will be a little less volatile. And as they gain more life experience, they will put upsetting situations into perspective much more quickly. The second time they have a crush on someone, for example, it will be a little different than the first. The second or third time a jealous friend puts them down, they will handle it a little easier. And the third or fourth time they get furious with a friend or teacher they will probably be a little clearer about how they want to respond. All of the needed emotional settling of adolescence, however, will not happen automatically. Your teenagers will need a little of your help, as they did as younger children.

You can do three things to help this maturing process move along. *First,* you can model mature ways of dealing with emotions. *Second,* you can help your teenagers contain their upsetting feelings and learn to feel more comfortable with them. And *third,* you can avoid letting your teenagers drag you into their emotional struggles in ways that complicate their already upset feelings.

Like Father, Like Son

Forest considers himself a pretty good father. Although he knows he is rather hot-tempered, he dearly loves his fifteen-year-old son, Mark. He spends a lot of time with Mark and has seen that he has plenty of opportunities for extracurricular activities at school and church. He regularly attends his son's baseball and basketball games and provides him a good allowance and all the clothes he needs. Recently, however, Mark has become irritable and combative with his father. He loses his temper and reacts violently whenever he is crossed or frustrated and he seems insensitive to other members of his family. Mark's tantrums caused Forest to bring his family to me for consultation.[7] A recent fight was typical of their interaction.

Forest gave his son a card for his fifteenth birthday and enclosed a sizable check. The card expressed Forest's love and pride in Mark's accomplishments. Mark was very pleased. Later that evening Forest noticed that Mark hadn't mowed the yard as he had promised, and he lost his cool. He clicked off the TV program Mark was watching and angrily told his son, "I'm sick and tired of you never doing your chores! I can't trust you to get anything done around here!"

When Forest stopped his rampage, Mark went into his room and retrieved his birthday card, stood right in front of his father and tore it into shreds. Not to be outdone, Forest steamed into his son's room, snatched the birthday check off the dresser, and tore it up. Mark got even madder, told his father he didn't want his "damned money," and stomped out the front door. By now it was obvious why Mark couldn't handle frustration. His father was as emotionally out of control as he was. Since Forest didn't know how to get his son to mow the yard by respectful means, he blasted him with anger. Like any normal teen, Mark returned the favor. Later, in my office, Forest told me, "I don't know what's the matter with me. When he keeps putting off his chores, I just lose it."

Forest and Mark's disaster isn't uncommon. Few things upset early and middle adolescents more than anxious, uptight, or angry parents. Since their feelings are so volatile or new, they need as stable an environment as possible. When a parent's unrestrained emotions are added to their own, it is simply too much to handle. Forest's angry reaction threw more fuel on Mark's emotional fire. As a proverb reminds us, "As charcoal to embers and as wood to fire, so is a quarrelsome man for kindling strife."[8]

If your adolescents return home late from a date, fail to do their chores, or do something else that upsets you, try this three-step procedure.

First, think before you act. Instead of jumping on them with accusative "you" messages such as, "You make me so angry," or "I've had it with you," bite your lip. These blaming messages throw more fuel on your adolescents' emotional fires. They create more anger and defensiveness and will probably escalate a minor or moderate problem into a major disaster. The Bible says, "A fool gives full vent to his anger, but a wise man keeps himself under control."[9] To stay under control, of course, Forest would have to come to grips with his own anger and impulsivity and inability to discipline his son consistently. This would take a willingness to look honestly at his relationships with his own parents and at his own upsetting emotions. Maybe his father treated him the same way he was treating Mark. The alternatives are clear. Either Forest will go through the next several years battling with his son or he will find a more mature way of handling his own upset emotions. Another proverb tells us, "Better a patient man than a warrior, a man who controls his temper than one who takes a city."[10]

Second, once you have restrained your first impulse, let your adolescents talk. Ask them a question or express your feelings and then let them respond. You might say, "I get frightened when you don't return home by the time we agreed upon," or "I feel angry when you keep putting off your chores." These messages express your concerns without blame and give adolescents a chance to explain themselves or apologize instead of having to fight you back. If Forest could tell Mark, "I'm reaching the end of my rope, son," or "I see you didn't mow the yard again," he would be off to a better start.

Third, after you have heard your adolescents out, discuss some ways of avoiding the problem in the future. Discuss some consequences, such as no television (or soccer or baseball) until the yard is done. This can be done quietly and rationally ahead of time instead of angrily and impulsively after the infraction. If you are too upset to do this calmly, simply tell your teenager you would like to set up a time to talk after you have calmed down. It is very difficult to resolve a problem in the heat of strong emotions, and even a night to sleep on it can put things into a much better perspective.

You can also help your sons and daughters handle their emotions by expressing yours appropriately. If you have had a hard day and are uptight and tired, don't wait until you lose your temper to tell them you are frazzled. Tell them ahead of time, "I've had a hard day and I really need some peace and quiet tonight." That lets them know they shouldn't blare their radios or hassle you that evening. It also shows your sons and daughters how to be direct about their feelings and their needs. That way, they can learn to warn you when they are feeling bad or upset.

Teenagers also need good models for expressing positive, enjoyable feelings. Some parents are bothered by their adolescents' enthusiasm and excitement. They encourage their teenagers to "relax" or "not get so excited." Others sit with a half-preoccupied look while their teenagers excitedly share about their activities and friends. And others are simply too depressed to enjoy their adolescents' adventures. Each of these reactions throws a wet blanket on a teenager's pleasurable and positive feelings. In fact, you can often see teenagers' excitement and joy progressively fade as they try to tell their parents about their day. They come in excited but become increasingly subdued as they sense their parents disinterest and gradually terminate the conversation and go off by themselves. Eventually they learn not to even bother trying.

Sharing joyfully in your teenagers' successes and experiences helps your sons and daughters attach deep positive emotions to their adolescent memories. Your joy is like a mirror held in front of your son's or daughter's face saying, "It's good to be happy," or "I'm glad you enjoy what you're doing." Your positive feelings validate your teenagers' happy emotions and help them integrate those emotions into their maturing personalities. Proverbs says, "A cheerful heart is good medicine."[11]

Be a Good Container

Ross was more successful helping his son handle his emotions than was Forest. His seventeen-year-old-son, Ed, had just taken a summer job at a local hardware store. After a few days on the job, Ed was assigned to the checkout counter where he had to balance his receipts each day. The first day he was short four dollars. The store manager seemed understanding but told Ed the company policy was that if a checker failed to balance his receipts three times, he was fired.

After Ed failed to balance his receipts a second time, he came home quite discouraged. He was trying his best but was afraid he wouldn't make it. One more mistake and he would be out of a job. Ross was concerned since this was his son's first venture into the adult world. He didn't want Ed to have a bad experience. But instead of anxiously warning Ed to be more careful and compounding the problem, Ross gave Ed a chance to talk about his feelings. "That must be tough," he said. "How can anyone balance it perfectly every day?" "I don't know," Ed replied, "but that's what he said." "That would really make me nervous," Ross sympathetically replied. "It does me too," said Ed. "I do my best but it just doesn't seem to be enough."

After they talked awhile, Ross told his son, "I can't believe they would really fire you if you are doing well and are only out of balance a dollar or two once more. If that happens, I would encourage you to go to the manager before he has a chance to come to you. Tell him you really like the job and think you are doing well and you really want to keep working there. It may be that their 'three strikes and you're out' rule is just to weed out people who don't have the ability to do the job or who are dishonest. I know you have the ability and you are honest and I'm sure your manager knows it."

Ed wasn't so sure, but was reassured by his dad's confidence and his suggestion on how to handle the problem. A few weeks later, he was out of balance again. But by this time the manager knew Ed was doing a good job. He told Ed, "Don't worry about it. It happens to everybody now and then."

Ed's dad had helped him over a difficult spot by being sensitive to his fears and helping him put them into perspective. In a way, he was serving as a kind of psychological container for Ed's upsetting emotions. Much as you might slip on an asbestos glove to pick up a red hot charcoal and place it in a box to cool, Ross listened calmly to Ed's upset emotions, held them in his own hands until they cooled off, and then gave them back to Ed when they had reached a manageable temperature.

You can do this for your children. If your adolescent is furious with a boyfriend or depressed over not making the cast of a drama production, don't tell her everything will be OK or offer her some quick advice. Listen to her disturbed feelings. Let her tell you how mad or sad she is. Try to put yourself in her shoes and imagine how she feels. Your empathic listening tells her, "I know you are upset but I'm not afraid of your emotions. I am confident that in time you will be able to handle them yourself." Your sensitive "holding," much as it did when they were infants, helps transform pain into pleasure, anger into tolerance, loneliness into companionship, and anxiety into peacefulness.

After you have heard her out and after she feels understood, she may be ready for a little advice or a different perspective. Even then, don't rush it. What she needs most is a listening ear. If you hear her out, she will probably find her own solutions and become more comfortable with her strong emotions. In time she will naturally integrate her feelings into her life in a rich and balanced way.

Of course, listening calmly isn't always easy. We parents have our own frustrations and our natural tendency is to react to our children's frustrations with anxieties of our own. If we come from homes where fighting and anxiety were the order of the day, it is difficult to react peaceably to our children's anger. And if we had painful or destructive experiences as adolescents, we may want to jump in and offer instant advice or try to avoid or quickly solve a problem. If you tend to react this way and have difficulty helping your teenagers contain their emotions, you need to take a look at your own reactions. To learn to listen more effectively and become comfortable with your adolescents' feelings, you may need to seek a counselor or a friend to help you put your own feelings into perspective.

Don't Get Sucked into Their Inner Struggles

Sixteen-year-old Jana was thinking about taking an after-school job. Several of her friends were working and she needed a little extra money. She also wanted to test out her abilities in the world of work. When Jana asked her mom what she thought about her taking a job at a local business, Jana's mother asked her if she thought a job might be too much along with everything else she was doing. Then she said she was concerned that Jana might not be able to keep her grades up.

Jana immediately hit the ceiling. She accused her mother of thinking she was irresponsible and of treating her like a child. No matter how her mother reassured her, Jana refused to listen. It was two or three days before Jana settled down enough to talk again with her mom.

This time Jana's mom started out by making it very clear that she was happy Jana wanted to take a job. She told Jana she believed she was a responsible person who could do well at a job. And she told her she was pleased by her willingness to consider working. Only after making her confidence in Jana clear did she say, "My only concern is that you don't take on so much that you wear yourself out and don't have time to enjoy life. You are only young once and I want you to have some fun and be able to keep up your other activities." After this clear explanation and some further talk, Jana finally admitted, "I'm worried about that too, Mom, but I think I can do it."

During their first encounter, Jana's mother hadn't recognized Jana's ambivalent feelings. Although Jana wanted a job, she too was afraid that work might interfere with her extracurricular activities. And she was also afraid she might do poorly. But instead of admitting her conflicting wishes and feelings, Jana seized on her mother's questions as an opportunity to externalize her own doubt. Instead of thinking, I want a job but *I'm* afraid I might fail, she thought, I want a job but *my mother* thinks I might fail.

Like Jana, many middle adolescents cope with their own unacceptable thoughts and feelings by projecting them onto a parent or another handy person. Instead of thinking, I want to eat this chocolate (or date this boy, or take this trip), but I also have some reservations, they think, I want to do it but my parents think I shouldn't. By attributing their doubts or negative emotions to someone else they try to convince themselves they have only mature thoughts and feelings and wishes. In this way, teenagers make you an actor in the theater of their minds. You play the role of the part of their personality they don't want to face right then. This creates endless conflicts as teenagers accuse their parents, parents feel unjustly attacked and become defensive or resentful, and teenagers become even more upset.

Most teenagers, for example, occasionally accuse their parents of treating them like children. Instead of being aware that they unconsciously feel afraid of failing as adults, they project their unacceptable feelings onto their parents' and loudly proclaim only their mature desires. This tendency for teenagers to project their unacceptable thoughts or feelings onto you is a remnant of the infant's tendency to confuse his thoughts and feelings with the feelings of his mother. Like the infant, your teenagers know those upsetting thoughts and feelings are present but they aren't sure whether they are located in themselves or you.

When your teenagers start to suck you into one of these inner dramas, watch out! Step back and realize what is happening. Listen carefully to your teenagers' accusations and see if there is some truth in what they are saying. Perhaps you are treating them a little like a child. Or perhaps you don't trust them. If you have some reservations, admit them and talk them over. Honestly telling them, "I get frightened when I think about you being out past midnight" is much better than "maturely" telling your sixteen-year-old, "We just know what's best," or "There's no reason for you to be out that late." A direct statement of your concern is always better than denying that you are a little worried or blaming your anxiety on your adolescents.

Once you are honest about your own feelings, you are in a better position to help your teenagers with theirs. Sometimes you can model an acceptance of ambivalent emotions and desires. You might say, "If I were in your shoes, I think I would have mixed feelings. I would want to take the job but I might also be afraid I wouldn't get it, or it might be too much." It can also help to say you were only asking the same questions you would ask yourself in a similar situation. These responses model the ability to look honestly at your own feelings or doubts without questioning theirs.

Your goal is to avoid two extremes. Don't let your teenagers force you to play a role that isn't you. If you are not an ogre, don't let them make you act or feel like one. But at the same time, don't try to stuff their upsetting emotions back down their throats. Let them know you hear their strong emotions. Be a good container. And after they have settled down, help them think things through. With time and patience you can help your teenagers acknowledge their mixed feelings and learn that they are manageable.

Chapter Highlights

This chapter is designed to help you help your middle adolescents grow out of their childish ways of understanding themselves and handling their emotions. If middle adolescence goes well, your sons and daughters will make major strides toward giving up their need to be protected by you, to be provided for by you, and to look to you as the major source of their security and the standard for their values. They will be feeling much more confident about becoming adults and they will have found a distance near enough to you to receive some support but far enough to feel increasingly independent.

By the close of middle adolescence, your sons and daughters will probably be less volatile and overwhelmed by their emotions.

They will be more able to handle their upset feelings by reflecting on the situations that triggered them and seeing some alternatives. They will be less likely to blame others for their upset emotions. They will also be more able to acknowledge their own contribution to a problem and more willing to take responsibility for their lives than they were even a couple of years earlier. Each of these abilities prepares them for the final stage of growing up—the years of later adolescence.

NOTES

1. Personal and clinical illustrations are by Dr. Narramore.
2. The fourth and fifth developmental tasks facing middle adolescents were described in chapter 9.
3. James 5:16.
4. 1 Thessalonians 5:11.
5. Dr. Lewis.
6. Dr. Narramore.
7. Dr. Lewis.
8. Proverbs 26:21.
9. Proverbs 29:11.
10. Proverbs 16:32.
11. Proverbs 17:22.

*Childhood
and the
prime of life
are fleeting.*
ECCLESIASTES
11:10 (NASB)

CHAPTER TWELVE LATE ADOLESCENCE: ALMOST GROWN

Remember our description of two- to three-year-old children who were completing their initial separation from their mothers?[1, 2] They were less anxious and less in need of your constant availability. They were outwardly more independent and assertive. And they had developed a relatively cohesive, stable, and independent personality. These changes reflected the maturing process psychologists call *consolidation.* Before your three-year-olds experienced this initial consolidation of their personalities, they first had to learn that they were mentally and physically separate from you, find out they could function on their own for brief periods, and develop a relatively stable set of memories of you that enabled them to feel less anxious when you were out of sight. They also had to learn that you would be available when they came looking for emotional support. Only after they learned these lessons were they ready to consolidate their own identities and become more independent.

Adolescents go through a similar process. During preadolescence, they learn that they are physically different from the opposite sex and mentally distinct from you. During early adolescence they practice separating from you and engaging in adultlike activities. During middle adolescence they gain increasing confidence to function on their own as long as they know you are available to support them. Their emotions become a bit more settled and they also experience some major changes in their understanding of themselves and others. But in spite of these changes, teenagers still don't develop a settled personality until late adolescence or young adulthood.

Early and middle adolescents are like an orchestra warming up for a performance. One personality characteristic hits a resonant note of maturity, another a flat note of childishness. Sometimes they stick responsibly with a job. Other times they excitedly begin a project only to give up a few days later. And sometimes they talk reasonably while at other times they throw a tantrum if they don't get their way. Their lives are a mixed cacophony of childish and adult attitudes and actions.

Between seventeen and twenty-one, your teenagers' psychological orchestra increasingly plays together. A previously stubborn or rebellious "No!" matures into a more thoughtful expression of a differing opinion. A livid blaming of others is given up in favor of a more responsible expression of anger and frustration. Infatuation and idealized romances are replaced by a growing ability to love maturely. A whirlwind of high school activities is pared down to fewer basic interests. And the naivete of early adolescence is replaced by more realistic thinking and ways of looking at the world. Your nineteen-year-olds' personalities probably won't sound like the Boston Philharmonic Orchestra, but neither will they be mistaken for your local junior high school band. They are more like a newly formed community orchestra that is learning to play together but will still take a while to be fully synchronized and musically mature.

As late adolescents consolidate their personalities they spend most of their time with friends outside the family. Many move out of their parents' homes or absent themselves so much that they are no longer a functional part of the daily family unit. They go away to college or take jobs with longer hours and greater re-sponsibilities. In various ways they keep replacing their previous dependency upon you with an increasing reliance on their own resources. In the process, your late adolescents will continue refining the attitudes and abilities they started acquiring in their earlier years of adolescence. Like budding musicians practicing to perfect their skills, they will continue solidifying their abilities to think for themselves by engaging in challenging dialogues with an ever-broadening range of people. They will keep growing out of their childish wishes to be taken care of by caring for more of their own needs. They will look more intently for someone to care for. They will continue growing out of their childish view of the world by facing more of both the hardships and pleasures of adult life. And they will become increasingly sensitive to their own emotions and experience them more maturely.

However good your teenagers' start on these abilities during early and middle adolescence, they need a few more years to fully incorporate these new ways of living in the world. Things that will eventually be second nature still create some worries for later adolescents. Many nineteen-year-olds, for example, still have trouble postponing an immediate gratification (such as a ski trip or new stereo) for a long-term gain (such as a car or an educa-tion). Some eighteen-year-olds experience incredible loneliness or depression if they go to college far from home. Other late adolescents are still testing their abilities to think independently of you by rebelling against your moral and spiritual values or challenging your economic or political views. They come home from college convinced that they know more than you. Still others are more emotionally volatile than they will be in a few years.

Late adolescence gives your teenagers a little more time to incorporate some new attitudes and skills into their lives before being completely on their own.

At the same time that late adolescents keep practicing skills they started learning in their earlier teenage years, they face the final two developmental hurdles of adolescence. *First* is their need to pull together their varied psychological resources into an organized, harmoniously functioning personality. *Second* is the need to consolidate their own unique personal identities. We will begin with a look at the organizing and settling process that generally occurs during the years from seventeen to twenty-one.

Pulling It All Together

Think about the last time you heard an orchestra warming up for a performance. The clarinets were running up and down the scale. Trumpets were testing their high notes. The trombones were practicing their slides and drummers were tightening or loosening their drum heads. The sounds were totally chaotic until the conductor tapped his baton on the music stand and suddenly the chaos turned to silence. All eyes focused on the conductor as he raised his baton, set the rhythm, and brought the entire orchestra beautifully together. From that time on, the conductor organized the entire performance and saw to it that the many talents worked beautifully together.

Every personality has its own conductor that brings order out of chaos. This conductor has been called the self or the ego. But whatever its name, it represents a set of psychological processes or functions that guide the personality and bring a sense of order and stability to the personality. These inner processes judge reality. They balance a person's immediate desires with long-term needs. They reconcile personal desires and needs with the needs and rights of others. And they balance their feelings with their thoughts and perceptions of reality. A well-functioning "inner psychological conductor" is one of the major results of your teenager's consolidation process.

Your children's "conductors" have been learning to lead their inner orchestra since they were born. When your infants cried to tell you they were hungry, they were trying to exercise a little influence over mother's section of the orchestra. When they pushed away from the breast after nursing they were telling you, "It's time to stop this number." As they began to walk and talk and say no, they discovered new instruments they could play. And when they first slept overnight at a friend's house, they learned they could lead the orchestra without mother watching every moment. Each time your children mastered a developmental task, they incorporated that new ability into their personalities and became a little stronger and more prepared to conduct their lives without you. This progressive integration of new abilities into their lives was the product of both their attachment to you and their ability to separate from you. Their closeness to you provided the emotional resources and models and training they needed to incorporate into their lives. Separating from you enabled them to test those resources and make them their own.

Although this consolidation process takes place throughout your children's lives, it is a special feature of the third year of life and of later adolescence. During these two periods children tend to pull together all the growth they have experienced up until that time and incorporate it into a more solid and stable personality. This process is a little like baking a cake. Before the cake is put in the oven, all of the appropriate ingredients must be added to the mix. Before your teenagers can consolidate their personalities they need all of the ingredients that were added at each earlier stage of development.

Infancy contributed their initial potential to love and feel safe with others. Toddler years contributed their ability to separate from you and begin to feel like independent individuals. Preadolescence contributed an awareness of their mental and biological distinctiveness. Early adolescence contributed confidence and joy in their ability to explore the world away from home. Middle adolescence contributed a more adult self-image and the confidence that they could cope with increasingly adult responsibilities.

And the entire period of adolescence contributed a more secure feeling about their masculinity or femininity. By late adolescence, these ingredients are ready to be mixed into an integrated and relatively mature personality. Instead of adding a lot of new ingredients, late adolescence is primarily a time for "baking" the ingredients that have been accumulating over the past twenty years of life. The end result of this "baking" or consolidation process will be the establishment of your son's or daughter's relatively mature and settled individual identity. That's the topic we will turn to now.

Who Am I?

Twenty-year-old Tom was a bright, creative child who never quite fit his parents' mold. From the time he was two or three Tom started asking all kinds of questions. In elementary school he was incredibly curious. As an adolescent he wore his hair longer than his parents preferred, dressed in a slightly off-beat style, spent a lot of time listening to rock music or practicing on his drums, and in general tried to tell his parents, "I want to be a little different." Tom tried hard to get his parents to recognize his special gifts and interests but with limited success. As he went through middle adolescence, Tom increasingly challenged his father's conservative political convictions. He criticized the "military and industrial establishment." And he complained about how naive most people were. His parents were sure he was about to become a radical.

When it was time for college, Tom decided to major in music and minor in philosophy. This upset his parents even more. They were sure he couldn't make a living with that education and encouraged him to find a major that would prepare him for a steady job. Tom persisted, however, and went merrily on his way. He continued exploring his liberal interests and dressed even more radically the first few times he visited home. He seemed to enjoy shocking and upsetting his mom and dad.

During his junior year, Tom's parents began to notice some subtle differences. Tom was beginning to wonder if he could make a living in music and philosophy. When he came home he was a little less provocative. The summer before his senior year he actually asked his parents' advice! More surprisingly, he seemed to listen—especially when they listened first. One day Tom told his parents, "I think I went into music for all the wrong reasons. I know I have some ability, but I wanted to do music so I could do my own thing. Now I don't know how I'll make a living." Another time he casually told his father, "I'm beginning to think the Protestant work ethic isn't all that bad." The next fall he called his parents to tell them about Rachael, a girl with whom he "had a lot in common." Then he said, "I think you'd like her more than you did Jessica" (his former girlfriend).

Tom's changes are typical of many later adolescents and young adults. He was rethinking his attitudes about his vocation, his values, and the type of person he might like to spend a lifetime with. In short, he was beginning to solidify his adult identity. Our identity is the sum total of who we think we are and what we value. It is all that is distinctively *me* in contrast to *you*. Once our identities are settled they become the central unifying core of our personalities. Everything we do is filtered through our understanding of who we are. Our identities include our moral, spiritual, and political perspectives and our answer to the question, Who am I?

If someone asks you, "Who are you?" you probably respond by giving your name. Then you might say where you live and what kind of work you do. Then you might tell a little about your family. And if you get to know the person better you might share something about your spiritual or political or social values and interests and commitments. We all define ourselves quite differently, but the chances are that after telling our names and where we live, we all would mention (1) what we do, (2) the significant people in our lives, and (3) something about our values and commitments.

These three areas are especially important in the formation of your late adolescents' identities. First, they must select a vocation and begin to see themselves as a productive (or soon to be productive) member of society. Second, they must come to see themselves as ready for a lasting, intimate relationship with a member of the opposite sex. And third, they must settle their values and spiritual and moral convictions.

When your children were young, their identities were largely wrapped up in you. They were "the Smiths' girl" or "the Joneses' boy." As they grew older they started building their own identities. They found out how they could compete with others. They discovered their unique aptitudes and abilities. And they found out what they liked and disliked in many areas of life. But as long as they were children, they still gleaned much of their identity from being a member of your family. When asked who they were, they might talk proudly about your job and values and friends. During adolescence your teenagers increasingly solidify their identities apart from you as they select their own values, decide their own likes and dislikes, and choose what they are going to do and be.

Your late adolescents' identity won't be totally new or different from what they have been becoming. In fact, there will be a sense of continuity tracing back to infancy as your sons' and daughters' inborn potential is creatively mixed with their past experiences with you, their long-standing feelings about themselves, their perceptions of their abilities and gifts, their spiritual and moral commitments, and their aspirations for their future. Adolescents need to answer three big questions as they solidify their distinct identities.

What Will I Be?

After her senior year of high school, Pam left home to work at a summer camp for children. At camp, she waited tables, cleaned cabins, and made new friends from throughout the state. She also put nearly all of her paycheck in the bank for college. Pam's best friend, Heather, stayed at home and took life easy. When they got together at the end of summer, Heather noticed a difference in her friend. "Pam," she said, "you've grown and stretched and made new friends and I've just sat on my rear end getting fat. I still haven't gotten out of my high school mode."

Pam hadn't changed radically in that three-month period but her friend could see a difference. By taking on the responsibilities of a job, Pam signaled a new phase of her life. She was more responsible for her finances. She had broadened her circle of friends. She had faced "the unknown world" beyond high school and found out that she could cope. In short, Pam was beginning to see herself as a competent and potentially productive member of adult society.

In an even more significant way, your sons' and daughters' eventual full-time educational and vocational choices will impact their personal identities. In order for them to consolidate their personal identities, they will need to think of themselves as teachers or musicians or parents or, at least, as in preparation for a definite career. Vocations have a much deeper meaning than simply how to make a living. They tell a lot about a person's interests and abilities. They reflect the kind of people we are and want to be. And they tell something about our values and commitments.

To take an extreme example, think of the vastly differing self-images of a lifetime thief and Mother Teresa, the great Catholic missionary to the poor of India. The thief, by choosing to steal, says, "This is the kind of person I am"; "This is how I look at life"; "This is what I think about myself and others." Mother Theresa's life of sacrifice reflects a totally different identity. She sees herself as a giving, caring person. She values others highly. She desires to serve the Lord. And she isn't interested in building financial or physical security into her life.

Selecting a career both helps late adolescents consolidate their personalities and is a result of some prior consolidation. Until your teenagers learn to face reality, engage in a little long-range planning, and feel comfortable about taking on adult responsibilities, they aren't ready to select a career. That's why most sixteen-year-olds (and some twenty-one-year-olds!) haven't decided on a college major or their life's career. But once late adolescents take a job or select a major, those decisions help them further consolidate their personalities. Since they are gainfully employed or working toward a specific career objective they feel more responsible and productive and gain more confidence. They also have a partial answer to the question, Who am I? They answer: I plan to be a salesperson, or a mother, a carpenter, a minister, a secretary, or a teacher. Once this question is answered, they feel a little surer about their personal identities.

Whom Will I Love?

As your late adolescents consolidate their identities you will see important changes in the way they relate to others. Since they are stronger and more independent than they were a few years earlier, they will be less likely to become enmeshed in dependent relationships designed to quell their anxiety over leaving home or their fears of failing as adults. Since they are emotionally more settled they will be less childishly excitable about the people they date. And since they have more clearly defined identities they will be increasingly ready for a long-term, intimate relationship.

When twenty-year-old Tom called his parents to tell them he had met a girl "with a lot in common," they sensed something was different this time. Tom wasn't commenting on how cute or how brilliant Rachael was. He also knew his parents would like her better than his last girlfriend. When Tom's parents heard this, they realized he was changing. They didn't know if Rachael would turn out to be "the one," but they did relax a little and feel a lot better about his potential choice of a marriage partner.

Your late adolescents' maturing capacity to love others will probably be reflected in a similar subtle change of attitude toward dating. Late adolescents still get anxious and excited and even infatuated. But their dating increasingly has a flavor of companionship or mate seeking, long-range planning or mutual sharing. Although early and middle-adolescent dating moves in these directions, it is still largely an exploratory or practicing stage. Middle adolescents tend to vacillate from one person to another or alternatively idealize and ignore or resent a particular member of the opposite sex. Since they haven't established their own mature identities they are often looking for someone to complete their personalities or help them break away from home. As important and necessary as these motives are, they do not make good grounds for marriage.

Since early and middle adolescents haven't consolidated their personalities they are still relating to the opposite sex partly as someone to fill the void created by emotionally leaving their moms and dads. They simply aren't ready to commit themselves to another person because their identities aren't complete. You can't commit half of a self or a dependent or needy self and expect an enjoyable, lasting relationship. Until your own personal identity is relatively settled, you are not ready to experience mature love and make the lasting commitments and compromises required in marriage. That is why more teenage marriages fail than marriages at any other age.

Some late adolescents date a variety of people to "play the field," find out what kind of people they enjoy being with, and just have interesting companionship. Others have one serious, long-term dating relationship that may ultimately lead to marriage. Others don't date much but still mature in their ability to relate meaningfully to the opposite sex. These late adolescents grow through their general friendships with members of the opposite sex or through "brother-sister" type relationships. No one of these methods is necessarily better than the others. They all provide late adolescents with increasing opportunities to spend time with the opposite sex, explore their mutual values and interests, and find out what kind of people they enjoy.

Many people have their "first loves" during middle or late adolescence. These friendships can have a lifelong impact—for good or ill. Many adolescents find the support they need to make the transition from feelings of childishness and dependency on mom and dad in these relationships. Not always to a parent's delight, many middle-adolescent boy or girlfriends encourage their dating partners to speak up more forcefully to their parents, to tell them to stop running their lives, or in some other way to step out on their own! These romantic friends also provide the emotional support to enable your teenagers to move further away from their past dependency on you.

Even the hurts that come when these relationships end can also be growth-producing. After a period of pain, anger, or mourning, most late adolescents can begin to see that the relationship had its weaknesses or potential problems as well as its strengths. In the meantime, they have taken in some more love (this time not from a mother or dad who was obligated to love them) and came to see themselves as more able to find their own relationships outside the home.

Some teenagers, of course, find these relationships difficult to give up. If it has been a lengthy one, if your adolescents idealized their boy or girlfriend excessively, or if your adolescents' needs were great, they may continue to be depressed or fantasize about their lost love for months or even years. Even after marrying someone else, they may compare their spouse to their first love. This can cause real problems in the marriage since it is impossible for a spouse to live up to the idealized fantasy of a past love. If your adolescents go through this experience, you can be of great help by listening sensitively and gradually helping them sort out their feelings.

What Do I Believe?

When Tom told his father, "I'm beginning to think the Protestant work ethic isn't all that bad," he was reflecting another shift in his understanding of himself and life. Tom's "liberal" adolescent values seem to have grown out of a combination of genuine sensitivity, youthful idealism, and rebellion against his parents. As he became more independent of his parents, he had less reason to react against their values. As he had more life experience, he began to see life more realistically. And as he started planning to make a living, he realized that he would need

a decent paying job. All of these developments came together to
help Tom experience a settling and maturing of his values. At
twenty he was more able to sort out the wheat from the chaff in
his parents' values. He neither had to naively swallow them all or
rebelliously reject them all. He could agree with some and
thoughtfully discard those parts that didn't fit with his developing
view of life.

Values and beliefs are an integral part of every person's identity.
They give meaning and purpose to our lives. They help define
who we are. And they provide the guidelines within which we live.
Spiritual commitments and faith in God help us make sense of life
and provide a unifying force and frame of reference. As your sons
and daughters pass through late adolescence they too will need to
rethink and solidify their moral and spiritual values and commitments. As psychologist David Elkind put it,

> Young people cannot attain a completely integrated sense of
> self and identity without an understanding of that which
> goes beyond self and society. . . . Religion provides a perspec-
> tive beyond ourselves and our world that helps us to manage
> the existential problem of realizing our significance and
> place in the universe.[3]

For Christians, faith goes beyond recognizing "our significance
and place in the universe" to having a personal relationship with
God who created us and forgives our sins. But the principle is the
same. Since teenagers are leaving childhood behind, it is a logical
time to ask themselves questions like, What is the purpose of life?
Why should I believe God exists? If he does, what is my relationship to him? Do I want to be conservative or liberal? How do I
make my life count?

For the better part of two decades your children have taken your
values and beliefs for granted. Now they need to think through
their faith for themselves. This rethinking creates a window of
opportunity when your children's lives are opened for a time of
special input and commitment. It provides one more opportunity

to add new ingredients as their personality "cake" is baking. But unlike in earlier periods of life, late adolescents don't limit their input to what they have been taught by you or a few teachers. Now they are free to explore new perspectives, seek new role models, and really think for themselves. They are able to move beyond, reject, or modify values they accepted as children out of respect for you. Now they must make moral and spiritual decisions on the basis of their own life experiences and understanding.

This can be a stressful time for parents. For the first time, your sons and daughters are fully free to structure their own moral and spiritual decisions. Since many late adolescents are away at college, in the military service, or in their own apartments, you can no longer monitor their actions—even if you want to. Even late adolescents who live at home spend most of their time out of the house. They are exposed to other values that they must consider and incorporate or reject. For the first time in their lives, your sons and daughters have the geographical distance, the physical and intellectual ability, and the psychological freedom to select their own values and behaviors no matter how much they might differ from your own. And for almost the first time in your children's lives, you have practically no control. Up until this time you could require them to abide by certain rules even when they didn't agree with you.

As your teenagers go through this reevaluation period, you may notice them becoming more dissatisfied with simple answers and black-and-white categories. They will discover that life is far more complex than they used to think and they will start searching for a more sophisticated way of understanding it. This is why most middle and late adolescents are so dissatisfied with rules. They see rules as childish and arbitrary and can't wait to challenge or break them. This is why students at schools with "codes of conduct" make a habit of rebelling against the rules. They realize that styles of dress, length of hair, and attendance at certain social activities are not the major issues facing our society and they want to know the real reason for these rules. They also sense someone is trying to control them, and that is something "real adults" don't like.

Late adolescents want to exercise their developing moral judgment, not simply abide by a set of rules that someone else established. At the beginning of adolescence, conscience is largely oriented to obedience. It is right to obey and wrong to disobey. By the end of adolescence your children's consciences will probably have matured to the point of seeing the deeper moral and spiritual issues and realizing that as well as black and white there are shades of gray.

To put this into biblical terms, late adolescents want to move away from the law or legalism toward a more mature, love-based set of moral commitments. They are realizing that moral decisions need to be made on the basis of respect for life and a love for others—not on an arbitrary code of do's and don'ts. This thinking may make you anxious, but remember that it is an absolute prerequisite for spiritual and emotional maturity. The apostle Paul said, "The entire law is summed up in a single command: 'Love your neighbor as yourself.' "[4] And Jesus Christ, when asked, "Which is the greatest commandment?" didn't reply, "Keep the law." He said, " 'Love the Lord your God with all your heart and with all your soul and with all your mind.' This is the first and greatest commandment. And the second is like it: 'Love your neighbor as yourself.' All the Law and the Prophets hang on these two commandments."[5]

Although laws are necessary and important, part of becoming a mature person is to look beyond specific laws or rules to see the needs of others or the principles behind the law. Once your teenagers can do that, they are a long way along the road to maturity. They will also be able to give a much better answer to the question, Who am I? since they will know their own values and commitments.

Character Formation

At the same time late adolescents are forming their adult identities and selecting their values and commitments, they are usually solidifying their character. Character includes their values and their sense of right and wrong, but it goes beyond that. It is a special part of one's identity. Once their character is formed they have a relatively stable and predictable sense of values. They experience remorse over wrongdoings but they don't berate or condemn themselves for failure. Instead, they feel a love-motivated concern for others or for the hurtful consequences of their actions.

Once your teenagers' characters are formed they no longer feel guilty for violating *your* standards. Now they feel remorse when they fall short of *their own* standards or the standards they believe God has for them. Their consciences, in other words, have become more independent of your values so they are free to determine God's will for their lives—not yours.

As your son's and daughter's character continues to mature, you will also see them more committed to making amends than to feeling miserable when they fail. Instead of blaming and condemning themselves for past failures, they try to make the future better. They also grow from their experience.

Taken together, these changes will make your adolescents much more responsible and mature. Their values may not always agree with yours, but you will see definite progress in the forming of their adult character.

Chapter Highlights

As your teenagers move through their later adolescent years, they will be integrating the growth they experienced in early and middle adolescence into their maturing personalities. They will continue learning to see reality more clearly. They will steadily develop a more balanced and settled emotional life. They will become increasingly more objective. And they will learn to delay some immediate desires in order to fulfill some long-term goals. Like teenagers of all ages, your children will pass through these maturing stages at different rates and in different ways. They will also have occasional setbacks along the way. But on the whole, they will be moving toward these more mature reactions.

The personalities of adolescents will become better organized and consolidated as they solidify their own distinct identities. These overlapping developmental accomplishments should result in a distinct settling and maturing of your late adolescents' personalities. During late adolescence most near-adults develop a clearer direction and purpose to their lives. They start thinking more seriously about their education, their vocation, and their philosophy of life. They become more ready for a lasting, intimate relationship with a member of the opposite sex. In short, their personalities become more stable and predictable.

Late adolescents still have a lot of growing to do and most of their lives still lie ahead. But as their personalities gel, their lives take on a much more settled and less changeable flavor. From that time forward, their growth usually comes by gradual maturing and slow changes in their personalities rather than by some radical or overnight alterations. Since their identities are more or less established they are no longer puzzling over such fundamental questions as, Who am I? or testing out all sorts of possibilities. Instead, they are busy living out what they have already decided they are going to be. By the end of this period of their lives they should have largely grown out of their need to be dependently taken care of *by you* and learned instead to be independent *like you*. Those are the basic features of late adolescence.

NOTES

1. Chapter 2.
2. Personal and clinical illustrations are by Dr. Lewis.
3. D. Elkind, *All Grown Up and No Place to Go* (Boston: Addison-Wesley, 1984), 215.
4. Galatians 5:14.
5. Matthew 22:36-40.

CHAPTER THIRTEEN
PARENTING LATE ADOLESCENTS

In professional basketball a player is credited with an "assist" when he passes the ball to a teammate who scores. Although the big scorers get the headlines, every coach knows his scorers couldn't produce without assists. Parents of late adolescents are a lot like assist players. If your children have successfully passed the developmental tasks of early and middle adolescence, they are nearly ready to consolidate their personalities and establish their own distinct identities. You won't be able to do this for them. You can look for every opportunity to pass the ball so they can score. And you may be able to serve as a coach who offers advice or as a cheering section which encourages them; but in most areas they will now have the major responsibility for finalizing their growth and maturation.

If you have been used to giving advice, setting limits, enforcing rules, and deciding the family game plan, you may have trouble adjusting to your new role. Becoming an assist-maker requires a different mental attitude toward yourself and your sons and daughters. You must accept the fact, for example, that you can no longer control many of their actions. They are now legally old enough to marry, live alone, buy alcohol, and go to war. You may decide not to give them money or a car or a place to live if they don't live the way you think they should. And you may require appropriate behavior around your home. But you cannot follow them around and control their actions—let alone their inner attitudes and values.

These changes stir potent feelings in many parents. Some feel abandoned as they watch their teenagers turn increasingly toward their friends. Others lose sleep or feel helpless because they fear their late adolescents will make disastrous decisions. Still others resent their late adolescents' efforts to assert their independence. A little of any of these feelings is normal. But be careful not to let them interfere with your ability to let your adolescents grow into adulthood. They must learn to make many of their own decisions—even if some of them are poor. The important principle to remember is: *your late adolescents still need you, but in a different way. Your goal is to love and support your teenagers in ways that foster the maturing and consolidating of their personalities and their unique identities.*

In this chapter, we will look at several ways you can assist your late adolescents. As we do, keep the two main developmental hurdles of late adolescence in mind. *First,* late adolescents need to pull together and organize their personalities by integrating all of the growth they have experienced by this time in their lives. This will mean that they learn to balance their emotional reactions with realistic perceptions of life, observe their actions from a more objective and mature viewpoint, and start planning for their future. *Second,* they will need to solidify their own distinct identities. They will do this as they increasingly think through their own values, plan their life's vocation, and prepare to establish an intimate relationship with a member of the opposite sex. Here are some ways that you can help.

Keep Listening

As late adolescents struggle to shape their own identities and consolidate their personalities, they need good listeners. Sensitive listening helps adolescents sort out their thoughts and feelings. Listening creates a sounding board that reflects back their various options and enables them to organize their thoughts and recognize the strengths and weaknesses of their logic. Many teenagers, after they have shared their ideas with a parent, suddenly brighten with recognition and say, "That doesn't make sense, does it?" Without saying a word, the parent's listening gave them an opportunity to hear themselves and to become more sensitive and objective.

Advice does just the opposite. It tends to rob adolescents of the experience of thinking for themselves. It perpetuates dependency and encourages them to unthinkingly adopt your views or rebel against them in order to find space to think for themselves. Even when late adolescents ask a question, there is a good possibility they aren't looking for advice. They are probably looking for an opportunity to clarify their options and their feelings.

If your high school senior asks you where you think he should go to college, don't tell him. And if your collegiate daughter asks, "What do you think I should choose for a major?" don't tell her either. Ask what they think and get them talking. A simple, "What have you considered?" or "What are your options?" forces them to think for themselves. You might suggest to your son that he write down a list of pros and cons of various college possibilities. Or you might ask your daughter what high school courses she has enjoyed or excelled in and which subjects turn her off. These exercises help narrow their choices without robbing them of the chance to practice making decisions for themselves. They also help your adolescents realize that they possess the ability to think things through. You don't need to make decisions for them. They just need to learn to consider their alternatives, to pay attention to their likes, dislikes, and abilities, and to find out where they can go if they need more information.

If, after some discussion, you think it could be helpful to offer your opinion about a major or a college choice, try to mention several possibilities. Tell your daughter, "You sure don't seem interested in history and English but you always do well in math and science. What majors would let you use those skills?" Or tell your son, "You seem excited about the possibilities at Georgetown." Then ask him about finances, geography, and some of the other reality factors involved. Broad, tentative advice gives your sons and daughters a little guidance without undercutting their responsibilities. It encourages them to keep on thinking and builds confidence in their decision-making skills.

Occasionally your late adolescents may both want and need your advice. When that is the case, don't hesitate to offer your more seasoned opinion. But first give them a chance to think the situation through for themselves. And when you do offer advice, offer it only as an opinion, not as some settled fact.

Well-timed questions can also help late adolescents cope with their personal struggles or conflicts or failures. If you can be sensitive and nonintrusive, questions such as "Why do you think your relationship with Sharon turned out like this?" or "This seems like a pattern. Do you have any idea what might be going wrong?" invite late adolescents to think for themselves or put their feelings into perspective. So do reflective statements such as, "This must have been brewing for a long time," or "Did you see this coming?" As long as your teenagers are ready to talk and you don't pressure them into disclosing more than they desire, well-timed questions can help adolescents momentarily step outside themselves and examine themselves more objectively.

Encourage Responsible Choices

Seventeen-year-old Rob[1] and his parents came to me for counseling because of their concern about Rob's rebellious attitude. Rob and his father were squabbling constantly, and his mother couldn't get him to do anything around the house. Rob complained that his parents kept treating him like a child. It turned out this family was suffering from a mixture of long-term problems aggravated by Rob's normal struggle to start thinking for himself, get out from under his parents' control, and take more responsibility for his life.

In our first counseling session, Rob told me how unhappy he was because he had no car. Since I knew he had a good paying job, I asked Rob why he didn't buy a car. He explained that he had recently paid several hundred dollars for a stereo, purchased some expensive tickets to a rock concert, and bought new skis for winter. I responded that it sounded like he could have had a car if he wanted one. "How?" he retorted. I pointed out that his stereo and skis alone cost more than enough for a down payment on a used car. If he had been willing to rein in his desires for immediate gratification he would already have the car he wanted so badly and wouldn't be so dependent on his parents.

Rob was defensive at such simple facts, but with a little discussing, he saw my point. In time he decided to draw up a list of priorities with a car fixed securely at the top. Then he started saving for it. Rob's parents also decided to help. They told Rob he wouldn't be able to drive the family car to school anymore because his mom needed it for her use. Forced to ride his bicycle to school for several days (very gauche in his circle of friends), Rob had even more incentive to curb his impulsive buying habits. Within six months Rob had his car.

Getting a car didn't solve all of Rob's problems but it taught him a lesson in long-range planning and gave him an increased sense of responsibility. It also helped him start breaking his passive dependent relationship with his parents and begin consolidating his own personality. Although Rob wanted his parents to pay his bills, he resented them for treating him like a child. Many late adolescents are trapped in this dilemma. They want to remain financially dependent but they resent any authority their parents exert or any limits they place on their life-style or behavior. You can help your adolescents avoid this trap by seeing that they take increasing responsibility for their own financial needs. Once they begin to earn their own money, it is easier for them to see themselves adultly and to have a stronger personal identity.

From the time Loren and Cheryl were in elementary school, their parents occasionally talked with them about their family's savings and investment decisions. They discussed the merits of putting money in a savings account compared to spending or investing it. Then they opened a small savings account for each child so they could put some of their birthday money in it. When Loren and Cheryl were middle and late adolescents, their parents added some money to the children's savings and told them they could leave it there or buy a few shares of stock. This forced them to read a little about the stock market and think through the merits of the safe but low yields of a savings account compared to the potentially larger profits but greater risks of the stock market. They weren't trying to turn Loren and Cheryl into expert investors, but they did want to teach them to think about the long-term consequences of their financial decisions. Even if they lost a little money in the stock market, they would gain some knowledge and decision-making experience.

Other parents help their adolescents learn to make decisions by discussing business problems, politics, or church issues. Any topic with two or more possibilities provides a chance to challenge your sons and daughters to think through the options and consider various possibilities. Don't burden them with heavy family decisions, but do involve them in significant family discussions and decisions. Coupled with the necessity of making choices on their own, they will find that these talks go a long way in preparing them for the responsibilities of adulthood.

Give Another Nudge

When Kevin started to attend a college twenty minutes from home, he thought it would be nice to keep on living with his parents. "It will save us money," he pointed out to his mom and dad. But Dan and Nancy quickly saw a potential problem. They had always been a close family, and although Kevin had a number of friends, he wasn't as socially active as he could be. He was content to spend most of his time around the house. Realizing that Kevin needed to expand his horizons, Dan and Nancy listened to his reasoning. Then they told him, "That's true. We could save a little money, but half the value of going to college is living in a dorm, meeting new people, and eating cafeteria food."

After listening to his parents' reasoning, Kevin somewhat reluctantly agreed to live on campus. The first few weekends he returned home as soon as classes were over on Friday. Then he missed a weekend or two. Soon he started coming home mostly on holidays or other special occasions. And when he came home, he often brought a friend. By the end of the year, Kevin was active in a number of campus activities and growing emotionally by leaps and bounds. He still came home and had good times with his mom and dad, but he was becoming a more independent and assertive young man. If Dan and Nancy hadn't pushed a little, he might have been happy to stay at home and drive to classes while remaining a passive observer of college life.

If your son or daughter needs a nudge to leave the nest, don't be afraid to give it. This doesn't mean all college students or high school graduates should live on campus or away from home. Sometimes that isn't possible or wise. But be sensitive to your late adolescents' need to venture out into the world and get out of a dependent rut. It is extremely difficult to consolidate your personality as an independent adult when you are still living off your parents. If your late adolescents want to live at home after high school, or need to because of finances, they should either be in college or have a full-time job. You can also give nudges by letting them buy their own cars, wash their own clothes, fix some of their own meals, and otherwise take care of themselves.

Don't Bail Them Out

Jack and Caroline were a financially successful couple in their early sixties. Growing up during the depression years of the

1930s, Jack's first job was in construction. He kept his eyes open for ways to increase his income and was eventually able to borrow money to buy a small piece of property. With his own hands, he built a warehouse on the property. Then he leased it out for commercial use. Before long Jack purchased another piece of property, and then a third. During the next thirty years he amassed a sizable amount of land and money through hard work and shrewd investing.

When I met Jack and Caroline they had three grown children. Their forty-year-old son had started several small businesses (with his father's money) but every one had failed. Their thirty-year-old son was married and had a low-paying job that he didn't take seriously. He was living rent-free with his family in a nice home that Jack and Caroline provided. Their twenty-six-year-old daughter was also married and living on one of the family properties. Her husband was an artist who was barely making enough to keep food on the table.

As Jack and Caroline poured out their concerns about their children, they told me, "We found out too late that we had given them too much." I agreed. Every time Jack and Caroline bailed out their older son, they prevented him from learning from his unwise business choices and fueled his fantasy of "hitting it big" without having to work like other people. By providing a house and a car to their younger children, Jack and Caroline allowed them to remain comfortably dependent. When I talked to Jack and Caroline, their three children were simply waiting for their parents to retire or die so they could live off their wealth. "If I had it to do over again," Jack told me sadly, "I'd give all my money away. It's been the curse of our lives."

Actually, Jack wouldn't have needed to go that far. All he needed to do was to help his young adults get through college or make a down payment on their first small house. He could have offered them an entry-level job like anyone else in his company. This would have started them on the road to financial stability while leaving them with the major responsibility for their own financial welfare. Jack might have also expressed his love with an occasional monetary gift or by starting a savings account for the grandchildren's college education. Or he could have paid for a family reunion every few years.

Jack and Caroline had fallen into the trap of providing things for their children that they could have earned themselves. This was a dangerous mistake. By giving their late adolescent and adult children things they could get themselves, they unknowingly reinforced their dependency and irresponsibility and prevented them from maturely consolidating their personalities. Even in their thirties and forties Jack and Caroline's children hadn't yet settled their vocational identities and their values were more like those of adolescents.

The tragedy of Jack and Caroline is that they loved their children deeply. They really wanted the best for them. But think about it. It was probably Jack and Caroline's struggles during the depression days that brought out their resourcefulness and helped them get ahead financially. By giving too much to their children, they unknowingly robbed their children of the very thing that made them successful.

Dan and Roberta handled their finances a better way. They offered their children jobs in their small business and helped them through college. But once they were married, the children were financially on their own. Dan and Roberta supported their church and other ministries generously and didn't give any large amounts to their children until after they retired. By that time, all of their children had responsible positions in the ministry or other work and had learned to handle their own finances. Dan and Roberta's gifts were now gladly welcomed, but they didn't come so soon that they deprived the children of taking responsibility for their own families.

When we help our children too much, or when we bail our children out of financial and other difficulties, we delay the day when they will learn to face reality, make good decisions, consolidate their personalities, and develop their mature identities. We keep them thinking, I am a person who has to be taken care of, instead of, I am a person who takes care of myself. Although it may be painful, we must progressively cut the financial cords that bind our adolescents to us. This doesn't mean we suddenly walk into our nineteen-year-old's room and announce, "Son, you are on your own!" It does mean that beginning in early childhood we look for opportunities to let our children make decisions. We occasionally let them learn from the school of hard knocks and we see to it that they learn to take responsibility for their allowances and their recreational activities. By late adolescence, we make sure they are experiencing the full consequences of most of their decisions and by young adulthood (twenty-one or so) they should have their own jobs and be providing for their own financial needs, with few exceptions.

Let Them Teach You

Nineteen-year-old Craig was a sophomore at a local university. He had grown up in an upper-middle-class Christian family and developed a set of moral, spiritual, and social values that were very similar to his parents'. He dressed nicely but not extravagantly, held a part-time job, tithed his income, and was thinking of a business career. During his freshman year in college, Craig roomed across the hall from a minority student from a low socioeconomic background. They struck up a friendship, and over the holidays Craig spent a day visiting his friend's house. Craig was shocked by what he saw in the ghetto. As a child, he and his family had driven through that area and he knew its poverty from a distance. His church even supported some Christian ministries in that area. But his middle-class upbringing had not prepared him for a firsthand experience with poverty.

Over the next year, Craig's cross-cultural experiences kept raising questions about what he now saw as his parents' comfortable upper-middle-class mentality. He started challenging his parents about their nice cars and expensive vacations. "How can you justify spending thousands of dollars on these things when millions of people are starving around the world?" he asked. Craig also criticized his family for spending so much on clothes and eating restaurant meals.

When Craig started confronting his parents about their values, they initially felt irritated and upset. After all, it was because they had a good income that Craig was driving a car, attending a fine university, and had the leisure to sit around and debate their moral deficiencies. Craig didn't help the situation by gently raising his concerns. One evening he sat down and rather obnoxiously attacked their "un-Christian" and "uncaring" values. "How can you spend a thousand dollars on a new television set when people are dying?" he asked. "And do you know that the money you spend on vacations each summer could feed five third-world families for a year?"

Craig's dad had just about reached his limit. He shot back, "Look, I'm paying for your education. You are driving a car I helped buy. And you never griped about the money we spent on vacations when you went along. I really resent your attitude." Then, just as their discussion was about to deteriorate into a real fight, Sam caught himself. He realized he was about to create a scene that wouldn't help their son at all. He also realized there might be a little truth in what Craig was saying. Could it be that he wasn't as good a steward as he thought? Did he have a larger responsibility to the underprivileged and the poor? And was his family wasting money that could be spent more wisely?

"Look, Craig," Sam said, "I'm sorry I got upset, but I felt you were attacking your mom and me. We've spent years trying to provide a good life for you and your brothers and now it sounds like you're throwing it all out the window." "No, Dad," Craig replied. "I appreciate everything you've done but I'm just realizing how many poor people there are in the world and I think we should do something about it." Then they had a good discussion about the problem. Sam realized that in Craig's visionary, youthful enthusiasm, he might be overdoing it. But underneath his criticism of his parents' life-style was a genuine concern about the needy. As Craig moved beyond his middle-class environment and faced the realities of life for millions of less fortunate people, he was adjusting his values to fit his new perspective.

After Sam apologized, Craig realized his dad was big enough to consider the possibility that he had become calloused to the needs of the poor. Sam even told Craig that he was willing to sit down and reconsider his priorities. Sam didn't agree with all of his son's arguments and he pointed out that although vacations cost money, the chance to rest and recuperate made him more effective in his work and his involvement at church. Even Jesus stopped to rest occasionally. Sam also made it clear that he believed it was his responsibility to provide for his family and to insure adequate income for his and Sandra's retirement. He pointed out the potentially huge medical bills they could easily face in their older years and explained that most people will need approximately 70 percent as much income to live on in retirement as they did while they were working. Since they might spend twenty years in retirement, they would have to save all of that while they were still employed.

Sam's willingness to consider his son's viewpoints let Craig know that his father believed he was a sensible young adult with ideas that deserved consideration. What more affirming experience can a fledgling adult have than finding out that his father can admit he might be wrong and his son right?

At the same time Sam helped his son by taking his criticisms seriously, he also helped Craig clarify his own identity by not agreeing with everything he said. In order to develop their own identities, teenagers and young adults need opportunities to push up against someone with different values. This helps them test out their own beliefs and learn to defend or reevaluate them. If Sam had given in to Craig's arguments, sold his house, and given all his money to the poor, he wouldn't have helped his son at all. But by both agreeing and disagreeing with his son, Sam helped Craig find out what it is like to challenge another adult and learn to give and take. He helped Craig gain confidence in his own perceptions. He helped him feel respected even though he held a differing opinion. And he helped Craig see a few weak links in his argument and strength in others.

Like Craig, all late adolescents need their parents to listen to their ideas and take them seriously. But they also need parents who can nondefensively articulate the reason for some of their opposing beliefs and values. This balance of sensitive listening and shared opinions provides late adolescents the greatest opportunity to think through their own opinions, to separate from their parents emotionally, and to consolidate their own unique and solid identities.

Stay Available

Late adolescents still have a lot of maturing to do and they face an array of important questions and decisions. They worry about dating, their college major, study, jobs, money, or their spiritual commitment. Although they can find ways to work things out without your participation, your listening ear and occasional help can reassure them and keep them from being overwhelmed by the new pressures and responsibilities. Eighteen- to twenty-one-year-olds aren't ready to be cut off from your encouraging support just because they are now largely directing their own lives. Like early and middle adolescents, they still periodically need to approach you again to share some new experiences, receive a little affirmation, or get some emotional propping up. They also need some occasional adult advice and opportunities to talk.

Charles was privileged to share meaningfully in his nineteen-year-old daughter Jodie's life. Although she had a full-time job and lived in an apartment thirty minutes away from her parents, Jodie regularly kept in touch. One weekend she talked to her father about two boys she was dating. "Kyle is really nice," Jodie told her dad. "And he's very mature and thoughtful. But sometimes he's almost too serious. Darryl is a lot more fun, but I don't know if he will ever get serious enough. I have a lot of fun with him, but I don't think I would want to marry him."

For two hours Jodie and her dad talked about Jodie's boyfriends and the kind of man she would eventually like to marry. Charles asked a few leading questions and affirmed both the strong points of the boys Jodie was dating and the importance of her concerns. He also assured Jodie that he believed she would eventually find someone who combined the best traits of both Kyle and Darryl.

Charles' talk with his daughter wasn't earthshaking but it did help her keep thinking through her values and the possibility of marriage, and it affirmed her attractiveness to men and her good judgment. It also helped her consolidate her personality and become surer of her own identity, her wishes, desires, and commitments.

Valarie did a similar thing for her twenty-year-old daughter Chris. After two or three bad experiences with men, Chris told her mother, "All men are jerks!" Valarie asked her daughter to tell her what happened and they had a long talk. Valarie agreed that some men were "jerks" but assured her that all of them were not. Then she shared a couple of her own young-adult experiences. Like Charles, Valarie helped her daughter keep a positive attitude toward the possibility of eventually finding a healthy, happy man and establishing a loving home.

If your late adolescents live at or near home, you may have similar opportunities to enjoy your young adult children and encourage them. If your daughter is in a public event at college, make a point of driving over to watch. If your son has a new job, drop by after he has settled into his routine. It is usually best not to come by the first day on the job. And don't check on them or hang out around their work since those kind of visits feel infantalizing. But do let them know you are interested and supportive of their new activities in life and do let them share their new adventures with you if they want to.

Once in a while your late adolescents may want to kick back and be a child all over again. They may long for you to fix that familiar Sunday dinner or play games like you used to when they were younger. If these times come, take advantage of them. They are sons' and daughters' way of saying, "I enjoyed those family times. They bring fond memories. Can we do them again?" Once in a while, late adolescents may even tell you they want you to take care of them as you did years earlier. In a mock childlike voice they may say, "Mom [or even 'Mommy'], will you read to me?" or "Can we play games after dinner tonight?" Their knowing look says, "I know adults don't act this way but for tonight I would like to be treated like a child again." These fun times reconnect your children with the happy times of their past and put one more deposit in their emotional bank.

Fill Up Some Holes

No children pass through adolescence without a few emotional bumps and bruises. And fortunately, even late adolescents are still open to the healing influences of loving parent-child relationships. When our own children were in their late teens, my wife and I found some good opportunities to solidify our love and give them a few things we hadn't been able to provide in earlier years. Although Richard (then Dickie) had gone with me to a lot of speaking engagements when he was a child, he still didn't have a clear picture of what psychologists do for a living. When he spent his first year at Biola University where I teach, he occasionally dropped by my office. We would chat about projects I was working on or I would let him read a few memos I had written or invite him to sit in while I talked with a student. We also talked about courses he was taking and the ones I was teaching. This maintained our connectedness and friendship at the same time he was gaining a clearer picture of what university faculty do. It is probably not coincidental that Richard is currently in graduate school preparing to teach on the college level.

When our daughter, Debbie, was seventeen, a friend told my wife about the novel *Anne of Green Gables*, an exciting story about an orphan girl growing up in eastern Canada in the first part of this century. It is written in vivid, descriptive, and romantic language. Although Debbie was finishing her junior year of high school and was in many ways an independent young lady, she asked her mother to read *Anne of Green Gables* to her one evening. Kathy read the first couple of chapters and they were hooked. Every night for weeks after that, no matter what time Debbie got home, she wanted Kathy to read her a bedtime story.

Sometimes when Kathy went to bed without reading, Debbie came knocking on our door with her book in hand and a mischievous smile on her face and reminded her mom, "Didn't you forget something?" Then she climbed into bed between us as she had when she was a little girl and Kathy read another chapter. Fortunately *Anne of Green Gables* has a sequel, so they kept on reading.

One weekend the three of us were driving to San Diego to watch Richard pole vault in his college track meet. Debbie and Kathy curled up beside each other in the back seat so they could read a few more chapters of *Green Gables*. Feeling a little shut out at one point of the trip, I asked Debbie if she wanted to drive awhile. But with a knowing smile and words that only a psychologist's child would use, she smartly replied, "Nope. Can't you see Mom and I are bonding?"

Even though Debbie was moving away from us in many ways, this period of intimacy with her mother was a renewing respite. It gave them a chance to bond again and to enjoy a nourishing quiet time together just as Debbie was becoming increasingly independent. A year later she was on her own, living away from home, and holding a challenging job.

Our experiences with Richard and Debbie at seventeen and eighteen were natural and easy. They allowed us to keep emotionally supporting our adolescents, even though they were already becoming young adults. As they neared twenty-one we were still able to be available, but in different ways. Instead of reading together or discussing my work, Richard and Debbie wanted to share their work, their plans, and their approaching choices. At various times we talked about a person they were dating, their college major, their future vocations, a job, politics, and faith. In each of these discussions we tried to be sensitive listeners who could draw them out while only occasionally offering our own perspectives. Our goal was to help them think through their own goals and directions, not push them into ours.

Sometimes late adolescence gives parents and teenagers a chance to start overcoming some longstanding problems or conflicts or misunderstandings. Older sons and daughters may be more ready for serious talks than they were a few years earlier. If you are sensitive to appropriate times, they may open up and share at a surprisingly deep level about their feelings or concerns. If they don't initiate this kind of conversation but you suspect they might like the opportunity, you can set the stage. One evening during a dinner together, you might start by reflecting on some experiences you had as a young family. You could recall some enjoyable or humorous time together and then a couple of difficult ones. If your teenagers respond with interest you might ask, "What were some of the happiest times you had while you were growing up?" Then you might ask, "What were some of the difficult or painful times?"

If you have an appropriate opportunity, you might say, "I'd be interested in knowing more about how you felt when you were growing up. Mom and I loved you a lot but we know we weren't perfect parents. We would be interested in some of the things that made life a little harder for you." You might mention that you nagged a lot or lost your temper or were too anxious. Or you might mention some period when you struggled in your marriage or were a workaholic during your children's developing years.

Current events or a movie you watched together can also trigger opportunities for meaningful conversations. Like all talks with adolescents, it doesn't help to force your way in, but most late adolescents love to talk if they know they will be understood and have their perspectives respected.

You can't immediately make up for all the troubles in your teenagers' growing years, but you can let your sons and daughters realize you know your family had some problems and that you all need to keep growing. Sometimes you can take specific steps to correct an earlier problem or fill in a few gaps in your relationship. If you were too busy to spend time with your children when they were young, for example, your seventeen- and eighteen-year-olds probably won't suddenly want to spend a week's vacation with you in a remote location or start having family fun nights together! But they might be interested in a weekend ski trip or other special outing—especially if they can bring a friend along and don't have to spend too much time with mom and dad. Some great family discussions have been carried out around the fireplace in a cabin on a weekend trip away from home or around the dining room table during semester break.

These talks can open your sons and daughters to seeing new aspects of their formative childhood years. They can also become a healing force in your relationship. Unless communication has been seriously ruptured, you may be able to listen to your adolescents' thoughts and feelings better than you did when they were younger. You are probably more mature and sensitive than you were a few years earlier and they will sense that. Don't expect any overnight changes, but don't assume your opportunities to help late adolescents grow are over. Many young adults have been able to change substantially as they learned to communicate more openly with their parents.

A thirty-year-old businessman I counseled had an important healing experience when his surgeon father admitted he hadn't been available to my patient when he was growing up. My patient had resented his dad for years because his work and his patients seemed more important than his son. Once the father admitted he had regrets about his failings as a husband and a father, my patient was able to start forgiving him and growing out of some destructive patterns.

Chapter Highlights

Late adolescents are nearing the end of their journey from the dependency of infancy to the independency and interdependency of adulthood. Along the way, you have been their primary source of love and nurturance and instruction. You may also have been their best friend and counselor. We can boil down many of the suggestions of this book to one foundational principle. Parents need to be *optimally present.* That is, we need to keep just the right degree of psychological closeness as our children mature. During infancy that closeness is almost totally complete; we need to be constantly available. As our children grow older, we need to give them more and more space while still being constantly available. And as our children pass through middle and later adolescence, they need more emotional distance from us while still knowing we are available and supportive when they need us. By young adulthood, they should be essentially on their own.

If you have been optimally present, your children will be able to make a shift from needing you to being like you. Instead of needing you to provide for them, protect them, set their goals, organize their lives, and establish their values, they need to reach the point of doing those things for themselves. At that point they become their own conductors and solidify their own distinct identities. They still have a lot of growing ahead but their foundation is strong for their future.

In 1942, a young Jewish girl, her family, and the family of her father's business associate took refuge from the Nazis in a hidden upstairs section of a warehouse in Amsterdam, Holland. For two years this little band of eight Jews lived successfully in hiding as the German invaders terrorized Holland, imposed harsh anti-Jewish measures, and finally began deporting Jews to prison camps for extermination. During her two years of hiding, Anne Frank wrote one of the most remarkable diaries of all time. In *The Diary of a Young Girl,* she detailed both the intriguing experiences of her family and her own rich inner experiences. Shortly before her family was discovered and she lost her life in a Nazi prison camp, Anne wrote these remarkable words:

> I have one outstanding trait in my character, which must strike anyone who knows me for any length of time, and that is my knowledge of myself. I can watch myself and my actions, just like an outsider. The Anne of every day I can face entirely without prejudice, without making excuses for her and watch what's good and what's bad about her. This

"self-consciousness" haunts me, and every time I open my mouth I know as soon as I've spoken whether "that ought to have been different" or "that was right as it was." There are so many things about myself that I condemn; I couldn't begin to name them all. I understand more and more how true Daddy's words were when he said: "All children must look after their own upbringing." Parents can only give good advice or put them on the right paths, but the final forming of a person's character lies in their own hands.[2]

Although she was only fifteen at the time, Anne's words reflect both the sensitive observations of a bright, creative mind and the adolescent processes of consolidating her personality and establishing her own identity. Notice several things about her.

• She "knows herself"
• She "watches her actions like an outsider"
• She faces herself without making excuses
• She knows what's good and bad

And most importantly, she realized "Parents can only give good advice or put them on the right paths, but the final forming of a person's character lies in their own hands."

Although the last comment is a little overstated in light of the tremendous, lasting influence of parents, Anne was clearly well on the road to taking responsibility for her own life and consolidating her personality. At fifteen years of age, she had moved beyond the exploring, practicing stage of early adolescence and the dependency-independency conflicts of middle adolescence. Her emotions were not on a psychological roller coaster and her many abilities and gifts were functioning quite harmoniously together. Certainly her difficult life experiences and her creative genius helped make her unusually mature for her age. But in their own way, all adolescents must experience a similar settling and maturing of their personalities.

You can help your late adolescents consolidate their personalities by:

- staying available
- continuing to listen
- encouraging responsible choices
- giving a gentle nudge
- not repeatedly bailing them out of difficult situations
- letting them teach you
- filling up some holes through honest discussions or renewing times together.

If growth goes well during these important years, your children should enter young adulthood with a relatively settled sense of who they are. They will feel moderately confident of their ability to tackle the real world. They will either have a full-time job or be ready to accept one. They will have a maturing set of values and beliefs. They will be more self-aware and sensitive to the needs of others. And they will be nearly ready to make a lasting, deep, and loving commitment to a member of the opposite sex.

NOTES

1. From Dr. Lewis's case files. Other personal and clinical illustrations in this chapter are by Dr. Narramore.
2. Anne Frank. *Anne Frank: The Diary of a Young Girl* (New York: Pocket Books, 1953), 234.

PART III

WHAT DO WE DO NOW?

PART III

WHAT
DO WE
DO NOW?

Son, why have you treated us like this? Your father and I have been anxiously searching for you.

LUKE 2:48

CHAPTER FOURTEEN
LETTING GO

Bill and Carol Woods were missionaries to South America.[1] When their eighteen-year-old son, Keith, left for the United States for college, Bill and Carol cried a little but were able to face the separation without too much difficulty. Keith made the separation easier by keeping in touch on a regular basis, and over the months Bill and Carol were able to emotionally release their son and enjoy Keith's growing independence.

A year later, the Woods' seventeen-year-old daughter, Cheryl, was scheduled to leave for college. Bill and Carol prepared themselves for Cheryl's departure, but they were shocked when their third child, fifteen-year-old Karen, decided she wanted to go to the States too. The Woods' first reaction was to refuse to let her go. They had coped with their son's departure and they were prepared to say good-bye to their older daughter, but they weren't ready to lose their youngest child and say good-bye to both their daughters at once.

Bill and Carol told Karen they would like some time to talk over the options before making a decision. First, they took some time by themselves sorting out their own feelings and desires. Was Karen old enough to go? Four thousand miles seemed so far! What if one of the children became seriously ill or had a difficult problem and they wouldn't be there to help? But as they talked it through, they realized that Karen would leave in a year or two anyway. They also realized their question shouldn't be, "What would we want?" but, "What is best for Karen?" Once they got this far, they were ready to listen to Karen's thinking and try to come to a decision.

That evening the family sat down to talk. Karen pointed out that she had few friends left in South America. All the older MKs (missionary kids) she ran around with would be leaving, including her best friend who had just graduated from high school. Karen also wanted to be close to her brother and sister. She reminded her parents that she would be sixteen when she left and that she had a standing invitation to stay with an aunt and uncle near her brother's college. "It will be fine, Mom," she assured her. "And the details won't be hard to work out."

After giving themselves a few more days' reflection, Bill and Carol decided they had given Karen a strong spiritual and emotional foundation and that with her aunt's and uncle's help, she probably was ready to make the move. The advantages seemed to outweigh the disadvantages.

That summer Bill and Carol flew to the States to help their children settle in. Bill returned to South America after three weeks while Carol spent the rest of the summer with the children. In September she checked them into school, said her good-byes, and was taken to the airport by a dear friend. When she arrived at the airport, it was more than she could handle. "I bawled for an hour," Carol told me later. "And even after I stopped bawling the tears kept streaming down my face. When I got on the plane, the whole front of my blouse was wet. The man on one side of me leaned away and stared out the window like I had the plague. The man on my other side finally said, 'Lady, who died?' 'I'm dying,' I said. 'I'm a missionary going to South America and I just left my three children in the States.' "

In spite of Carol's pain, Bill and Carol let go of their children beautifully. They resisted their first urge to force their daughter to stay at home, admitted their fears to each other, and talked their way through to a wise decision. They reminded themselves they still had each other and that they could keep in touch by letter and an occasional phone call. They also consoled themselves by remembering that Joseph was separated from his family in Egypt[2] and that Daniel was sent from Jerusalem to Babylon[3] as a young man, and they both did quite well! By letting go when their children were ready, Bill and Carol gave their children a beautiful gift. They expressed confidence that their children could make it away from mom and dad. Keith, Cheryl, and Karen felt their parents' confidence and knew they were loved and committed to God's care as they began their separate lives.

Few of us will have to say good-bye to three children at the same time. But in one way or another, we all will have to say good-bye to our adolescents. Throughout history, parents have told their sons good-bye as they went off to war, or to another part of the world, not knowing if they would return alive. And in less painful ways, all parents eventually face the time when their children take that final step from home. Sometimes it is a small step across town. Sometimes it is halfway around the world. But regardless of the physical distance, it is never a small step emotionally. Once our children step out on their own, something changes forever. They are suddenly more responsible for their lives—and we are a bit less necessary. They are more independent—and we are more alone. They are busier with other activities and friends—and our homes are a little quieter and our lives a little emptier. In some ways, we have become ex-parents. This can require as much adjustment on our part as it does our children. If our children are off to a good start, seeing them go can be an exciting, joyous time.

But even then, most parents feel at least a tinge of sadness as their children go.

The Thompsons had a harder time letting their children grow up. When their son Kevin wanted to attend an out-of-state college, they promised to buy him a new car if he went to a local university and lived at home his first two years. When Kevin tried to transfer out of state after his freshman year, they threatened to take his car away. And when he married, they offered to pay a hefty down payment on a home "if you will move close enough for us to see our grandchildren."

After the Thompsons' daughter, Katie, graduated from high school, she continued living at home. Even after she had a good job and could support herself financially, she had a hard time breaking away. When Katie decided to marry a man her mother didn't like, her mother only grudgingly attended the wedding. But the year after Katie and Don were married, Katie's parents offered to pay for Katie and Don's vacation on one condition—that they go to Hawaii with her mom and dad. Another time Katie's mother tried to bribe Katie into a family vacation by offering to purchase her and her husband some clothes they badly needed. Needless to say, Kevin and Katie had a hard time separating from their mom and dad. And even though they eventually did, it cost a lot of guilt and struggle—and on Kevin's part a lengthy period of rebellion.

In this chapter, we look at some of the feelings you may face as your children grow up and leave the nest. We will also look at some ways you can prepare for that stage of life and avoid the problems that come from trying to hang on to your children after they are ready to go.

Facing Your Loss

Remember when Jesus was twelve and Mary and Joseph took him to Jerusalem for the Passover celebration at the temple? After the Passover they headed back to Nazareth and assumed that Jesus was somewhere in the crowd of relatives. But a day later, they couldn't find him. You can imagine their fears. Was he lost? Hurt? In danger?

With these questions on their minds, they hurried back to Jerusalem. And when they found him, they reacted like any parent. "Son," Mary said, "why have you treated us like this? Your father and I have been anxiously searching for you."[4] Or to put it in our vernacular, "Your father and I have been worried sick!"

If Jesus' mother, who had been told by an angel that her son would rule from the throne of David,[5] worried about Jesus, it is not surprising that we worry about our adolescents. From the time our children are very young, most parents worry a little when they are out of sight or away a little longer than expected. We also have mixed feelings as they become more independent and less in need of us. Remember the first time your two-year-old stubbornly told you, "No! Mommy (or Daddy), I do it!"? You may have felt pleased or amused by his growing confidence and ability, but weren't you just a little irritated that he was taking so long or insisted on doing it by himself? Or weren't you a little sad that he didn't need you quite as much? And if that was a strictly happy occasion for you, didn't you feel a twinge of sadness when you watched your child walk down the sidewalk alone to his first day of school? Did you feel a little apprehensive the first time he went away for a week at camp, or the night of her first date, or the day she got her driver's license or took a part-time job? Although we feel pleasure and excitement in seeing our children growing up, we can also feel a little anxious, rejected, or even angry at them for leaving us.

If you have been aware of some feelings of anxiety or loss during your children's growing years, you will probably find their adolescent separation relatively easy. You won't be surprised by either your teenager's efforts to move away or by your own misgivings. Like Bill and Carol, you will be ready to face your mixed emotions. But if you were unaware of the little losses you experienced as your children progressed through childhood or felt overwhelmed by them, you may have a tougher time helping your teenagers leave. If this is true of you, now is the time to sit down with your spouse or some friends and think back over your children's earlier years. Talk over their accomplishments and little moves away from you and try to recall your feelings at those times. Your best preparation for letting go will be your awareness of your feelings, whether they are excited and happy, anxious and sad, or any combination.

Since their early years, my own children have been relatively independent. Kathy and I have tried to nourish and guide Richard and Debbie, but we also allowed them to tackle new experiences as soon as they were ready. They occasionally slept over at friends' houses and left us for weekend trips and summer camps from the time they were six or eight years old. When Richard was seven, he flew to Arizona to visit his cousins and spend a week attending school with them in the farming town where I grew up. When he was fifteen, he traveled to Indonesia by himself to visit some missionary friends. When Debbie was sixteen, she spent a week in Mexico working in a local church with other teenagers from our church youth group. They both worked part-time as middle adolescents and they have both purchased their own clothes (from a set allowance) ever since they were ten years old.

These experiences assured us that Richard and Debbie had become responsible young adults who could handle life away from home. They also helped prepare Kathy and me for their eventual departure from our nest. Still, we will never forget the days our children moved out of the house for college.

On those days, three years apart, they each packed their things. We helped them check their lists so we were sure they had everything they needed. Then we went out to their cars to say good-bye. We hugged them, told them we loved them, prayed together, and wished them well, as we wiped away a couple of tears. Richard and Debbie were affectionate and thanked us and told us they loved us, but they weren't particularly emotional. After all, they were only going thirty minutes away and could come back any time they wanted.

Kathy and I had an entirely different reaction. We knew an era had come to its end. We were no longer parents of dependent children. We were no longer needed to tell them good night and encourage them during the day. And we were no longer physically close. In short, our children were leaving us. As Richard and Debbie happily drove down the road to college, we put our arms around each other, walked into the house, and cried.

When Richard left, it was hardest for us. He was our first child and our close-knit family was breaking up. For several minutes we alternated between crying over our loss and laughing at ourselves for bawling like babies. But our crying wasn't "babyish" at all. In fact, it was an adult thing to do. We were expressing our grief over losing Richard and we were affirming how much he meant to us. We were also crying because we were happy for him and affirming his adulthood. We weren't crying because we were neurotically attached or immaturely hanging on. And we weren't crying because we felt like failures. We were thrilled with his progress and happy with our relationship with him, but we weren't going to deny our loss and act like it didn't matter. When you have invested eighteen years in a relationship, it is abnormal not to feel a loss.

When Debbie left, it was a little easier. We still felt some sadness, but her departure was more gradual than Richard's. We had also been through it once before. Other parents have the opposite reaction. They have the hardest time letting go of their youngest because he or she is the last child.

Once Kathy and I allowed ourselves to experience our loss, we were ready to start enjoying our children's newfound independence—and our own. Human emotions are like that. Once we face our painful feelings, we can enjoy our positive ones. In the case of departing adolescents, if we aren't aware of the loss we feel, we may try to hang on in ways that are hurtful to our children as well as preventing us from moving happily into the next stage of our lives.

For some parents, grieving a departing child can be a little like grieving the loss of a loved one through death. First we try to deny the loss. We glibly say, "They are just going across town." Or "We haven't lost a daughter; we have gained a son-in-law." But true as these comments may be, they are only part of the picture. Even though you have gained a son-in-law, you have also lost your daughter. And though she is "just across town," things will never be the same.

After an initial round of denial, parents may then feel some resentment toward their departing young adults. We may say (or want to say), "How can you do this to me?" Or when our children drop by the house just long enough to wash their clothes or clean out the refrigerator, we squeeze them with comments like, "Why don't you stay long enough to talk?" or "You *never* spend any time with us anymore." These feelings are normal, but don't let them get the best of you. If you try to handle your feelings of rejection by pressuring your children into spending time with you, you are likely to create resentment and drive them farther away. Remember how you felt repelled when your mother reminded you, "You never write anymore," or "You never spend any time with us"? Chances are you felt a twinge of guilt or irritation and you may have made a silent resolution to do better. But if you were like most young adults, your behavior didn't change. In fact, you may have distanced yourself even further while feeling guilty the entire time.

When you feel like pressuring your departing adolescents with guilt-inducing comments, step back and take an honest look at your own feelings. If you are feeling unneeded or abandoned, don't deny it. But don't blame your feelings on your children either. Share them with your spouse or a friend to get a better handle on them. Put yourself in your children's shoes and remember your departure from your parents. Was leaving home easy or difficult for you? What made it that way? What did your parents do that helped? What did they do that made it harder? Were you thrilled or sad to leave or both? Did you allow yourself to feel any loss or were you totally wrapped up in your new endeavors? And once you had been away awhile, did you start missing mom and dad? In short, what did you need and feel when you were their age? By recalling your own feelings and experiences, you may find it easier to identify with your adolescents and help ease their transition to adulthood.

Staying Connected

Lest I be misunderstood, I am not suggesting that the moment your late adolescents move out of the home you should suddenly never want to see them again. Of course you will want to see them often. I am simply suggesting you relate to departing late adolescents as the young adults they are.

Most late adolescents and young adults enjoy dropping by or being invited home to dinner occasionally. If your collegiate or working young adult seems to drop by your house only to get something, take advantage of that brief time. If you think you need a little more time, don't sit idly by, feeling hurt or resentful. Express your desire for some time together and come up with a couple of specific suggestions. You might tell your college-age son, "We know you are busy at school and we are glad for that. But since you are only an hour away, we wish we had a little more time together. Since you come home every couple of weeks, do you think we could plan a Sunday dinner or work out another definite time when we can sit down and talk awhile? We don't want to cramp your style and we know you are busy. But we would like to have a time that we could look forward to once in a while." Or tell him, "We would like to see your campus and take you out to dinner sometime." Specific statements like this are much more helpful than complaints, such as, "You *never* spend any time at home," or "You *never* talk to us anymore." They are also more helpful than general statements such as, "*Sometime* I need to talk with you."

If your young adults aren't willing to agree to an occasional planned time, don't force it. They may be telling you they need more space. Pressuring them won't help. The only exceptions I would make to this are when you are still paying their college bills or when your young adults are coming home for you to meet some of their needs. If they come home to wash their clothes or eat, it is fully appropriate to ask them to spend a little time with you in exchange for the service. And if you are paying for their education, you deserve an occasional report on how your investment is going.

But even then, work out those times mutually rather than pressuring and coercing them.

Parenting Is a Temporary Job

Parenting is a high calling that takes enormous energy and commitment, but it is not our only responsibility, nor is it a lifetime task. The very first time children are mentioned in the Bible, the parent-child relationship is pictured as eventually giving way to the intimacy of the husband-wife relationship: "For this reason a man will leave his father and mother and be united to his wife and they will become one flesh."[6] The marriage relationship is to be the enduring one, not the parent-child. Although we want to enjoy our children's companionship throughout life, our primary responsibility is to launch them into adulthood.

From the time her first child was born, Frances threw herself into motherhood. Within five years, Frances and her husband, Dave, had three children. Dave worked long hours at his job and had little time for the family. Before long their marriage became dull and unfulfilling. When he was available, his mind was usually on his work. Sensing that Dave wasn't about to change, and not knowing how to express her needs to him, Frances soon made the children the center of her life. She developed few interests outside her home and spent hours chauffeuring the kids from one activity to another. She helped with their homework and school projects and assisted in several clubs for children. To many people, Frances was a supermother. She worked tirelessly to meet her children's needs and sacrificed so much for them. When her children hit adolescence, Frances continued her active involvement in their activities. She served as a band mother. She was on the parents' council at her children's high school. And she was at all of her teenagers' athletic games and other school activities.

When Frances' older two children finished high school and went to work across town, she felt some emptiness but quickly immersed herself in her remaining child's activities. Six months after her youngest left the nest, Frances started slipping into a depression. At first, she didn't know what to do with herself. Then she started becoming irritable. When she tried to get some support from her husband, he was still too busy. Before long, Frances started experiencing serious depression. She was crying a lot and spending hours in front of the television. When she started thinking of taking her own life, Frances finally sought out professional counseling.

During therapy, Frances uncovered the roots of her depression. She had grown up on the wrong side of the tracks and had been physically and verbally abused. She married at seventeen to get away from home. Vowing to protect her children from an unhappy childhood like her own, she threw herself into motherhood. And though she was dissatisfied with her marriage, she said little to her husband since their marriage was better than her own parents'. Instead of communicating her needs to her husband, Frances filled her life with her children's activities. When the children moved out, she was left with a stale marriage, unresolved childhood feelings of loneliness and depression, a certainty of being unneeded, and no job skills to seek employment outside the home. She was trapped emotionally and socially.

As Frances faced her depression and the way she had been using her children to avoid it, she was gradually able to turn her life around. Even though her husband was unwilling to work at their marriage, Frances became happier and more productive. She started by developing new friendships. Then she found a half-time job that employed some skills she had acquired in her volunteer activities. Within a couple of years, she had regained her confidence and was functioning well.

Like Frances, many women pour their lives into their children. While some of this is good, it can be overdone or done with the wrong motives. Some parents attempt to overcome the loneliness or rejection they experienced as children by investing in their children. Some are compensating for their dissatisfaction with their marriages. Others, like the frustrated athlete or musician, are trying to relive their lives through their children. But whatever the reason, if you have overly invested in your children, now is the time to start looking to your future. Your children need it so they can leave you without guilt or fear, and you need it so you can find other sources of fulfillment.

Children need parents who don't need their children. Parents who give to their children in order to meet their own needs give with strings attached. This binds children to the parents or makes them an extension of their parents. Mature parents give with no strings attached because they are giving out of a full cup. Since they have relatively sturdy self-concepts and their basic needs are met, they are able to give to their children and to enjoy their growing up and eventual departure. They are also prepared for the empty nest.

There *Is* Life After Children

I realize all your children haven't left home yet or you wouldn't be reading this book. I also realize you may be looking forward to some peace and quiet, an extra bedroom, the car in the driveway when you want it, and food in your refrigerator where you left it. But that isn't the whole story. You will soon have a relational vacuum where your children used to be. And your home—which has been filled with sounds of childhood—can suddenly seem awfully empty unless you are prepared for the next phase of your life. If you haven't done so already, think about these questions:

- Is your marriage strong enough to nourish and fulfill you?
- Are you involved in enough church or community activities to keep you challenged and busy?
- Might you want to go back to work after the kids leave?
- If you have been working to put your children through school, will you want to cut back?
- Do you have plans for increased time together as a couple?
- Will you want to make new friends and expand your social network when your children leave the scene?

Questions such as these can help you prepare for the departure of your children. If you are prepared, the post-parenting years can be an exciting time of life. In fact, many people find these are some of the most enjoyable years. Since your children are well launched, you can have both the fulfillment of a job well done and more time and money to do some things you have wanted to do for years. Travel, friends, new jobs, more education, a business venture, or more time to be involved in church or social activities can be exciting and fulfilling. But those things won't happen without some planning. Start getting ready now.

Enjoy Your Memories

Several summers ago, my wife and I returned to our favorite vacation spot, the island of Kauai, Hawaii. During previous years, we had spent several beautiful times there with our children. For the first time since our honeymoon, we were there without Richard and Debbie. We wondered if we might be lonely for our children. As we drove around the island, we found ourselves reminiscing about different experiences with our children. We remembered where Richard caught his first fish. We remembered where Debbie learned the hula. We revisited Brenneke's Beach where our children had spent so many hours boogie boarding in the surf. And we recalled the hiking and camping we had done along the Na Pali coast. These memories vividly brought back the happy times our family had shared together. In a very real way they filled the void created by our physical separation from our children.

In chapter 9 we described the way your children's emotional lives were first nurtured by your loving care and later by their memories or inner mental pictures of your care. Memory is the pen that etches your love in your child's mind and the conduit that keeps communicating that love across the miles and years. As your middle and late adolescents increasingly move away from you, they will be sustained by these memories as well as by their developing abilities and newfound friends. Even if they are many miles away, they will know you love them and have their pictures of you tucked safely away in the recesses of their minds. Those memories will keep nurturing them and reminding them that they are capable, loved, and competent to cope with life.

In much the same way, you have gone through a psychological process of internalizing memories of your children. During your children's growing years you too took in a vast gallery of pictures of your times with them. You remembered their infant days, their toddler years, and each period of their lives. Like your children, you internalized the pictures of both good times and bad. When your children leave, you may have some regrets over your failures, and some sadness over your loss. But you will also have a lot of fulfillment and pleasure from your many positive memories and emotions. Just as your children take you with them in their minds, you now take them with you. Those memories can fill your lives long after your children have left the nest, and they are one of God's great provisions for parents. Combined with other resources and friends and activities, they can enable you to look as expectantly to your own future as your children do to theirs.

Face Your Failures

Not all of our memories, of course, are pleasant. All parents have at least a few regrets over their relationships with their children. Some look back and see some serious mistakes. Some of us realize we let those years slip by too quickly. Others see our young adults struggling and wish we had been more helpful to them. Loving our children as much as we do, our having these regrets can be normal and even healthy. But how should we react to our failures and regrets?

First, let's face them directly. None of us were perfect parents. When my wife and I look back at our children's early years, we realize we could have done better. Kathy was more anxious than would have been ideal, and I was too busy at work. When our children started misbehaving, neither of us was as patient and sensitive as we could have been. Especially with Richard, we lost our tempers when he was slow to cooperate. We sometimes found it easier to try to frighten Richard into obedience than lovingly to lead him there. We knew our anger wasn't helpful but couldn't seem to get a handle on it. By the time Debbie was born, Kathy and I had learned enough about ourselves and our children to be less anxious and irritable. We wish we had been more that way with Richard, but we weren't. So, when Richard was older, we talked with him about the impact of our anxiety and anger.

At the same time we face our regrets and failures, we should avoid unrealistic guilt and blame. What's done is done. Rather than mire ourselves in guilt or condemnation, we need to admit our shortcomings, acknowledge the extra stresses they have created for our children, experience some genuine regret, and move on into the future. Condemning yourself for being less than the ideal parent actually makes it harder for you to let your children grow up. Instead of allowing you to happily watch them mature, your guilt can make you hang on while you look for one more chance to fix the past. But by the time your children reach young adulthood, they have to find their own ways of coming to grips with their problems, just as you did with yours. If they seek you out in that process, great. If not, there isn't much more you can do. The best strategy is to accept your strengths and weaknesses and be honest about them with your children. That gives them the best chance of maximizing their own strengths and growing in their areas of need.

Remember Whose They Are

Christian parents can have either an extra resource or a special difficulty in letting adolescents go. For us, our children's spiritual choices are not simply a matter of being morally upstanding members of society. We believe their choices affect them for all eternity. This causes some Christian parents to be overly anxious or attempt to hang on too long or control too much. When their teenagers start rebelling or questioning their faith, these parents panic. Fearing for their children's eternity, they pull out all the guilt or fear that they can muster to keep them in the fold. Unfortunately, these maneuvers only compound the problem. As important as your teenager's faith is, overcontrol and pressure in this area is as hurtful as in any other.

On the other hand, Christian parents have an extra aid in letting go. We know we have never "owned" our children. God placed them in our homes for a limited time so we could nurture and prepare them for adulthood. From the very first, our job was to equip them to be healthy, happy people who love God and want to serve him and his world. Once we have done our part, we can step back and let other influences do their work.

It also helps to remember that God is not powerless to work beyond what we have done. God doesn't ask us to do the job of parenting by ourselves. Church, teachers, and friends play important roles. Your children have the freedom to make decisions of their own. And in adulthood God will continue to guide your sons and daughters if they ask for his direction.[7] Your continuing prayers, your years of love and training, your children's own maturing judgment, their friends or spouse, and the power of God will be working together to keep them moving toward maturity.

Chapter Highlights

Letting go is a process that begins at birth. It is being sensitive to your children's unique needs, interests, and abilities and encouraging them to make choices, try things, and step out on their own at every stage of life. Some parents find this easy. Others struggle because of their own needs or fears. The best way to feel good about your children's growing up is to:

- affirm their increasing maturity and skills
- face your own mixed feelings about their growing up

WHAT DO WE DO NOW?

- maintain an appropriate ongoing contact
- prepare for the years after they will leave
- enjoy your memories
- face your failures and regrets
- remember God is not finished with them yet.

With these suggestions for handling our own emotions and feeling good about letting our children go, we turn next to a discussion of some of the experiences and dynamics that can make it difficult for children to let go and leave maturely.

NOTES
1. Illustrations are by Dr. Narramore unless otherwise indicated.
2. Genesis 37–42.
3. Daniel 1:1-21.
4. Luke 2:41-50.
5. Luke 1:26-33.
6. Genesis 2:24.
7. Proverbs 3:5-6.

Teenagers need both to cleave to their parents and to leave. Any family pattern that blocks consistent nurturing or prevents them from leaving on schedule makes it difficult to mature emotionally.
THE AUTHORS

CHAPTER FIFTEEN
ROADBLOCKS TO MATURITY

Each of the developmental hurdles children and adolescents face is designed to help them grow up and become more responsible and mature. Like runners preparing for a race or weight lifters getting ready for a competition, children need to stretch and strengthen their emotional and mental muscles. If the difficulty or height of each successive hurdle is gradually increased as your teenagers prepare to meet a challenge, they are able to grow through the experience. Each time your sons and daughters clear a new hurdle, they become a little stronger and more ready for the competition of adult life.

Whether that challenge is becoming aware of their mental distinctiveness from you during preadolescence, developing friends outside the family during early adolescence, or learning to face reality and overcome their dependency strivings in middle adolescence, your teenagers grow by successfully meeting new challenges. Each successfully navigated hurdle strengthens their personalities and helps them consolidate more mature identities. But just like young athletes, teenagers can be confronted with challenges that are too sizable or overwhelming and they need a lot of support and encouragement in the process. If an aspiring athlete tries to run a marathon his first day of practice, he is doomed to fail. And if an aspiring adult runs into obstacles that are too formidable or if he doesn't have sufficient help, he is likely to give up trying or find a devious way to complete the course. As the parent of teenagers, your responsibility is to see that as much as possible your sons and daughters encounter their developmental challenges with the right preparations and appropriate resources and training. If you don't, their growth can be delayed and their personalities can develop weak links or become distorted.

In earlier chapters we have incidentally mentioned several experiences that make it difficult for teenagers to meet confidently the challenges of adolescence and move smoothly on toward adulthood. Now we want to detail a more complete picture of the potential roadblocks adolescents can encounter. We will do that in this chapter and the next by looking at five experiences that can delay or derail your adolescent's normal maturation processes. These experiences are (1) problems in attaching or bonding in infancy and childhood, (2) clinging parents and other barriers to separating on schedule, (3) problems individuating and developing a solid personal identity, (4) premature separations from parents, and (5) physical and sexual abuse. In this chapter we will talk about the first three potential barriers to your adolescents' smooth departure. In chapter 16 we will look at the latter two.

Barriers to Attachment

Teenagers cannot become independent, mature adults until they first receive plenty of emotional nurturing. In a nutshell, children and adolescents need a deep feeling of belonging and

being loved. They need parents who are consistently available.
They need to play and have fun. And they need to be understood
and to learn to communicate freely with their moms and dads.
Taken together, these experiences provide preadolescents with
the full tank of emotional fuel they need for their trip through
adolescence. Anything that interferes with this nurturing process
makes it more difficult for teenagers to grow up happily and
healthily.

Some infants and toddlers, for example, have trouble bonding
with their mothers. Through no fault of their mothers' or their
own, some children are born colicky or restless and unable to
attach securely to their moms. Others are hospitalized for several
months immediately after birth because of physical illnesses. And
still others have trouble bonding because their mothers are ill for
lengthy periods or are too anxious to care calmly for their infant
children. Children whose mothers go back to work soon after they
are born, children whose mothers go through a severe period of
postpartum depression, and children under three years of age
who spend most of their daytime hours in day-care facilities may
also have trouble gaining the sustained material nurturing they
need.

Brian had this problem long before his teenage years.[1] Shortly
after Brian was born, his father started having an affair. Brian's
mother, Pat, learned of the affair and became distraught. She
spent so many of her emotional resources fighting her husband
and "that other woman" that she had little left for her infant son.
When Pat's husband finally left her four years later, she started
putting her life back together. But by then, Brian had missed out
on a lot of emotional nourishing that comes from the mother-
infant bonding. Pat told me, "I was physically present, but I wasn't
emotionally available. I remember just letting him cry in his crib
because I felt I couldn't comfort him. And when he wanted to play,
I was just too drained. I was so preoccupied with my own problems
I couldn't pay attention to Brian's needs." The departure of Brian's
father created an additional emotional void for this sensitive
four-year-old.

When Pat brought Brian for counseling, he ran up to me and grabbed me around the waist. When I sat down in my chair, he kept hanging on. And when his mother tried to move him to the waiting room, Brian would not let go. Pat told me, "That's the way he always is. He hugs even strangers because he feels so insecure." At seven years of age when his friends were mingling with peers and gaining confidence to relate outside the home, Brian was clinging to any available parent substitute. If he had not gotten help through counseling, he would have continued to seek intimacy and care obsessively or would have eventually turned away from all people to avoid further hurts and disappointments.

Later childhood and adolescent experiences can also make it difficult for children to feel as loved and nurtured as they need to be. Divorce, separation, or ongoing parental conflicts undermine the security of an adolescent's love. So do passive, uninvolved parents or workaholic parents who are physically present but emotionally absent or unavailable. Adolescents whose parents give a lot of advice but aren't sensitive listeners may know their parents are concerned about their actions or successes but wonder if they care enough to understand their needs and hurts and feelings. *These teenagers may be loved, but unless they experience their parents' interest in their lives in practical, daily ways, they may not feel loved.*

Some teenagers sense that their parents are interested in their achievements and activities more for the parents' ego than for the teenager's good. Even though parents like this seem extremely involved in their children's activities, the teenagers still feel isolated and unsupported because they sense that their parents' interests are selfish. Teenagers whose parents don't show an interest in their high school activities and their friendships and experiences can also feel less supported than they need to be.

Here is a list of other experiences that can make it difficult for children or adolescents to attach securely to their families and receive the emotional nourishment they need in order to grow up on schedule.

- Physical or temperamental factors present in the child at birth
- Physically absent parents (whether through death, divorce, or separation)
- Emotionally absent or preoccupied parents
- Anxious parents who find it difficult to calmly relate to their children
- Parents who are uncomfortable with intimacy and emotional closeness
- Family fights and conflicts that interfere with a sense of togetherness and make closeness frightening
- Parental inability to enjoy their children and communicate respectfully (this makes it harder for children and adolescents to feel connected and understood)
- Serious parental illnesses or accidents that force adolescents to take care of their parents

This last barrier deserves additional explanation. Teenagers whose parents become ill or who have serious accidents or emotional struggles may be prematurely placed in the position of having to care for that ill parent. Instead of receiving their parents' calming, loving influence, these teenagers must step in to help their parents. In the case of lengthy physical illness or injuries, some early and middle adolescents are forced to work in order to help support the family. Others have to give up most of their free time to help around the house. Teenagers with seriously depressed parents or parents with conflicted marriages can also feel like they have a responsibility to make their parents happy or help them solve their problems.

Although some adolescents seem to accept these heavy responsibilities, they can also suffer serious problems later. Deprived of their childhood, they may develop an overly acute sense of responsibility, find it difficult to relax and enjoy life, or find it hard to separate from their injured or ill parent enough to develop a life of their own. Since they have to give before they have received, they may learn to take care of others' needs but not their own.

Although this may seem mature—or even biblical—it isn't. The

Bible says mature giving comes after one has received what he or she first needs. Christ told his disciples, "Freely you have received, freely give."[2] And the apostle John wrote, "This is love: not that we loved God, but that he loved us. . . . We love because he first loved us."[3] The ability to love and give is a response to being loved. Until teenagers have grown inwardly strong, they are not ready to nurture and give a lot to others. The apostle Paul showed a sensitivity to this when he told the church at Corinth, "Children should not have to save up for their parents, but parents for their children."[4]

Although we parents have needs and hardships, it is not our children's responsibility to take care of us. Teenagers need to share responsibilities around the house, handle their own schoolwork and church and school activities, and be prepared to offer extra help in emergencies. But they should not be deprived of a normal period of adolescence by being responsible for their parents' health or happiness or security. When a crisis hits, or when parents are sad or anxious, we should seek encouragement and help from our mates or other adults—perhaps a physician or counselor—but not primarily from our children. After our adolescents are grown, they will have enough of their own inner resources to help us in our times of need. But as teenagers they still need to be on the receiving end of care. If they are, they will be prepared to return the favor when our resources and health start failing in our later years.

Barriers to Separating

Once children have attached securely to their parents and received the initial nurturing they need, they are ready to start becoming less dependent. Any experiences that bind your children to you after they are ready to start asserting themselves can become a second barrier to their growing up.

Henry and Helen Almajian moved from Europe to the United States after they were married in the early 1930s. Recent immigrants, the Almajians prided themselves on their U. S. citizenship, their family history, and their ethnic background. They determined to share their heritage with their only child, a daughter, Lisa. To do this, they celebrated all of their ethnic holidays as a family, attended a small ethnic church, and taught Lisa a good bit of their mother tongue at an early age. Henry worked long hours in his small family business and Helen carefully reared their daughter to be a good citizen, a committed family member, and a dedicated Christian.

The Almajians had strong convictions about politics, morality, and Christianity, and they tried to protect Lisa from what they saw as the negative influences of the world. They feared non-Christian friends might drag her down, so they rarely allowed her to play with neighbor children. She wasn't allowed to sleep over at friends' homes because "we don't know those people." And when their family socialized, it was always with a tight circle of friends from their church. Lisa's mother often told her, "When you are in trouble, you can't count on anyone besides your family."

Henry and Helen closely regulated their daughter's behavior from early childhood. Helen was a compulsively clean and orderly woman who wouldn't allow Lisa to go into their formal dining room without her parents' permission. She dressed Lisa like a doll and carefully saw to it that she didn't get dirty. By the time Lisa was four, it was clear that her mother was also highly anxious over sexuality. Helen would no longer let her sit in the lap of any man except her father. She never talked with Lisa about her body. And she didn't allow Lisa to watch any television programs except the news because "most of them are dirty." When Lisa got older, she wasn't permitted to cut her hair or wear any but the slightest makeup. Her mother said, "That will make you look like a 'woman of the world.' " And when Lisa wanted to wear slacks or jeans as a junior higher, her mother told her, "How could you think of doing that? It will just make men stare at your rear end." Consequently, Lisa always had to wear a dress to school.

Lisa wasn't allowed to date until she turned eighteen and even then her parents wanted to select her boyfriends. Although this practice was common in her parents' native country, in the United States it alienated Lisa further from her peers and tied her even more closely to her mother. When Lisa wanted to go to the state university several hours away from home instead of to a local college, her mother made her feel guilty about desiring to leave. She repeatedly told her, "You want to go away from home, don't you? You want to leave me." One day she remarked, "I think you want to hurt me. You'll go away and have a good time at college and I'll be the one who's sad." Torn between needing to get away from her controlling, engulfing mother and feeling guilty over leaving, Lisa somehow managed to get the courage to go away to college. But as soon as she arrived at school, her mother started phoning and writing to tell her how lonely and sad she was without her daughter. After fighting guilt for an entire semester, Lisa gave up and returned home to attend the local college.

Back home, Lisa's mother continued her efforts to control. Over a period of years she pressured Lisa into breaking off two prospective marital relationships. And when Lisa finished college, her parents talked her into doing the accounting for her father's business. Now in her late thirties, Lisa is taking care of her aging parents, trying to talk her father into finding a buyer for his business, and regretting the years of living she has missed. Her friends periodically urge her to get out before it is too late, but she can't stand the accusations of betrayal that would bring. Her conscience, echoing her mother's indictments, would reproach her for being such an unloving, uncaring daughter.

Lisa's story could be entitled "Ties That Bind." Although the Almajians meant no harm, they bound their daughter to them as much as if they had put her in a prison. She was imprisoned by bars of fear and guilt. We could describe Lisa's dilemma this way: Although she received a lot of love from her parents (especially her mother), that love was filled with anxiety, control, and guilt. It was "smother love" designed to meet her mother's needs for a caring daughter, not love that was given for Lisa's benefit. Consequently, at each stage of adolescence, Lisa had trouble mastering her God-given developmental tasks.

When Lisa reached preadolescence, for example, she should have been learning to think differently from her parents. But how could she? Henry and Helen weren't comfortable letting her think for herself so they made Lisa feel as if she were a bad child if she questioned or challenged their judgments or decisions. During preadolescence, Lisa also wasn't enabled to feel good about her dawning sexuality and her physical differences from the opposite sex. Every one of her attempts to feel good about her body and her femininity were squelched by her mother's anxiety or guilt. So instead of feeling a healthy pride in her physical development, Lisa felt guilty and ashamed.

When Lisa reached the practicing stage of early adolescence, she wasn't allowed to practice being adult by starting to separate from her parents as her peers did. She wasn't allowed to sleep over at a friend's house. She wasn't allowed to go to the social functions that help most early adolescents begin to break away from their moms and dads. And she certainly wasn't allowed to practice relating to the opposite sex.

When she reached middle adolescence, Lisa couldn't grow by facing the usual developmental hurdles that most adolescents encounter—trying to cope with the adult world while still having some desires to remain dependent on their parents. Lisa couldn't even entertain the thought of doing most of the things her friends did. She wasn't allowed to drive a car, vacation with a friend, take a part-time job, or just have some free time with her friends. She was to go to school and church, come home, and be part of the family. Since she could never test out her ability to function in the world beyond her home, she could not outgrow her dependency and develop feelings of confidence and self-assertiveness.

Even when Lisa reached late adolescence, her parents kept preventing her from growing up. She couldn't go happily off to college like many later adolescents. She couldn't get an apartment of her own. She couldn't date whomever she pleased, and eventually she ended up working for her father. When it came time to solidify her identity in later adolescence, all of this left Lisa with a serious problem. Who was she? What was her own unique identity? How could she think about leaving her parents to eventually marry and become intimate with another person? How could she select her own vocation and feel good about her ability to compete in the world of work? And how could she develop a mature set of her own moral and spiritual values since she had never been allowed to think for herself? Since Lisa didn't have these inner strengths and abilities, she could only develop an identity as a dependent helper who sacrificed her own life for others.

If Lisa had had a brother (or a sister) he might have taken precisely the opposite route. Instead of giving in to his parents' control, he likely would have rebelled against his parents, left home at an early age, and rejected all that the Almajians stood for. And if he married, he would probably be afraid his wife would try to control him and run his life the way his mother had. So to avoid that, he would either keep his distance or try to control his wife before she controlled him.

Our discussion of Lisa's family isn't intended to blame her parents. Any of us can unknowingly erect barriers that make it difficult for our teenagers to separate on schedule. The Almajians' tenacious clinging grew out of their own emotional needs and conflicts. For some reason Helen was extremely fearful of being left alone. She apparently felt so emotionally fragile or impoverished that she needed her daughter to fill her void. And she also must have felt incredibly anxious and guilty over her own sexuality. Like each of us, the Almajians brought their own needs and problems to their job as parents. But we can learn from their mistakes. Here is a list of the type of barriers that can interfere with any adolescent's progression toward mature independence. Notice how many of them Lisa's parents displayed.

- Parental overprotection or control (this makes it difficult for adolescents to learn to make independent decisions and feel confident about their abilities)
- Insufficient opportunities to test out one's ability to cope with life outside the home

- Inadequate opportunities to shift their dependency from parents to peers (friends should serve as a transition from dependency toward independency)
- Inadequate parental modeling of how to function competently in the world
- Lack of opportunity to learn skills that might lead to a vocation
- Guilt and fear motivation (this binds teenagers emotionally to their parents)
- Lengthy illnesses which deprive adolescents of opportunities to practice coping outside the home and force them to remain dependent
- Parental discomfort with their own or their teenager's sexuality (this makes it difficult for adolescents to feel good about their sexuality—a requisite for leaving home and anticipating a meaningful relationship with a member of the opposite sex)
- Parental inability to validate their adolescents' developing sexuality
- Parental illness or unhappiness that forces teenagers to care for their parents
- Parental discomfort in allowing adolescents to think for themselves

Adolescents whose parents hold on too long react in one of two ways. Some cease their struggle to grow up and resign themselves to remaining a child. Like Lisa, they remain overly tied to their parents, controlled by fear or guilt, and unable to develop their separate emotional lives. Throughout life their parents continue to manipulate their decisions, evaluate their actions, and set the limits of their freedom.

To avoid this perpetual bondage, other young adults break away and vow never to return. Fearing engulfment, they stay angry and distant to avoid being sucked into their parents' controlling ways. These are the adult children who rarely call or visit their parents or who avoid all but the most essential family gatherings. Since their being around their parents stirs up so much guilt and anger, they purposely avoid them. And while these children may be better off than their siblings who remain at home, their lives are still not free of their controlling parents. Since they must always keep an emotional distance from their parents, they are unable to be emotionally close or relaxed around them. And since their ways of coping with their parents tend to carry over into other relationships, they usually have trouble establishing intimate relationships with their own spouses and friends. They are always afraid someone will intrude on their space, violate their autonomy, or manipulate them through guilt.

Spouses of such adults know exactly what we mean. There is always a wall, a fear of getting close. The same needs for emotional safety and autonomy that drove them from their parents make them fearful of being close and vulnerable with their spouses. They develop an exaggerated, self-assured style or silently withdraw to protect themselves from being swallowed up or becoming too dependent on a needy, controlling person.

Barriers to Individuation and Identity

As we saw in earlier chapters, becoming a mature adult involves more than just becoming emotionally independent of your parents. It requires a four-step process of first attaching, then separating gradually, then developing one's own individuality, and finally establishing one's own stable identity. Each time your teenagers take a step away from dependency on you, they have another opportunity to develop their individuality and move closer to establishing their own unique identities. Anything that prevents them from testing and strengthening their gifts and interests and decision-making skills makes it harder for them to eventually consolidate their personalities and establish mature adult identities.

Ron had a serious problem in this area. He grew up as the oldest child in a hardworking, middle-class family. His father had dropped out of college and given up a promising career in order to get married. Consequently he was determined that Ron would get an excellent education. When it became apparent that Ron was a very intelligent child, his father started encouraging him to set his sights on becoming a physician or an engineer or some other kind of professional. Every evening from the time Ron was in the second grade, his father sat down and reviewed his studies with him. He grilled Ron on his mathematics tables, quizzed him on spelling, and saw to it that all of his work was complete. Although Ron complained a little at first, he soon accepted his dad's involvement in his studies.

Before long, Ron didn't need his father looking over his shoulder. He came home right after school and went to his room to finish his homework before he went out to play. By the age of thirteen, Ron had decided to be a surgeon. From that time on he rigidly disciplined himself, read everything he could on famous physicians, and became an outstanding student. He took everything in life quite seriously and rarely dated. When he did, it was with girls of similar levels of "seriousness" and "maturity."

Ron went through college the same way—and eventually completed medical school and a surgical residency. He worked long hours and studied longer. He rarely relaxed with his fellow students because he thought that was frivolous. After finishing his medical training, Ron married a young woman who had been an outstanding and serious student herself. Then he joined a well-respected group of medical practitioners in his home town and soon he was doing very well. His parents were very pleased, but problems were brewing underneath Ron's external success.

Although he was married and had a lovely daughter, Ron continued his workaholic life-style and found little fulfillment in anything besides work. Eventually even that became routine and boring. Ron wondered if he was in the wrong line of work. He liked the money he was making and took pleasure in knowing he was helping others. But his future looked totally predictable and uninteresting and he started longing for some variety and freedom in his life.

About that time Ron met a woman a few years younger than himself. She was warm and playful in a way his wife had never been. Before long they were having an affair. In time, Ron divorced his wife, married his lover, and started a new career as a real estate investor. I met him a few years later in my office when he sadly told me, "I'd had it up to here with being responsible. As a kid I had to always be mature. I never had time to play and enjoy life. In some ways I think I never had a childhood. If I had it to do over again, I would never select medicine as a career."

Ron is typical of many adults who were forced to shape their lives according to someone else's expectations. He missed out on the opportunity to gradually find out his own gifts and interests as a child and adolescent. Consequently, when it was time to consolidate his personality and establish his identity in late adolescence, he didn't have access to major portions of his personality. He couldn't incorporate a fun-loving side of life because it was shut out. And he couldn't incorporate an intimate, loving side because those feelings had long been pushed underground. His only option was to solidify his personality as a workaholic physician.

Some adolescents shape their lives this way because they lose a parent and are forced to take on too much financial responsibility in the family at an early age. Others, like Ron, have parents who drive them incessantly to become doctors or lawyers or missionaries or athletes. Some are pressured to take over the family business. And others simply seem to latch onto a childhood ideal too tightly. They let it shape their educational decisions and choice of a vocation before they have had a chance to discover their own unique gifts and interests. Whatever the cause, these adolescents have one thing in common: although they may function very well on the outside—in fact, may be leaders in their schools or churches—they are neither fulfilled nor happy. They are like rosebushes trying to become magnolia trees. Everything they do runs against their innate, God-given potential and gifts. That takes the enjoyment out of life and turns their work into a boring routine.

Some of these "prematurely adult" adolescents also have another thing in common. They are prime candidates for midlife crises. They are likely to suddenly wake up in their forties and decide they want out of their jobs, life-styles, marriages, or other "shackles." So twenty years after they should have been adolescents, they turn back to recapture their lost youth. If they had gone through a normal adolescence and young adulthood, they could have avoided these tragic solutions.

Other teenagers distort their personalities in a different way. Instead of trying to live up to their parents' or others' vocational expectations, they try to conform their values and beliefs rigidly to those of parents or other important people. Fearful of losing their parents' approval, they conform in order to keep it. They become extremely polite and learn to avoid all confrontations with their parents. They adopt all of their parents' social or spiritual or political values. And they consider anyone who disagrees with them "naive" or "stupid." If they do disagree with their parents, they don't dare do it out loud. Their motto is "Don't rock the boat." These adolescents experience a kind of pseudomaturity or false sense of identity.

Your teenagers need you to have some expectations for them and they need to know your values. Your goals and hopes and aspirations let your sons and daughters know you have confidence that they can become successful adults. But there is a vast difference between helping your children succeed by holding out realistic, age-appropriate expectations and trying to vicariously live out your own wishes or goals through your adolescents. Parents who were dissatisfied with their own achievements as adolescents can unknowingly push their own teenagers to succeed in order to meet the parents' frustrated wishes. This makes teenagers an extension of their parents and creates feelings of guilt and failure when adolescents fail to live up to their parents' expectations. It also binds the adolescents to their parents and causes distortion in their development.

Whatever the reasons, anytime teenagers try to mold themselves to someone else's image of themselves instead of becoming the unique individuals God created them to be, their emotional development suffers. They live with undue pressure, lose their spontaneity and joy in life, become depressed or workaholics, or in some way bear the scars of their developmental struggles.

Here is a summary of several experiences that make the process of becoming a distinct individual with a solid identity difficult for some adolescents.

- Angry, impulsive discipline (this makes adolescents fearful of asserting themselves)
- Unfavorable comparisons to siblings or peers (this makes teenagers feel bad for being themselves; they feel they shouldn't be unique)
- Parental criticism (this undermines self-confidence and can limit exploration, risk taking, and decision making)
- Overprotection or other experiences that limit their opportunities to compete and develop their own abilities
- Lack of parental modeling and teaching of ways to handle adult responsibilities such as driving, balancing a checkbook, cooking, cleaning the house, or fixing the car
- Unavailability of a competent, loving, same-sex role model (this makes it harder to develop confidence in their masculine or feminine roles)
- Parental inability to accept a teenager's competitiveness with their eighteen-foot giants (this makes teenagers feel small or bad for wanting to be as intelligent or confident as their parents)

As you look back over this list, you will notice that each of these experiences tends to undercut your adolescents' ability to feel good about themselves as unique people with their own interests and abilities and choices. The apostle Paul gave a good antidote for avoiding this skewed identity formation. He pointed out that the church, like the human body, has many different parts or members. Each member of the church should develop and use his or her own gifts, not try to become like someone else. Paul put it in a humorous way: "If the whole body were an eye, where would the sense of hearing be? If the whole body were an ear, where would the sense of smell be? But in fact God has arranged the parts in the body, every one of them, just as he wanted them to be."[5] God created us with different abilities and interests. Our task as parents is to help our children identify their unique capabilities and to support them in fulfilling their own unique potential, not try to shape them into our image. Only when our adolescents have these opportunities to grow will they both fulfill their God-given potential and best find their niche in society.

NOTES

1. Personal and clinical illustrations are by Dr. Lewis.
2. Matthew 10:8.
3. 1 John 4:10, 19.
4. 2 Corinthians 12:14.
5. 1 Corinthians 12:14, 17-18.

*Which of
you, if his
son asks for
bread, will
give him a
stone?*

MATTHEW 7:9

CHAPTER SIXTEEN
DISTORTIONS OF IDENTITY DEVELOPMENT

In *All Grown Up and No Place to Go,*[1] psychologist David Elkind shows how many American teenagers are being forced to grow up too quickly. From the time they set foot in junior high school, pre- and early adolescents are pressured to look and act "maturely." Eleven- and twelve-year-olds have to make decisions about alcohol and drugs. Peer pressure to become sexually active is incredibly strong. News media fill teenagers' homes with daily reports of murder, rape, and other human tragedies. Homes have to be carefully locked and secured and few neighborhoods are safe from break-ins, theft, drugs, and other problems. Threats of nuclear and environmental destruction also loom on the horizon to give even children awesome potential worries and concerns.[2]

On top of this, the rapid increase in two-career families and single-parent homes means that millions of teenagers come home to empty houses. They have less parental guidance, less available parental role models, more unsupervised time, more social freedom, more need to take care of themselves and to make more solitary decisions than ever before. Teenagers also face a rudderless society with relativistic values that gives them few guiding norms. This places adolescents in a precarious position. They face far greater pressures at much earlier ages than their counterparts of a generation or two ago. They also lose their childhood innocence much earlier and no longer have a relatively protected period of adolescence in which they can gradually grow up, solidify their values, and consolidate their personalities.

This combination of increased pressures and lessened support at earlier ages forces many teenagers to grow up without the necessary emotional resources. Instead of progressively taking on more responsibilities, facing life's pressure, solidifying their own values, and separating from their parents, they have to start making life-influencing decisions in early and middle adolescence. Instead of turning to their parents for encouragement and support, they have to tough things out alone. Instead of gradually thinking through their moral and spiritual values within the context of a supportive church or family, they are left to choose by themselves from a smorgasbord of possibilities. And instead of gradually developing confidence in their masculine or feminine identities by identifying with their same-sex parents, and having a variety of dating relationships, they test out their sexual identities through premature sexual encounters. They also turn almost totally to their peers or to the media for their role models instead of balancing that influence with continued identification with their parents. They are like children thrown into a river and told to sink or swim.

Some swim; some sink under the tides of destructive peer pressure; most struggle on by themselves and try to act mature and "put together." The combination of premature pressure and insufficient support leaves many adolescents with a distorted and fragile sense of personal identity. Although they may look adult on the outside, inwardly they have empty places in their personalities. They are a little like decorative eggshells that have had their insides blown out through a pinhole and their outsides painted beautifully. Although they look wonderful, they are actually very fragile and unsettled. They are vulnerable to future stresses and pressures, more likely to turn to various forms of escapism, and are poor prospects for establishing healthy, intimate relationships with a marriage partner and later with children.

These cultural pressures and potential problems can be offset by parents who take the time to be actively involved in their adolescents' lives and to help them grow up gradually. Sometimes, however, family dynamics actually compound these stresses. In this chapter we will look at two experiences that have the potential to create serious distortions of an adolescents' personality. These experiences do more than merely slow down your children's growth toward maturity. They actually push teenagers to consolidate their personalities in unhealthy, defensive ways. Those experiences are: (1) premature separations from parents and (2) physical and sexual abuse. In some ways, these occurrences are simply variations of the roadblocks to attachment and individuation that we discussed in chapter 15. But they are so potentially serious that we have chosen to discuss them separately.

Premature Separations from Parents

Ruth Van Reken is a third-generation missionary who spent her childhood years in Nigeria, Africa. Like many missionary children, Ruth was separated from her parents for lengthy periods at an early age. When she was six years old, she left her mom and dad for boarding school three hundred miles away. She attended there two years, seeing her parents only at Christmas and in the summers. Then she spent the next four years with her parents. When she was thirteen, she came to the United States for high school and was separated from her mom and dad again.

Ruth wrote a moving book about her separation from her family.

Without blaming her parents and while recognizing the many rich experiences of her life as an MK (missionary kid), she describes the trauma of growing up away from her parents and the impact of that on her adjustment as an adult. In her book, *Letters I Never Wrote*[3], she writes the letters to her parents she wished she could have penned when she was a child. On her first day of high school in the United States, Ruth wanted to write this letter to her parents in anticipation of their leaving her to return to Nigeria.

> Dear Mom and Dad,
> My first day of high school. . . .
> I think I'm already beginning to withdraw from you again. I remember the pain of first grade. I see the same thing coming at me like a steamroller that can't be stopped. I want to jump up in front of it and scream "STOP, STOP." But I know there isn't a thing in the world I can do to make it change its course. Even while I stand there screaming, it will surely flatten me.
> My mind understands just fine. I know many other families are worse off than ours. They have parents who are divorced, or don't love them, and some even are dead, but none of that knowledge comforts my heart.
> When I try to express the pain, I always bump into the reasons of what it's all about. That locks me up. Somehow I need to get my feelings out. Maybe it hurts you too, more than you dare show.
> I sense that all of us have our private pains that make it impossible to bear each others'.
> I'm sorry, for I've never needed you more and been less able to express it.
>
> Ruth Ellen

Four years later, on the night of her high school graduation, Ruth wanted to pen these words to her parents.

> Dear Mom and Dad,
> Tonight I graduated from high school. You weren't there to see me make my speech as class vice president. Some

twinges of pain almost popped out, but my technique is pretty refined for handling that by now. Within seconds I was back to: "No, it doesn't bother me. I'm used to it."

Actually by anyone's standards I would say I've had a very successful high school career. . . . Besides being class vice-president, I was also voted "Girl Most Likely to Succeed" by my class. . . .

I've worked very hard to keep you proud of me. So far you haven't had to come home on my account. But do we know each other anymore?

There were times I did write out my feelings, especially about my first crushes that were not reciprocated, or when some boy liked me that I didn't like back and I didn't know how to handle the situation. I appreciated every good letter in response, but when they came a month later, I hardly remembered what you were writing about. The situation had long since been resolved one way or the other. After awhile, I didn't write very much about that kind of thing. It seemed useless.

Your letters have been as faithful as they were years ago in boarding school. Thanks for both of you writing each week. I know I couldn't have asked for more. You always tell me what you do, I tell you what I do, but rarely do we talk about how we feel.

I'm not worried about recognizing you physically as I was in first grade. I have pictures all around, but it's still the same question:

Will I *know* you?

Love,
Ruth Ellen

Ruth's experience is common for teenagers who are separated from their parents for lengthy periods of time. Although she knew her parents loved her and did their best by writing her each week, that didn't remove Ruth's loneliness and pain. To cope, she had to hide her feelings, tell herself that she was better off than some kids, and convince herself that if God had called her parents to serve him, she had no right to miss them or complain. Those rationalizations helped push her hurts temporarily beneath the surface, but they didn't make up for the lack of nurturing during key stages of her development. In fact, denying her feelings soon became part of an elaborate strategy Ruth employed to compensate for the loss of her mom and dad.

From the time she arrived at boarding school she started hiding her feelings. On her very first day at the tender age of six, the personnel at Ruth's mission school encouraged her, "Try to be big and brave like your sister. She's not crying." Soon after that, Ruth found out that children who cried or sucked their thumbs were ridiculed by other children. These and other experiences led her to hide her needy feelings and start acting strong and independent.

Ruth also coped with her inner longings by becoming a conforming and achievement-oriented person. Instead of feeling needy, she set out to show how competent and successful she could be. That occupied her time, gave her less opportunity to think about the parents she was missing, and reassured her that she could cope with life alone. By the time she reached high school, Ruth had become an outstanding achiever. She earned National Honor Society recognition and ranked ninth in her graduating class of three hundred and sixty-five. She continued that success in college and nursing school and eventually became a productive missionary herself.

Ruth's strategy was commendable and some of her success was healthy. Without it, she probably would have gone into a severe depression as a very young child. But its long-term effects weren't positive. Ruth cut herself off from feelings and stunted her ability to form open relationships with others. Although she longed to share her love and thoughts and feelings, she was prevented by fear of added pain. Even on her wedding day she couldn't tell her father her true feelings. Listen to that unwritten letter.

Dear Dad,
I heard you come into my room this morning, while you thought I was asleep. I realized you stood there watching me

for awhile and were probably thinking of the fact this was my last morning as just your daughter, not someone else's wife.

I felt your love and wanted to open my eyes and respond, but something stopped me.

I didn't know what I wanted to say or do. I guess I would have liked to have told you the things I appreciate about you as my Dad, but I think if I had told you them, or shared how I'm feeling today, the wall would have been down and it might have made the leaving tonight unbearable.

So I waited with my eyes closed to see what you would do. Would you wake me and say something? Should I open my eyes and let you know I knew you were there?

Neither one happened.

You kissed my forehead and walked away. My eyes stayed shut and the moment was lost forever.

I'm so very sorry.

Love,
Ruth Ellen

You can see the invisible barrier Ruth formed by years of closing off her feelings. She couldn't even allow herself a tender moment with her father. Years later, after she was married and had three daughters of her own, she still found herself struggling with depression, negativism, and anger. She felt as if she had "a deep, unfilled hole" in her life as the feelings she had pushed down for years rose up to frustrate, discourage, and upset her.

Ruth's experience is like that of many adolescents who are prematurely cut off from their parents' daily support. In some circles in the United States and Europe, early adolescents are routinely sent away for four or five years of prep school. There they receive the very best education money can buy. But no amount of money or education, or even friends, can replace the loving nourishment of a mom and dad. No one can console an adolescent girl about her first crush like an understanding mother. No one can strengthen a young man's sense of masculinity like his father. And no one can share a teen's excitements and successes like a parent. A counselor at one of those prestigious schools recently told me their students frequently try to escape their unhappiness and loneliness through alcohol, drugs, or suicide, or by throwing themselves excessively into their studies.

We realize that parents who send their children away to school want the best for their children. We also realize the painful struggles missionaries face when sending their sons and daughters off to boarding school. But most adolescents simply are not ready to leave their parents for extended periods of time. Children who leave home before late adolescence or young adulthood are often forced to live for years with feelings of depression because they never learned to feel comforted and reassured during their formative teenage years. Some wander aimlessly through life never quite fitting in or feeling "at home." They feel an emptiness or have unfinished emotional business that never lets them come to rest and feel satisfied. Others, like Ruth, survive by creating a strong, self-reliant exterior that masks their inner needs. And still others rebel against their parents or Christianity in order to protest their emotional abandonment.

Because of the serious damage that premature separations can cause to an adolescent's personality, we rarely recommend sending children away for schooling. In most cases, teenagers need to be with their parents at least until they are off to college or the military or ready to take a full-time job away from home.

We believe that some mission agencies need to rethink carefully their personnel and educational policies in light of the emotional needs of missionaries' children. Since missionary parents and agencies are God's representatives, they ought to exemplify God's way of relating to his children. "Never will I leave you; never will I forsake you," he promised.[4]

Some adolescents make their own decisions to leave home prematurely by running away. Although this is very different from being sent away to school, it creates similar kinds of problems. Like adolescents who are sent away from home, these teenagers are cut off from their parents' emotional support. Since they haven't had time to consolidate their personalities by gradually learning from their parents and taking in all of their needed emotional supplies, they enter adulthood with serious emotional gaps.

Many lack an inner sense of solidity and strength and a clear-cut personal identity. Some have lasting feelings of loneliness and isolation. Some develop a pattern of escapism. Once they have run from home, they try running from every difficult situation through alcohol, drugs, or promiscuous sexuality. Others develop a pattern of toughness or irresponsibility. And still others remain excessively dependent or seek out one companion after another to take care of them because they are unable to stand up by themselves. When these solutions fail, some tragically turn to suicide, the ultimate effort to escape.

Teenagers who consistently turn to these coping patterns are different from normal adolescents who go through brief periods of rebellion or experimentation with alcohol or drugs. Teenagers who have their parents' support can grow out of those difficult stages. As adults, they may look back at those times as painful, crazy, or risky, but they don't consider them a lasting portion of their lives. By contrast, prematurely separated adolescents tend to incorporate their faulty patterns of coping into their ongoing personalities. Tendencies to avoid feelings, run from difficulties, or fight authority become enduring personality characteristics that are stubbornly resistant to change. Their settled identities become "I am a person who escapes when things are difficult." "I am tough and don't need people." "I am dependent and can't handle life on my own," or "I don't fit in anywhere."

Adolescents who marry early can suffer similar distortions of identity. Feeling anchorless, unappreciated, or misunderstood at home, they latch on to someone who seems to understand them and offer an answer to their problems. For the first time in years they feel accepted. But beneath their "love" another story is unfolding. That is the story of two needy people who have not grown emotionally strong enough to leave their childish needs and ways behind. Instead of gradually growing out of their dependency needs, they have simply transferred them to their mate. Once the honeymoon is over, the hidden problems surface. The very conflicts that pushed them into early matrimony now become the central problems in their marriage.

If these teenagers had proceeded through a gradual separation process, they could have worked through many of their conflicts and potential problems. With their parents' sensitive support, they could have learned to feel good about themselves and others. They could have worked through their doubts about their ability to be competent adults. They could have outgrown their dependent tendencies and their propensity for blaming others. They could have solidified their sexual identities. And they could have had a couple of moderately serious dating relationships that helped them learn to give and take and meet another person's needs. Lacking those experiences, they were pressured into consolidating their personalities with patterns of escapism and blame-fixing that are more appropriate to early and middle adolescents than they are to happily married adults.

Making It on Their Own

Some teenagers who run away, drop out, or marry prematurely do eventually get their lives together—especially if they had moderately healthy and happy experiences in early childhood. We all know couples that married in middle or late adolescence and were able to continue growing and adapting to each other. We also know people who ran away or dropped out of mainstream society who eventually made their way back in. That happened to many American college students in the 1960s and early 1970s.

Raised under the banner of permissiveness, and disillusioned with the Vietnam war and materialistic middle- or upper-class living, a large segment of young adults literally took off for Europe, Canada, and other places. In London's Piccadilly Circus and in the Damrak Square in Amsterdam, you could find a "sea of adolescents" with no place to go. If you asked what they were doing, most shrugged and said they had just "dropped out of an intolerable society." Their goal was to get away (separate) from the establishment, find some freedom, and become their own persons.

Eventually many of these young adults made their way back to America and consolidated into mature personalities. After running into near starvation and the ravages of drugs and promiscuous sexual encounters, they realized there was no Garden of Eden. They also realized that all the problem wasn't their parents or America. They would have to take some positive steps to "get their acts together."

A colleague told me[5] of a scene he witnessed on board a ship returning to America from Europe during that time. Three hundred of these young people were on board returning from self-exile. The night before they sailed into New York, the captain announced that the passengers would be able to see the Statue of Liberty topping the horizon if they got up at dawn. Sneers of disdain for such a display of patriotism came from the young travelers. Yet the next morning when my colleague hurried above deck to glimpse the "lady of liberty," he could hardly make his way to the bow because the mass of young people were there ahead of him. When the symbol of America came into view, their sham of toughness fell away and he heard whoops of joy and saw tears on young faces that he would never forget. The children were returning home.

Many of these young adults had outgrown their adolescent sense of omnipotence and their unrealistic view of reality. Although they bore scars, they were more ready to complete the consolidation of their personalities than they were before they left. Life experience helped their growing up. Premature separations from parents are never advisable because they can distort an adolescent's developing personality, but like these young adults, some eventually manage to consolidate their personalities in mature ways.

Abusive Relationships

Now we come to perhaps the most damaging experience a child or teenager can undergo—physical or sexual abuse. Although we used to think abuse was far removed from most families, we now know better. A recent study in Los Angeles County estimated that as many as one in four women will be sexually abused by the age of twenty-one. In New York City 60,000 cases of child abuse are reported annually. Even many Christian families are devastated by this problem. Parents who were victims of abuse or parents who can't control their anger or their sexual impulses are not limited to those outside the church. We have counseled several women who were sexually abused by religious workers or physically and sexually abused by their minister fathers.

Sexual abuse freezes a child's growth and ties a rigid, tangled cord around a growing person's capacity for intimacy. Adolescents who are sexually abused feel violated and like pawns for others' pleasures. They have difficulty drawing boundaries saying, "This is me and this is what I want or need." Some victims of abuse turn to prostitution or reckless promiscuity. Others experience such self-hatred and confusion that they are unable to trust anyone—including their spouses. How can you feel good about yourself and trust other people when you have been secretively betrayed and exploited?

Many abused children are too frightened or confused to tell their parents, so they suffer in silence for years and years. Many have been threatened against "ever telling anybody what we've done" and feel guilty about identifying their abuser. Tragically, when some abused children do tell a parent or other adult, they are not believed or the abusing person is protected. Having their confusion and hurt denied, these victims then try to convince themselves that the offender must have been somehow justified. But if the abuser is justified, the victim must be to blame. So these innocent children end up concluding there is something wrong with them. What a tragic solution—to go through life blaming yourself because you were sexually molested by a disturbed adult!

One young adult who was sexually abused by her father from the time that she was seven years old described her anguish in this poem titled "Daddy's Home."

WHAT DO WE DO NOW?

The sun goes down
upon our house
all is quiet
all is calm.
The night has come
Daddy is home.
You know me
I'm Daddy's little girl.
Secrets
in the night,
traitors,
in the fight
Nightmares
I never tell
The rain poured down
the tears fell
Daddy's here
I must be in hell.
Don't you know me, mama,
I'm the one
that you despise.
You're the traitor
in the fight
you know the secrets
of the night.
The sun comes up
upon our house
and we see the actors
upon the stage
with the lines
that we all make.
I lie alone,
all alone again.
Daddy's gone
and I'm here
to live with the pain
to live with fear.
Won't you please
love me
like you did before?

Won't you please
hold me
and tell me once more?
I'm all alone
in the fight again
So all alone
in love
that I don't
understand.

This woman's description of abuse as hell, the secrecy and fear and pain, and her mother's betrayal by not stepping in to protect her, are nearly universal feelings of abused children. What she doesn't include are the years of depression and self-hatred she endured until she gained release through a lengthy period of psychotherapy. Physically abused teenagers experience similar emotional pain. Cruel or abusive same-sex parents discourage teenagers from identifying with their appropriate sex role model and push them toward homosexuality or other distortions of their sexual identities. Many abused children follow their parents' example and become abusers themselves. Just recently in Los Angeles a six-year-old boy beat his infant sister to death with the same belt his parents had used on him!

An Ounce of Prevention

Although many experiences can scar an adolescent's personality, none are so severe or lasting as abandonment and abuse. Adolescents who are sent away from their parents or physically attacked or sexually abused are like children who ask for the bread of love and understanding but are given instead a stone of abandonment or abuse.[6] When the time comes to consolidate their personalities and solidify their identities during later adolescence, these children have major problems.

Instead of holding memories of being loved and cared for, they bring memories of toughing out life alone. Instead of reflecting on happy times shared with parents, they recall boarding school experiences far from their distant parents. Instead of a rich store of emotional nurturing, they bring forced efforts to be prematurely independent. And instead of having memories of being valued and respected, they bring vivid or repressed recollections of being abused. As they solidify their identities, these warped memories are cemented into their ways of thinking and feeling about themselves and others. Their unmet needs linger on in their unconscious lives, yearning to be fulfilled. But the barriers they erected to keep others from hurting them more and the traits they developed to manage their pain prevent the very intimacy they crave.

Here are a few suggestions for avoiding those potentially destructive and distorting experiences:

- Communicate your love freely and openly
- Make your family life enjoyable
- Let your children leave you when they are ready—don't leave them
- Learn what healthy children need and do your best to provide that
- Commit to meeting your children's needs, not to having them meet yours
- Be sensitive to your children's maturing abilities and don't force them to be prematurely adult
- Support your children's growing up by encouraging age-appropriate independent behavior
- Protect your children from potential sources of abuse
- Get help if there are serious problems in your family

Chapter Highlights

In the last two chapters we have looked at five potential roadblocks to a child or adolescent's emotional development. Those roadblocks are: (1) problems attaching intimately to mother and later to the entire family; (2) difficulty separating from mom and dad on schedule; (3) inability to find one's own unique gifts and potentials and to solidify their identities; (4) premature separations from parents; and (5) physically or sexually abusive relationships.

Although most teenagers don't encounter extreme roadblocks, all teenagers run into at least a few minor barriers. They have to struggle with parents who are too busy to get involved in their daily lives, too anxious to listen patiently, too preoccupied to draw out their feelings, too desirous of seeing them grow up in predetermined ways, too prone to hang on too long, or too fearful or domineering to let them learn to think for themselves.

If you are struggling with patterns in your life that may create barriers to your adolescents' growth, seek out a wise friend or a professional counselor before a serious accident occurs. It is impossible to offer your teenagers the nurturing they need while you are struggling with unresolved attitudes or unmet needs from your own childhood days. Trained counselors can help you resolve the barriers you unwittingly erect to your adolescents' growth by helping you get a handle on your own emotional or family struggles.

NOTES

1. David Elkind. *All Grown Up and No Place to Go* (Reading, Mass.: Addison-Wesley Publishing Co., 1980).
2. Personal and clinical illustrations are by Dr. Narramore unless otherwise indicated.
3. Ruth Van Reken. *Letters I Never Wrote* (Oakbrook, Ill.: Darwill Press, 1985). A new edition titled *Letters Never Sent* has now been published by David C. Cook Publishing Co., Elgin, Ill., 1988.
4. Hebrews 13:5.
5. Dr. Lewis.
6. Matthew 7:9.

Hope deferred makes the heart sick, but a longing fulfilled is the tree of life.

PROVERBS
13:12

CHAPTER SEVENTEEN TOO YOUNG TO DIE

Every 100 minutes a teenager in the United States commits suicide. About 100 more make "unsuccessful" attempts. Suicide is the third leading cause of death among teenagers, exceeded only by accidents and homicides. Nobody knows how many more "accidental" teen deaths may be suicides in disguise, and a very significant portion of teenagers have at least fleeting thoughts of taking their own lives.

Because of the wrenching pain of teenage suicide, we hesitate to write this chapter. Parents who have lost teenagers through suicide don't need to be reminded of the grief and confusion and despair they suffered. They need to move on and rebuild their lives. But the frequency of teenage suicide and the prevalence of temporary periods of depression among many adolescents urge us to try to understand why some teenagers are vulnerable to this drastic action and what can be done to avoid it.

In reading this chapter, we encourage you to avoid either of two extreme reactions. Don't minimize the problem and confidently conclude, "It could never happen to us," or "It always happens in other families." Nearly every parent of a suicidal adolescent has had the same thoughts before the tragedy. On the other hand, please don't be frightened and jump to the conclusion that a substantial proportion of teenagers take their lives and that your son or daughter is likely to be one of them. In spite of the large numbers of teenage suicides, the actual percentage of adolescents who take their lives is very, very small.

We hope your reaction will fall between these two extremes. First, we hope you will gain a greater understanding of all teen-agers as we discuss the struggles of adolescents with severe depressive moods and suicidal thoughts. Second, if you see some warning signals, we encourage you to seek out professional counseling. Find a well-regarded psychiatrist or psychologist and discuss your concerns. It is better to take extra precaution than to wait too long. Teenagers who are hurting can be helped through moments of despair, and no cost is too great at these crucial times of life.

Why Do They Do It?

Research is shedding a lot of light on adolescent suicide. Although no single personality type is especially prone to suicide, several studies reveal clear connections between suicide and certain life-styles and experiences. There is, for example, a high frequency of drug and alcohol abuse among young suicidal vic-tims.[1] One study found that more than half of young suicidal victims were drug or alcohol abusers at the time of suicide.[2] Another research project found that nearly one in four adolescents who run away from home attempt suicide, and that one in five adolescent homosexuals have attempted suicide. Another found that 12 percent of teenagers who are assaulted, threatened, or arrested attempt suicide within one year.[3] These figures show that suicide is part of a larger picture. It reflects major emotional pain and is often tied to conflicts in relationships and follows other attempts to escape the pain.

The only universally common feature among adolescent suicide victims is that they have lost hope. The Bible says, "Hope deferred makes the heart sick."[4] In suicide, hope has not only been deferred, it has been lost. No matter how outwardly successful or "together" these adolescents seem to others, they are wracked with emotional pain that seems too great to bear. Suicide is their attempt to find relief. It is a way of bringing an end to their depression, confusion, or despair.

Four types of teenagers seem to be most prone to the painful emotions that can lead to suicidal attempts. In the pages that follow, we will take a close look at these susceptible teenagers, at the most common causes of teenage suicide, and at some ways of identifying adolescents who are at risk for suicidal attempts. Then we will discuss some principles of prevention.

The Lonely Adolescent

One especially suicide prone teenager is the lonely adolescent. Although these young people may be well-mannered and cooperative, inwardly they don't feel socially or emotionally connected. A few are social "loners" but many are friendly and even outgoing. Inwardly, however, they feel cut off and isolated from others and do not believe they can turn to anyone in their darkest moments.

Marlin was a lonely adolescent.[5] His father abandoned his family when Marlin was ten. Although Marlin had always been attached to his mother, she became increasingly protective and controlling after Marlin's father left. Using Marlin to make up for her lost husband, she unknowingly bound him to her in neurotic ways. When she was worried about finances or her job she turned to Marlin for encouragement. When she was sad, she looked to Marlin for consolation. She often told him she didn't know what she would do without him, and when he planned his own activities, she often told him she really needed him around the house.

When Marlin reached middle adolescence, he started complaining about his mother's closeness and struggled to find some relief from her pervasive influence. He took a part-time job. He stopped telling his mother about his daily activities. And he started disagreeing with her and occasionally getting into angry arguments. Working, withdrawing, and fighting were the only ways Marlin could distance himself from his mother's engulfing personality. But when he stopped talking to his mother as much, she told him, "We never talk anymore." And each time Marlin lost his temper, he felt so guilty that he soon asked his mother for forgiveness and promised not to hurt her again.

Marlin's needy mother quickly seized on his "confessions" as a way of binding them closer. Instead of accepting her son's anger or withdrawal as a signal of his need to separate and begin his own life, she effusively "forgave" him, said she knew he didn't want to hurt his mother, and expressed her confidence that he wouldn't do it again. This reinforced Marlin's feelings that he was bad and that he wasn't entitled to his natural feelings. It also made him increasingly angry and despairing of ever establishing a life apart from his mother.

When Marlin was sixteen, he started dating Lisa. He had practically no other friends, and she quickly became his only source of emotional support besides his mother. Since Marlin could not ask for emotional nourishment from his mother without being sucked into her enmeshing dependency, he turned increasingly to Lisa. In her he found an understanding person who helped him feel less like mama's boy. Before long he was spending hours at her house and rarely went anywhere without her. After several months of dating, they began to talk of marriage. This gave Marlin another hope for separating from his mother and he soon started pinning all hopes for his future on his relationship with Lisa.

In time, Marlin's excessive need for closeness caused Lisa to edge away. She told him she wanted to spend a few weekends by herself and do more with her other friends. Finally, Lisa broke off their relationship. Her rejection was more than Marlin could handle. He wrote a note telling Lisa life wasn't worth living without her and then took his life.

Marlin's suicide grew out of both his longstanding problems and his middle-adolescent crisis. He was programmed for loneliness and depression by his father's abandonment and his mother's controlling need to bind her son to herself. These problems were accentuated by his normal adolescent struggle to separate from his mother and master the rapprochement tasks of middle adolescence. Like all middle adolescents, Marlin was struggling to find a balance between independence and dependence. He needed to feel increasingly adult and independent while still having his parents' support. But since his father wasn't there to help and his mother kept thwarting his efforts to grow up, he had no one to turn to except Lisa. When she left he didn't have the inner strength to go on by himself, and he couldn't go back to his mother since she would use his loneliness to bind them even more inseparably together. Caught between childish dependency and total isolation, suicide seemed to be his only answer.

In retrospect, Marlin was actually doing to Lisa the same thing his mother was doing to him. Both Marlin and his mother were trying to fill their own deep emotional loneliness by attaching themselves possessively to someone else.

Self-hatred

Marlin's suicide reveals another reason some adolescents take their lives—anger and the search for revenge. His suicide note left the blame at Lisa's feet. At one point he wrote, "If we were together I would be alive today." Some suicidal adolescents express their anger by choosing violent means of killing themselves. Others don't even know they are angry and feel only loneliness or depression. These potentially suicidal adolescents turn their anger on themselves. "I can never be what you expect" is replaced by "I can never be what I expect." And "I hate you" becomes "I hate myself." The Bible refers to this connection between anger and depression when it says, "Fathers, do not embitter your children, or they will become discouraged."[6]

Remember the inner images your children developed in their formative years?[7] As they take in your standards and expectations, they gradually combine them with their own to form an ideal picture of how they ought to be. They also develop strong feelings about themselves and their success in living up to those expectations. If they feel quite inferior or inadequate, they can literally hate themselves for failing to live up to their unrealistic expectations. In killing himself, a severely depressed teenager is saying in part, "I quit!" "I can never please you (or my own internal expectations)." "I hate myself and I hate you."

Most suicidal adolescents don't understand these feelings and have no one to talk to. If they did they would find out their rage is normal, their hurts are real, and they can be understood. But as long as they keep their feelings hidden, they shut themselves off from the very help they need.

Terry and Melvin may have prevented a suicide attempt by their thirteen-year-old son. David was locking himself in the bathroom for an hour or more after losing his temper and fighting with his father. After a few sessions with a counselor, David said he was so angry he had to get away from his dad or he might hit him. He also admitted that on more than one occasion he looked through the medicine cabinet for something lethal to "show" his parents and "make them sorry." Killing himself was the best way he knew to hurt his dad and get back at him. As the family continued counseling, David learned to express his hurt and anger more directly and his parents learned to understand. If they hadn't faced their problem early, they might have encountered a disaster.

Pressured Teens

Twenty-two-year-old Ken was in his last semester of college. A good student who was respected by faculty and peers alike, Ken had been elected president of his senior class. The entire college community was shocked to hear that Ken had hanged himself in his dormitory room just a few weeks before he would have graduated. Ken is typical of another group of adolescents who sometimes turn to suicide. They are apparently happy and often very successful and well liked, but they live under immense internal pressure.

Ken had always been considered a "good kid." He had no history of drug or alcohol abuse, got along well with adults and peers alike, and seemed to come from a fine family. Ken's father was a success-ful minister who had built a large church from scratch. He was highly regarded in the community, and although he was somewhat of a workaholic, he was no different from many successful busi-ness and religious leaders. Ken was the youngest of his parents' three children and both of his siblings were married and doing well. His mother was a talented person who loved her children, didn't work outside the home, and was supportive of her husband.

Inside this apparently ideal family, however, a crisis was brew-ing. Although Ken's father was a fine man, his personality created problems for his extremely sensitive son. Ken's dad could cope with anything and never seemed to have a problem. He didn't allow himself to appear weak to his family or friends. He never showed any feelings of discouragement or worry. When he encoun-tered a problem, he prayed about it, attacked it with a determined attitude, and worked it through. When his wife or children brought problems to him, he would listen briefly and then offer some advice. He didn't take time to draw them out and understand their fears or hurts and he certainly didn't let them know he ever had any feelings like that.

Ken's older brothers managed to do rather well in this environ-ment. They grew up to be a lot like their father and became achievement-oriented businessmen. Ken had a harder time. From early childhood, he was more sensitive and bothered by things that didn't upset his brothers. He had a tender spirit and needed more patience and understanding. Although he admired his father, he also felt terribly inferior to him. Since his father seemed so much bigger than life, it was hard for Ken to feel that he could ever grow up and be successful like his dad. For years, these feelings of inadequacy and self-doubt festered without attention under his polite personality, his cooperative attitude, and his excellent school performance.

During adolescence, two normal developmental hurdles compounded Ken's pain. When he started struggling with his sexual feelings, he felt intense guilt. But since he was sure no one else in his "perfect" family struggled with these feelings, he couldn't share them with a soul. He also couldn't reconcile them with his father's preaching on moral purity.

Coupled with this sexual guilt was Ken's adolescent need to compete favorably and prove himself to his peers and parents. Although Ken did very well in college, his approaching graduation signaled that he must move into a world inhabited by people like his successful older brothers and his father. This intensified his feelings of inadequacy and fears of failure. Since Ken never shared his doubts, he didn't realize his feelings were entirely normal. Most adolescents would feel similar pressures in his home, and many college graduates have serious doubts about their entering a competitive world.

Unlike Ken, however, most late adolescents don't have such a "perfect" father. And most late adolescents are able to share at least a few of their doubts about their ability to cope with life. Living as the "perfect child" of a perfect eighteen-foot giant, Ken didn't have that option. A teenager struggling with his sexual feelings and depression and self-doubt wouldn't fit with his pastor father's view of himself at all. Even after his son's suicide, Ken's dad told me he couldn't think of a single thing that might have caused the tragedy except that the boy "temporarily lost his mind." The father's abhorrence of weakness and his inability to come to terms with his own hidden guilt forced him to once again deny any responsibility for his son's problems.

Like Ken, a surprising number of suicidal adolescents are well liked, high achieving, and outwardly successful. But beneath their success they are never satisfied with their performance. The tyranny of unattainable perfectionism drives them to do better and better but it is never quite enough. The temporary satisfaction of each new success quickly dissipates under the relentless accusations of their demanding consciences which echo their parents' impossibly high standards or their own unrealistic expectations. These adolescents' pressures are usually fueled by their low self-esteem, the fear that they can never do enough, and their family's inability to face directly their personal problems and openly share their hurts or struggles. They usually feel their parents don't really know or understand them and many feel quite unloved even though their parents care.

Some of these parents want their children to fulfill their expectations so they are very sensitive to their children's performances and behaviors. But they aren't sensitive to and involved in their children's emotional lives. This gives the child a very confusing message. From all appearances the parents seem very kind and loving. But at an unspoken level the child senses the parent's lack of genuine emotional availability and involvement in his life.

The Acting-Out Teenager

Another high-risk group for suicide is made up of socially active adolescents who are partying, using alcohol and drugs, or periodically in trouble with school authorities or law officials. Unknown to many parents—and even to their friends—a significant number of these adolescents are frantically searching for pleasure or excitement to ward off underlying feelings of depression. These adolescents suffer a variety of lonely, depressed feelings common to suicidal victims, but they also have a history of escaping from their pain. Unlike the solitary or perfectionistic teenager, they try to ward off their inner emptiness through round after round of partying.

Jeff was this kind of boy. He got low grades at his high school though he had the ability to do better. He spent most of his free time listening to his stereo or partying with friends and seemed proud that he didn't take his schoolwork seriously.

Jeff's father's work took him out of town frequently and his mother was preoccupied with her own activities. In his senior year of high school, Jeff's parents found him dead in his car from an overdose of drugs. A brief note revealed his underlying depression and confusion: "Life is senseless."

Although Jeff's life-style seemed to say he didn't care about anything, his "don't give a damn" attitude masked a corrosive suffering. He was badly hurt by the fact that his parents seemed too busy to love him and help him make sense out of life. And he apparently felt deeply the absence of meaning and purpose in a family life-style devoid of spiritual interest. Jeff's wandering life-style was his way of avoiding the pain of loneliness and depression he would have to feel if he admitted he cared. But once his escapes became routine, his despair caught up with him.

Suicide and the Adolescent-Separation Process

Adolescents and young adults can be especially susceptible to suicidal feelings because normal struggles with depression or failure or loneliness are aggravated by the stresses of adolescence. The pressure to adapt to a threatening world, for example, and the fear of giving in to feelings of dependency are both scary for adolescents. So is the pressure to be accepted by their peers and the desire to live up to their peer groups' expectations. Finding spiritual meaning and purpose in life can be another heavy burden. Since teenagers are moving away from the love of home but have not yet established their lasting relationships, they are also living between vital support systems. This makes them more vulnerable to depression than they will usually be in later life.

All of these struggles can be intensified since adolescents have difficulty viewing them objectively. Early and middle adolescents are prone to impulsive decisions until they develop emotional control and long-range planning. Since adolescence is a kind of boot camp for adult life, they also don't yet have enough experience handling stress. A lot of the struggles we had as teenagers seem less serious to us now, and many adults would relish the chance to go back and live adolescence again with their current knowledge and experience. As one person put it, the trouble with adolescence is it comes too early in life!

When you combine normal adolescent feelings of inferiority, pressures to cope with the adult world, the loss of past intimacy with parents, undeveloped coping resources, a short-term view of life, and a tendency toward moodiness and impulsiveness, you can better understand why suicide sometimes seems to be the best way out for adolescents. If you add in longstanding family problems, a serious lack of self-esteem, or hidden rage toward the parents, it can be extremely difficult for some adolescents to put things into perspective and see a glimmer of hope beyond their current despair.

Warning Signals

Perhaps the biggest question on many parents' minds is, How can we know if our child is at suicidal risk? Although it is impossible to always recognize a potential suicide victim, some advanced signs are nearly always given. Here are some danger symptoms that should alert you to be concerned about your adolescent. These warning signals are not always indicative of suicidal feelings, but they are significant and need to be addressed. After each behavior, we try to state in your teenager's words what that behavior means. If your teenager exhibits one or more of these, we strongly encourage you to seek professional help.

Running away: "Life at home is too painful. I have to get away. If running away doesn't solve it, I may try a more permanent solution."

Drug and alcohol abuse: "My life is meaningless or miserable. I have to have an escape."

Changes in eating and sleeping patterns: "My whole life pattern is upset and I don't value myself enough to take good care of myself."

Talking about death or suicide: "I am curious about people who die or what death means. It might be a way out of my pain."

Signs of depression: "I'm no good. I'm a failure. Life isn't worth living."

Sudden withdrawal from family or friends: "No one cares about me." "I don't want to hurt anyone."

Taking unusual risks: "I don't care anymore." "So what if something happens?"

Giving away possessions: "I won't be needing these. I want someone I love to have them."

Chronic low self-esteem: "I'm no good no matter how much I accomplish."

Avoiding Tragedy

In addition to being alert to potential danger signs, what can parents do to rear children who won't be pushed toward depression? Actually, everything you do to meet your teenagers' needs, communicate your love, and help them prepare for adult life will minimize the possibility of serious depression or suicidal feelings. Happy adolescents don't entertain thoughts of ending their lives. Helping teenagers become aware of their distinctiveness, develop confidence in their abilities, separate from parents while building new friendships, and outgrow their conflicts between dependency and independency—all makes them stronger and healthier and less susceptible to periods of depression and suicidal thoughts. The dynamics of suicide we have discussed in this chapter, however, make certain principles of parenting especially important.

First, *be sure you find ways of expressing your love so that your children can feel it and believe it.* Most parents of suicidal victims love their children, but love is not enough. We must be sure we communicate our love in ways our children understand. This means being involved in their lives, seeing things from their perspectives, and putting ourselves in their shoes.

Next, *be sensitive to your adolescents' hidden feelings.* Don't assume that because your sons or daughters are achieving well or behaving well that everything is fine. Be alert to their hurts or hidden feelings of failure or isolation. Learn to pick up on their subtle clues that they aren't feeling well. Although pushiness and prying won't help, sensitive listening will. If you have some regular uninterrupted times together, most teenagers will open up and let you know how they are feeling.

Third, *beware of excessive pressure.* Many teenagers are under intense pressure to achieve in school. In Japan, for example, it is not uncommon for teenagers who fail to pass the college entrance exam to commit suicide. Although this pressure has produced high academic achievements, it has become so unreasonable that many adolescents believe their life is destined to be a failure without a college education. Since unachievable expectations drive some youths to suicide, be careful not to lay unrealistic expectations on them. Help your teenagers set realistic goals that allow time for fun and friends and recreation. More important than academic success is your teenagers' attitude toward themselves and others. Teenagers who feel good about themselves and others will succeed even if they don't get a great academic start. But no matter how well your children do in school, they can be burdened for life by nagging doubts about themselves if they haven't learned to relax and enjoy life and set realistic, attainable goals.

A fourth suggestion is to *learn to share your own weaknesses and struggles.* Your teenagers' feelings of failure are often magnified when they compare themselves to you. If you act as though you have no problems—and never did as an adolescent—you make teenagers feel even worse. My wife and I worked at this with our two children.[8] We learned to be clear about our awkwardness and problems when we were teenagers. I reminded Richard and Debbie that I got my share of C's in high school and that I wasn't even a very serious student in college. We also told Richard and Debbie about some of our spiritual and psychological struggles before our lives started coming together and some of the feelings of inadequacy we still felt as adults. These talks let our children know it was normal to have some anxieties and problems and concerns.

Next, *encourage your children to express their negative emotions.* This includes their anger at you. As we saw in chapter 11, teenagers need help in coping with their strong emotions. Since depression is partly the result of repressed anger, the best prevention is to encourage children to be honest about their feelings. Rather than squelching your adolescents' angry attacks or criticisms with rebukes such as, "Don't talk to me like that!" listen to the hurt behind your adolescents' anger. Statements like, "That really made you mad, didn't it?" or "I'm sorry I hurt you. Can you tell me what I said that was so upsetting?" show that you are more interested in understanding your teenagers than in defending yourself. They also reassure your teenagers that their angry feelings are normal and needn't be destructive. The same is true of anxious, excited, and depressive feelings. Your teenagers need to have their feelings heard and understood.

Christian parents have an added resource in raising healthy children. Teenagers who know that God loves them are better able to cope with the identity and separation struggles of adolescence. Faith gives teenagers an extra resource for finding security, support, and purpose in life. It provides a framework for understanding the world and a loving relationship with our Creator. A biblical understanding of forgiveness can help your teenagers find a solution to guilt. Your church youth group can provide a loving community where your sons and daughters can share their joys and sorrows. And a Christian world view can help your children make sense of some of the hardships and struggles of life. Christian teenagers, of course, are not immune to severe problems such as suicide. Normal adolescent struggles, feelings of depression, and family problems can blur anyone's view of God and make it difficult to feel his love. But a vital faith in God can be a powerful resource for your maturing adolescents.

Chapter Highlights

Teenagers who turn to suicide have lost all hope of being understood and coping with their problems. You can protect your family from this tragedy by becoming sensitive to your children's needs, picking up their cues of distress, helping them feel better about themselves, and supporting their meaningful relationships with others. If you see any potential danger signals, don't overlook them. Find a way to talk to your adolescents about how they are feeling, and if they are having a lot of inner pain seek professional help quickly.

NOTES

1. R. C. Fowler, C. L. Rich, and D. Young. "San Diego Suicide Study I: Young vs. old subjects," *Archives of General Psychiatry* 43: 577-582, 1986.
2. R. C. Fowler, C. L. Rich, and D. Young. "San Diego Suicide Study II: Substance abuse in young cases," *Archives of General Psychiatry* 43:86 962-965.
3. "Questionnaire may help deter teen suicides." Associated Press, *The Dallas Morning News,* March 15, 1987, 4A.
4. Proverbs 13:12.
5. Clinical illustrations are by Dr. Lewis.
6. Colossians 3:21.
7. Chapter 9, "Internalization."
8. Dr. Narramore.

Sex for teenagers is a health hazard. Teenagers are too vulnerable, too available for exploitation.

SOL GORDON

CHAPTER EIGHTEEN TEENAGE SEXUALITY

According to several recent surveys, the average American male is sexually active at the age of fifteen and the average female at sixteen. Many start much earlier. Approximately three-fourths of college students report they have engaged in sexual intercourse. The United States has the highest rate of teenage pregnancy in the Western world—more than twice as high as teenagers in Canada and England. Every day in the United States nearly three thousand teenage girls become pregnant. Each year more than one-half million babies are born to teenage mothers. And each year more than four hundred thousand adolescent girls have abortions. Yet these statistics are only a portion of the story. Behind them lies the struggle of millions of teenagers to come to grips with their maturing sexuality, to learn to relate intimately and lovingly to the opposite sex, to select their moral values, and to prepare to spend adulthood in a meaningful, life-enhancing relationship with another person.

Your sons' and daughters' sexual adjustment will be determined by three separate but intimately related developmental processes. The first is their social and psychological adjustment. Although this aspect of your children's development is not sexual in the narrow biological sense, it provides the foundation for their attitudes about themselves and their ability to relate to members of the opposite sex. If your teenagers don't feel good about themselves and others, their dating experiences will be a tangle of anxiety, conflicts, or misunderstandings.

The second decisive aspect of your sons' and daughters' sexuality is their understanding of their biological sexuality and their comfortableness with their bodies. Your teenagers need to feel good about their bodies and their sexual feelings and they need to integrate their sexuality into their total personalities.

The third vital ingredient of your teenagers' sexuality will be their moral and spiritual values and commitments. Your teenagers need to have a clear understanding of the meaning of human sexuality, of God's perspective on sexual intimacy, and of appropriate means of expressing their sexuality.

Since your sons' and daughters' attitudes toward themselves and their sexuality develop throughout the entire span of adolescence, we have not discussed this important topic in depth at any stage of adolescence. Instead, we have reserved most of our discussion of sexuality for this chapter. We will begin with a brief review of the important psychological developments your children need to have gone through in order to be prepared for the arrival of their biological sexual maturity at puberty. Then we turn to some specific ways of helping adolescents feel good about their maturing sexuality and learn appropriate ways of expressing their feelings of love and affection.

Sex Begins at Home

The foundation of your sons' and daughters' ability to relate to other people was laid down during their first few years of life. Although a mother's loving care seems far removed from adult or adolescent sexuality, it was in those earliest months of life that your children first learned how it feels to be with other people. When you tended your crying infants or held or fed them, you were establishing a basis for trust and intimacy that would impact all of their future relationships. As they started separating from you during their toddler years, they increased their capacity to be healthily independent—another requisite for happy interpersonal relationships.

At three or four years of age, your children took the next step in developing their attitudes toward themselves and others. During those years, your children began to look to their same-sex parent in order to learn what it meant to be a man or woman. Chances are your sons were big on being like daddy and your daughters wanted to be like mommy. They dressed in your clothes, played "teacher" or "fireman," got ready to go "off to work," and in many other ways imitated you or your spouse. During this critical period, your sons had a special need for their dad or a father substitute to affirm their developing male identities. Girls needed the same thing from their mothers. They didn't need perfect "models," but if the same-sex parent was absent or distant or hurtful, the children had a harder time identifying with and patterning their life after that parent.

Although the development of homosexuality is complex, it is frequently rooted in the rejection of one's biologically given sex role because of the absence of or abuse by a same-sex parent. A sensitive boy may look at his austere father and conclude: "Men are cruel. I don't want to be like them. Mother is nice. I want to be like her." Or he may unconsciously decide, "Since I never had a father, I am going to keep looking for a man I can be close to." In this way, the choice of a homosexual partner sometimes reflects a hidden search for the desired father. In contrast, children with loving and available same-sex parents look forward to growing up and becoming like those parents. Their enjoyable, idealizing relationship with their same-sex parent enables them to feel good about their developing sexual identities.

This doesn't mean that children of single parents or children whose same-sex parent has some problems are doomed to disturbed sexual identities. None of us have perfect parents, and many children from one-parent families turn out very well. Some find positive sex role models in adult relatives, older friends, or teachers. Others find support through literature or fantasized relationships. But all things being equal, a girl with an understanding, loving relationship with her mother and a boy with a healthy, friendly relationship with his father are more likely to feel good about their feminine and masculine identities than children who lack those models.

Mommy's Boy, Daddy's Girl

At the same time children need a same-sex role model to aspire to be like, they need a parent of the opposite sex to relate to affectionately. Girls need fathers who love them and validate their femininity and boys need mothers who appreciate their efforts at being manly. A special recognition of their developing competence from the opposite-sex parent gives a big boost to their tentative feelings about their budding masculinity or femininity.

Around four or five years of age, boys especially want to be admired by mother for their "manliness." And while teenage boys want their father's validation of their school work, their athletics, or their other successes, they also want an admiring mother who appreciates their "manly" endeavors. By their example, fathers tell their sons, "This is the way you can be a competent, sensitive man." By their approval and appreciation mothers say, "You are doing a great job at becoming a man."

Four- and five-year-old girls and early-adolescent girls want their mothers to help them dress up for special occasions or to prepare for a scholarly or social activity. But the real plum is hearing father say, "You're beautiful!" "You were fantastic," or "That's a tough job you handled very well." After all, if the most important man in your life thinks you have what it takes to be a successful woman, you are bound to feel encouraged and affirmed! For both boys and girls, the opposite sex parent plays an important role in their maturing sexual identities. Same-sex parents provide models of masculinity or femininity and opposite-sex parents affirm their success in reaching toward that goal.

The Expanding Years

By the time your children began elementary school, they should have formed a good beginning identification with their same-sex parent. Combined with their biological endowments, their relationships with you and your spouse had already begun to shape their sexual identities and accompanying gender roles. During their elementary school years, your children expanded their social interactions beyond the family, developed their language and learning skills, and learned to relate to a variety of adults and peers. They also continued to solidify their earlier identifications with their same-sex parents by spending most of their time with same-sex peers.

That's why six- to ten-year-olds spend most of their time with same-sex friends. Since their feelings of masculinity or femininity are new and fragile, they aren't about ready to walk up to a member of the opposite sex and say, "Me, Tarzan. You, Jane. Let's get acquainted." In fact, most eight- and nine-year-old boys are a little afraid of girls. During those years, boys continue defining their budding masculinity by saying, "I am like Dad" and "I am like other boys," while girls define their femininity by saying, "I am like Mother and my girlfriends." It will take a few more years before their sexual identities are strong enough for them to relate closely and confidently to the other sex.

As the first decade of your children's lives reached its close, your sons and daughters should have made major progress in the development of their sexual identities. If things went well during those years, they approached adolescence with a sixfold foundation for their future adult sexuality. That foundation included:

- The ability to experience loving, close relationships with others
- An awareness of their own uniqueness or distinctive identities
- The ability to be somewhat independent and stand alone when necessary
- A basic identification with (and desire to be like) their same-sex parent
- A love and respect for the opposite sex—especially as embodied in relationships with their mother or father
- An identification with their same-sex peers

Changing Attachments

With the onset of puberty, your children's progress in establishing their sexual identities has to be tested in a broader arena. The first time around, they learned to attach intimately, think for themselves, separate healthily, and relate to members of both sexes largely in the safety of your family. Now they must test out these abilities outside the home.

During preadolescence, ten- to twelve-year-olds still spend most of their time in same-sex groupings. Although they are beginning to become aware of the opposite sex, and while they are increasingly involved in mixed social interactions, their heterosexual interests will still be limited. Ten- and eleven-year-old boys especially prefer the company of their own sex. They avoid close contact with their more quickly developing female peers while they keep on solidifying their masculine identities with their male friends. Preadolescents of both sexes, however, start to become more acutely aware of their physical distinctiveness from the opposite sex, and they begin to compare their physical development more carefully to their peers.

By twelve, many preadolescents start showing more interest in the opposite sex. For example, when our[1] daughter, Debbie, was on an eighth grade class trip to Washington, D.C., she phoned us one evening. After excitedly chattering about the trip and the sights they were seeing, she said more quietly and seriously, "Dad, I've got a question." "Sure, honey," I replied, "what is it?" "I was wondering if Andy and I could go around together."

Since I had never heard of either Andy or "going around together," I asked her about both. Debbie reminded me I had seen Andy at a school function and explained that "going around" wasn't dating. "It means—well—just kind of going around together at school." I asked Debbie a few more questions and after receiving satisfactory answers, told her that was fine. She said a great big "Thanks" and was on her way. This type of interest in the other sex becomes increasingly frequent as preadolescence nears its close.

During early adolescence, several changes will take place in your sons' and daughters' social relationships. They will probably develop one or two close friends of the same sex. Those friendships will help lessen their anxiety over leaving you and are a little like the security blankets they held onto so dearly when they were toddlers. Early adolescents also begin to pay a lot more attention to the opposite sex. Daydreaming or talking with friends about possible opposite sex relationships starts about this time. "Going around" and pairing up at social gatherings are also common at this practicing age, and some early adolescents begin to date. Serious relationships with the opposite sex should still be a few years down the road. Unfortunately, many unsupervised early adolescents have their first sexual encounters at this age.

By middle adolescence your teenagers are ready to take the next step toward maturing heterosexual relations. They may spend hours talking to a special friend at school or on the phone. Although these friendships may be with either sex, they are increasingly likely to be heterosexual. These relationships help teenagers continue separating from you by giving them sources of love and support outside the home. They also help middle adolescents keep defining their own identities. Lengthy conversations enable them to test out ideas, share perspectives, and debate the pros and cons of all sorts of issues and decisions. Even when these relationships are not romantic or even heterosexual, they expand your teenagers' confidence and their abilities to relate to others.

During middle adolescence, most teenagers make a decided turn toward heterosexual interests. Same-sex friends remain important, but the level of interest in the opposite sex and the ability to act on those interests pushes your sons and daughters into a new era of relationships. Their first serious or prolonged dating often happens at this time. Jealousy toward same-sex friends is common as young men and women compete for the attention of members of the opposite sex. And when dating begins, many teenagers show a sudden increase in their masculinity or femininity and take renewed interest in their looks and dress.

You may also notice an increase in your middle adolescents' tender, giving concern for others and a lessening of the self-centered love so characteristic of many early adolescents. Instead of looking for companions to help them separate from you or to complete their personalities, middle adolescents start developing more intimate and giving friendships. By sixteen or seventeen many teenagers are beginning to share vocational and intellectual interests and are able to love others in a more mature manner. There is still a great deal of idealism and naivete in their understanding of love, but they are moving in the direction of maturity.

Competition and anger at the same-sex parent often peaks during middle adolescence. Much as four- to six-year-olds try to become like mommy or daddy, middle adolescents try to define their masculine or feminine identities by being like father or mother. But not only do they want to be like their mom or dad, they often try to prove their maturity by being better than their same-sex parent. This triggers the conflict with the same-sex parent we mentioned in chapters 9 and 11. By cutting you down or pointing out your weaknesses, your sons and daughters try to shore up their own shaky images of themselves as competent men and women.

During the later stages of middle adolescence and the entire period of late adolescence, most teenagers move beyond the practicing and transitional relationships of early and middle adolescence. They also move beyond the excitement of dating just to have a date and become involved in a serious, ongoing relationship with one member of the opposite sex. For the first time in their lives, your sons and daughters may now experience a glimpse of adult love that isn't based on childish need.

Although these "first loves" generally do not lead to marriage and can be the source of deep hurts, they are very important to your adolescents' development. They are usually the place your children first seriously consider being permanently attached to a specific person. They are also the first time most adolescents start thinking seriously (although still somewhat idealistically) about marriage, education, jobs, renting or buying a house, and having children. These relationships provide a lab experience in learning to share more intimately, engage in long-range planning, and find out how to give and take and care for another person. Although most late adolescents need a few more years of experience to prepare for marriage, they have most of the basic psychological ingredients by the time they reach their early twenties.

This concludes our overview of some of the key psychological and social developments that prepare children for relationships with the opposite sex. If these developments have progressed smoothly, your teenagers should reach young adulthood with positive and realistic attitudes toward themselves and others. That will provide a solid foundation for relating meaningfully to the opposite sex and integrating their maturing sexuality into their total personalities. The following chart summarizes these ingredients.

Be Open and Direct

Now that we have traced the social and psychological background for your sons' and daughters' sexual maturation, we turn to ways of helping them cope with their specifically sexual desires

CRUCIAL STEPS IN THE DEVELOPMENT OF SEXUAL IDENTITY AND INTERPERSONAL RELATIONSHIPS

Age	Contribution to Adult Sexuality & Gender Identity
Birth—1 year	Capacity for intimacy and closeness is first established in relationship with mother
6 months—2 years	Initial awareness of distinctiveness from others comes as infants realize they are separate from mother
10 months—3 years	Rudimentary development of separate, independent identity as toddlers start moving away from mother and asserting their own desires
3—6 years	Identification with same-sex parent and loving relationship with opposite-sex parent lays the psychological foundation of sex role identity
6—10 years	Stabilizing of sexual role identity through relationships with same-sex friends and continued identification with same-sex parent
10—12 years	Growing awareness of physical distinctiveness from the opposite sex
12—14 years	Growing interest in the opposite sex; practicing relating to opposite sex; idealizing relationships help separate from parents and serve a transitional function
14—17 years	Deeper relationships of a less selfish and more giving nature; confirmation of sexual identities through dating and other friendships with the opposite sex
17—21 years	Personality is consolidated so there is a growing readiness for marriage and commitment and mutual love and giving

and attitudes and values. We will focus on ways of helping teen-agers, but since many of these principles relate to children of all ages, we will include a little discussion of younger children as we go along.

The starting point for your children's effective sexual education is learning about their bodies and human sexuality in very natural ways. From your children's early years, body parts such as the penis, vagina, and breasts, should be referred to as naturally as hands, nose, and ears. Your children should be encouraged to ask questions about their bodies by your attitude of openness. In a natural way, they need to learn how their bodies function and the rudiments of sexuality. Pregnancies of friends, family members, and even puppies and kittens can provide spontaneous opportunities to teach your children the basic anatomical facts of sexuality.

As puberty approaches, your sons and daughters need more explicit information. A small book or pamphlet or readings from a class can serve as a catalyst to enlarge your children's knowledge and provoke discussion. So can television programs, a newspaper article, or some event around the neighborhood. Be on the lookout for teachable moments when your children ask spontaneous questions or evidence curiosity. If you don't know everything you need to answer your adolescents' questions, don't sweat it. Simply tell them, "I don't know exactly how that works, but I'll do a little reading (or check with a friend or doctor) and find out." Your attitude is the important thing, not your intricate knowledge of human biology and reproduction.

Teenagers need to know that absolutely no question is out of bounds. They should feel free to talk about AIDS, venereal disease, homosexuality, premarital intercourse, or anything else that crosses their minds. When your adolescents ask a question about their bodies or sexuality, give direct answers that convey accurate information. If they want to know how you practice birth control or what you think about homosexuality, answer them. It is usually good to first ask, "Why do you ask?" or "What do you think?" to see what is on their minds. But once they have shared their concerns or perspectives, forthright answers will be most helpful. Also be on the lookout for opportunities to place your answers in a moral or spiritual context. Teenagers don't need a sermon, but they do need a biblical perspective on their sexuality and insight from your own experience and convictions.

At each age, your teenagers will have a slightly different set of questions. Preadolescents want to know things such as:

"When will I get my period?"
"What happens when my period starts?"
"What's a condom?"
"What's intercourse?"
"How do babies live inside their mother?"

Early and middle adolescents have questions such as:

"Is the size of my breasts normal?"
"Is my penis normal size?"
"Will I ever catch up with my friends?"
"How does an abortion work?"
"Is masturbation sinful?"
"Can I masturbate too much?"
"Why are some people homosexual?"
"Do I have homosexual tendencies?"
"How can I tell if I'm in love?"
"Is intercourse painful?"
"Is it OK to pet if you don't have intercourse?"
"What should I do if my date wants to go farther than I do?"
"Is sex wrong when you love someone?"

By late adolescence most teenagers have found some type of answer to these questions. If they have not received them from you they have at least picked up some factual details and opinions from television, their friends, or school. If late adolescents talk with you about heterosexual issues they are more likely to ask about a specific person, the type of person who would be good for them, the timing of marriage, how to juggle college or work and marriage, your attitudes about abortion, or premarital sexuality. Their concerns are shifting from the biological aspects of sexuality to long-term relational or ethical issues.

If your teenagers don't ask questions about their bodies or

sexuality, don't assume they have none. They simply don't know how to ask or are too embarrassed. If that happens, initiate the topics yourself. Well before a girl begins menstruating and before boys begin to have wet dreams, they should have a clear understanding of the normality and significance of these processes and know that you are happy to talk with them about their bodies and their sexuality.

If you are comfortable with your own sexuality, you should find talking with your teenagers relatively easy. But if you feel anxious or uncertain, don't worry. If your parents didn't talk easily about their sexuality, it is natural for you to feel a little awkward in return. If you are, talk with your spouse or a couple of friends who have already gone through this stage. Spend time catching up on your own sexual knowledge. Don't be afraid to rehearse a little either. If it feels awkward to say penis, vagina, intercourse, condoms, or masturbation, practice with your mate until it feels more natural. If you still feel anxious, don't be afraid to tell your teenagers, "Frankly, I feel a little awkward talking to you about sex. My parents never talked with me and we all felt embarrassed by the topic, but I want to be more helpful to you." You are never too old to learn, and preparing to talk more freely with your teenagers can be as good for you as it is for them.

It's the Attitudes That Count

By now it should be clear that we believe that the most important part of sexuality is not biological. Sexual education begins in the crib, not in the bathroom or the bedroom. Your attitudes toward sexuality and the quality of your relationship with your teenagers are far more important than their grasp of their biological functioning. Through scores of interactions, your sons and daughters will see your attitudes toward marriage, sexual intimacy, and sexual promiscuity. They watch the way you dress, the way you treat your husband or wife, and the way you get along with those outside the family. They see your reaction to films or television programs and remember your discussions of the values you saw reflected there. Even without sitting them down for a heart-to-heart talk, they will know whether you believe the intimacies of sexual intercourse are beautiful and enjoyable or embarrassing and slightly guilt producing and if they are intended for marriage or not.

When your teenagers begin to date, you will need to have some discussions about values, dating standards, and sexuality. But long before that time their basic attitudes toward sexuality will already be established. Christian parents have a special resource for helping their adolescents develop positive attitudes toward their sexuality. The Bible shows the beauty of physical attraction, the joy of sexual intimacy in marriage, and the wisdom of limiting sexual intercourse to the lasting, loving commitments of marriage.

The very first chapters of Genesis teach that Adam and Eve were created for mutual love and intimacy. God's very first instruction to the first human couple was "be fruitful and increase in number; fill the earth and subdue it."[2] And in case anyone might jump to the conclusion that sex is intended only for procreation and not for pleasure, God gave us the entire Song of Solomon. Solomon wrote, "How beautiful you are, my darling! O how beautiful!"[3] Then he went on very explicitly describing his lover's physical beauty. These and other passages clearly show the beauty and naturalness of sexual intimacy as part of God's grand design for men and women.

At the same time children are learning the naturalness and beauty of sex, they should be understanding that beauty in its proper context of values and its deepest meaning. God created human sexuality for pleasure and enjoyment, for reproducing the human race, and as a means of expressing the deepest feelings of intimacy and oneness in marriage. The Bible says a husband and wife "become one flesh."[4] Sexual intercourse is a life-enhancing "oneness" experience that involves the total person—physical, spiritual, social, and emotional. It opens us up in an intimate and vulnerable way that is intended only for a life-long relationship.

Within that lasting commitment in marriage, sexual intercourse deepens and enhances a relationship. Outside of marriage, it violates the very oneness it was designed to enhance. Sex becomes a temporary pleasure in which some physical and emotional parts of one's life are shared without the commitment of the total personality.

After intercourse, two people feel differently about themselves and each other. After intercourse in marriage, partners feel renewed, enhanced, and closer. But after intercourse outside of marriage, this fulfilling oneness is either not present or vanishes quickly. That is why many people feel guilty or defrauded or used after engaging in intercourse outside of marriage. When God prohibited premarital sexual intercourse, he wasn't being arbitrary or capricious. He was giving us instructions on how to maximize the fulfillment in our lives and how to avoid the hurts that come from the misuse of our sexuality. If your teenagers can see both the beauty of sexuality and its purpose in marriage they will be off to a great start in developing healthy attitudes toward their sexuality.

Validating Their Sexuality

In order to get the message that their sexuality is a gift from God, your teenagers will need continuing affirmation of their developing sexuality. They will need to be complimented on their more adult or mature ways of dressing. They will need your interest in their athletic or musical or social activities. They will need your affirmation of their ideas and plans. And they will need your approval of their increasing interest in the opposite sex.

Since early and middle adolescents are just beginning to test out their ability to relate to the opposite sex, they are extremely sensitive to criticisms or comparisons. Any hint of teasing or a put-down of themselves or their newly chosen friends can trigger hurt or anger. Joking about their interest in a boy or girl or an upcoming date is out. Instead, find occasions to naturally affirm your teenagers' increasing interest in the other sex. Treat them like budding adults, not little children.

When your adolescents start planning for their first date, be especially sensitive to their feelings. Your daughters will probably want you to share their excited feelings. For them, dating is a sign of approaching maturity—another exciting minipassage on the road to adulthood. Your sons probably will not want you to make a big deal of it. In fact, they may become upset if you act as though their first date or first girlfriend is something special. They think "real men" are "cool" so they act like dating is no big deal. For them, being an adult male means not being giggly and excited like a girl.

Since your teenagers will show varying amounts of enthusiasm and concern about dating, don't be too quick to jump in and excitedly talk about their dates. But don't just sit back and be disinterested either. Let them take the lead and be prepared to give them just as much interest as they need. If they want your excitement, give it. But if they want a casual, offhand acknowledgment, give them that instead. In either case, be sensitive to the concerns and anxieties they may have.

Part of validating your sons' and daughters' sexuality involves letting them know you want them to appreciate their bodies. When children are young, your comfort with your own body and your direct answers to their questions tell them, "Our bodies are good. We should take care of them and be happy with them." They should not be made to feel guilty when they explore their bodies and find that touching gives them pleasure. As your sons and daughters move through the adolescent years, they need to know you want them to be aware of their sexual feelings and their desires to give and receive affection. They should know that you believe some physical expression of affection with a boy or girlfriend is healthy but that some limits are equally as important. Teenagers who don't feel this parental approval of their sexuality become confused or guilty or frightened by their desires for affection and their sexual feelings.

Be Aware

When your middle adolescents begin to date, you should
know who they are dating, where they are going, and when they
will return. Although fifteen- and sixteen-year-olds need increasing freedom, they are not yet ready to go wherever they want with
whomever they please. Ideally they also should not be coming
home to empty houses after school. Many adolescents now have
their first sexual experience in the privacy of their own homes
when both parents are away at work. Most middle adolescents are
still too vulnerable to their awakening sexual feelings to withstand
unlimited freedom and pressures.

If you have good communication with your adolescents, you will
already know many of their friends and where they spend their
time. You may, however, occasionally sponsor a social activity in
your home or encourage your teenagers to bring friends to the
house so you can keep in touch with their activities and relationships. It is important to know something about the young people
your teenagers want to date before they go out. You don't have to
grill them like the FBI, but you certainly should have a fair idea of
who they are and what they are like before you allow your teenagers to go out with them. It is also appropriate to meet their date
if you don't already know the person.

If you have a party at your house, welcome your teenagers'
friends and let them know you will largely stay out of sight, but that
you may exercise the prerogative to walk through a couple of
times. Expect the same kind of nonintrusive supervision when
your early or middle adolescents go to a party at a friend's home. It
isn't necessary for fifteen- and sixteen-year-olds to go to a party
where the parents aren't home or where they fail to offer adequate
supervision.

In chapter 7 we mentioned the wisdom of having most teenagers
wait to begin solo dating until around the age of sixteen. That is
partly because most practicing early adolescents aren't prepared
to make good decisions under the impact of either their awakening
sexual drives or peer pressure. Ninety-one percent of teenagers

who begin dating at twelve end up having sexual intercourse before marriage. Only 20 percent of teenagers who begin dating at sixteen do. For those who begin dating at thirteen or fourteen the statistics are between 53 and 56 percent. And for those who begin dating at fifteen, the percentage is 40 percent.

You also need to know that the high school scene has changed dramatically in the past twenty years. Peer pressure to become sexually active is incredible in many schools. Being a virgin is no longer seen as a virtue and friends may ask girls and guys who refrain from sex, "What's your problem?" or "Are you gay?" In the absence of other clear-cut passages into adulthood, having intercourse has become one of the newly accepted passages by many adolescents.

The way sex is presented in the media doesn't help this pressure. The average teenager sees several thousand actual or implied acts of sex on television every year. Ninety percent of those are outside of marriage and most of them are in the middle of very brief encounters. Television and movies rarely take the time and effort needed to display the beauty of sex in marriage or the lengthy time people need to build a deep companionship and love. They also rarely show the painful consequences of pre- and extramarital intercourse. Instead, they present a picture of sudden love or a brief encounter triggered by some mysterious, sudden vibes or physical attraction. Recently the media seems to be becoming a little more responsible as I have seen a few television shows in which teenagers actually struggled with being virgins and made that choice. Unfortunately, these programs are still clearly in a small minority.

As your children approach late adolescence, they need fewer limits. But as long as they are in high school, it is appropriate for teenagers to have an agreed time to return home and for you to know where they are going and who they will be with. A few limits can help teenagers avoid making some bad decisions and maximize their opportunities for positive experiences at the same time they are stretching the cords of independence to an increasing length. Although your teenagers may not appreciate your limits at the time, they will sense your caring and accept them if they are appropriate and grow out of your adult wisdom—not excessive parent anxiety.

In Search of Balance

Teenagers today have a more difficult time finding an appropriate balance in expressing their sexuality than their counterparts of earlier generations. At the close of the last century, girls in the United States didn't experience the onset of their menstrual cycle until fourteen years of age and they generally married by seventeen or eighteen. Now the average girl experiences menarche at thirteen and doesn't marry until after twenty. That expands the average period of nonmarital biological sexual maturity from approximately three years to more like seven or eight. This lengthened period creates increased frustrations for young adults who desire to wait until marriage for the full expression of their sexuality.

This also creates a dilemma for parents: how do you tell your children that sexuality is a pleasurable gift of God to be enjoyed in marriage but not to be fully participated in until that time—especially when their glands are operating at full steam and they have the complete physical capacity for sexual intercourse? The general lowering of sexual standards and the media's flooding of society with images of carefree, commonplace sex don't help. Neither does the increasing frequency of intercourse among even twelve- and thirteen-year-olds. Outside of their families, most teenagers will not find spiritually and emotionally mature models who both value and enjoy their sexuality and are committed to reserving its fullest expressions for the intimate relationship of marriage.

You can help your sons and daughters by avoiding either of two extremes. Don't leave your adolescents to themselves and appear to condone any sexual activities they please by your silence. And don't talk to your teenagers as though you think they should totally turn off their sexuality until the day they marry. The first approach opens your adolescents up to untold hurtful relationships—not to mention the possibility of unwanted pregnancy or sexually transmitted diseases. The latter approach encourages your teenagers to deny their God-given sexuality and can create intense feelings of guilt and confusion over their sexual desires and interests. But how do you find a balance between guilt-producing repression and unhelpful permissiveness? And just where should your teenagers draw the line? There is no single answer for all adolescents. Some things that may be appropriate for eighteen-year-olds, for example, are dangerous for thirteen-year-olds. And some things that are appropriate for one sixteen-year-old aren't suitable for another sixteen-year-old. The age of your teenager, the stage of their relationships, their emotional maturity, and their ability to say no or to draw a line limiting their physical involvement are all vitally important. But in spite of these individual differences, there are a few clear guidelines that help steer your adolescents through this maze.

First, your adolescents need to know that you welcome their sexual maturation and want them to feel good about their bodies and their developing sexuality. *Second,* they need to know that you want them to develop positive relationships with the opposite sex. *Third,* they need to feel an inner permission to feel good about their sexuality. *Fourth,* they need to know God designed the human personality so that the full expression of sexual intimacy should be reserved for marriage. *Fifth,* they need to know that they will have to draw some lines and make some clear decisions about expressing their affection and their sexuality before marriage.

Although these guidelines are broad, they do set some parameters that can anchor your efforts to help your adolescents come to grips with their maturing sexuality. The most difficult line to draw is the one between having permission to accept their sexual feelings and express some physical affection without engaging in heavy petting and sexual intercourse. Our position is this: your teenagers should know that you believe it is normal and healthy to show physical affection. They should know that you believe that hand-holding, hugging, or kissing with one special boy or girlfriend is appropriate for middle and late adolescents as long as they know how to set some limits. But they should also know that the farther they go, the harder it is to stop. And they should know the time to set their limits is before they go out on a date.

Ginny was able to help her sixteen-year-old daughter with her limits. One evening Fran confided to her mother, "Bill keeps pushing me to be more physical." Ginny sat on her impulse to overreact and calmly (on the outside) asked, "What do you mean?" "You know, Mom," Fran replied, a little embarrassed, "he wants to do more than hug and kiss." By now Ginny was even more anxious and curious about what Bill wanted to do and how far they had already gone. But she sensed Fran didn't want to be any more specific right then so instead of probing for more details, she asked, "How do you feel when Bill pressures you?" Fran replied, "I feel bad. I like Bill a lot, but I wish he would respect me more." Then she said, "I feel confused. I don't know how far I should go. Sometimes I think there's something wrong with me; then sometimes I think there's something wrong with Bill."

As they continued talking, Ginny let Fran know that her struggle was entirely normal. "I had the same problem with a guy I dated. Sometimes I didn't know if I should give in or tell him to forget the whole thing." Fran seemed surprised that her mother ever had those feelings; but it helped to feel more understood. Then her mother reminded Fran that sex was a gift of God and she should enjoy her sexual feelings but that we all need to set some limits before marriage.

She also told Fran, "It sounds like you and Bill are both normal teenagers. Sometimes boys are able to set some limits on their physical involvement, but it looks like you are going to have to be the one who does that in your relationship with Bill." Then they talked about ways that Fran could do that. When they finished their long discussion, Fran hugged her mother and said, "Thanks, Mom. You are really here when I need you." All teenagers need this kind of help.

Just Say No!

The best way to help your teenagers establish limits on their sexual expression is to talk frankly with them when they begin to date. Begin by telling them you are pleased they are starting to date, then talk directly about some of the questions or problems they may face. You might begin by saying, "I know these aren't things that worry you now, but sometime in your dating you will probably have to face them. Dating is fun and sometime you are going to meet someone you really like. When you do, you will have to decide how physically affectionate you are going to be." Then ask if they have given that any thought. You may be surprised that many early and middle adolescents are way ahead of you: they already know they don't want to kiss on their first date, or don't want to get involved in petting, or don't want to have intercourse before they marry.

If your teenagers haven't thought about some guidelines and standards, you can suggest a few. Talk to them about the progression from hand-holding to hugging to kissing to heavy petting to intercourse. Point out that the key is control and the farther they go the more difficult it will be to stop. And let them know that the time to make those decisions is not on the spur of the moment on a date, but before they go out. A firm commitment made ahead of time is much easier to keep. It also sets a tone for the whole relationship. Encourage your teenagers to work on the total relationship with their boy or girlfriend. Remind them that they need to learn to communicate and have fun and share their friends and interests and commitments.

You might let them know it is good not to put themselves in a situation where it will be hard to set limits until they know they can say no. You can also tell them that some middle adolescents decide, "No passionate kissing and no fondling." You can talk to your son about the myth that it should be up to the girl to set the limits. And you can tell your daughter (and your son), for example, that they should not be surprised to run into some peer pressure to become sexually active or to be pressured by a date.

Introduce them to lines such as, "If you really love me, you will go all the way with me," "Prove you love me," or "What's wrong with you? Are you afraid?" To answer each of these lines you can prepare your teenagers to say, "No, I really care for you, but I am waiting until I marry to have sexual intercourse," "Do you expect me to fall for that old line?" "Do you think I'm that naive?" "If you really love me, you will respect my values," "No, I'm not afraid. Do you have something you need to prove?" or "No. Can't you control your hormones?" You can also encourage them to share directly with their date and close friends why they are choosing to wait for marriage: They believe sex is beautiful as part of an enduring, committed relationship in marriage and they are saving themselves for that time and person.

Preparing your teenagers this way helps them feel more confident and assertive about setting their own limits and boundaries. If you have good rapport with your teenagers, these discussions can sometimes even be lighthearted and humorous at the same time you are communicating about some very vital issues.

Masturbation

Many parents and teenagers have serious questions about the appropriateness of masturbation. Some parents consider self-stimulation sinful. Even in our generation, they threaten teenagers with guilt or tell them masturbation causes mental illness or other problems. One patient with sexual problems in her marriage recalled how, when she was fifteen, her mother pointed to a severely mentally disturbed adolescent and told her, "That's because he plays with his sexual organs." She quickly stopped masturbating, repressed all signs of her sexual desires, and developed a terrible attitude toward sex. Even after years of marriage, she continued feeling sex was dirty, unenjoyable, and bad.

We can understand a parent's concern. Sex is a powerful experience that is frequently abused in our society. Teenagers can get carried away by their sexual passions, and the Bible does warn us to "flee the evil desires of youth."[5] Biblically, however, sexuality is presented as a gift of God, and masturbation isn't even mentioned, let alone prohibited. Over 95 percent of teenage boys indicate that they masturbate and approximately 50 percent of teenage girls. Given the explicit biblical descriptions of sexual attraction in the Song of Solomon and very clear teachings about extramarital sex and homosexuality, it would be a curious omission if God had simply "forgotten" to add masturbation to the biblical list of immoralities.

God created us with sexual desires just as he created us with desires for food and love. All of those desires need to be filled at the appropriate time and in appropriate ways. The problems come when we attempt to satisfy our desires inappropriately or when they become obsessions. Self-control and appropriate expression of desire is the biblical standard.[6] Whether it relates to food, money, work, exercise, or sex, the question for parents becomes, How can I help my children meet their needs appropriately and develop self-control?

The answer is: people develop self-control when they feel good about themselves and are emotionally healthy people. Teenagers who become obsessed with sex or masturbate compulsively, just like teenagers who become obsessed with money or status or food, are usually teenagers with underlying problems. They may have lacked opportunities to talk freely with their parents about their bodies or to develop good attitudes toward themselves and their sexuality. They may be sexually ignorant. Or they may feel so inferior to the opposite sex that they are afraid to date and become obsessed with masturbation as a private consolation.

By contrast, teenagers who feel good about themselves and have a good knowledge of human sexuality are not riddled with inappropriate feelings of guilt or undue curiosity. Consequently, they are able to healthily integrate their sexual feelings into their developing personalities. These adolescents do not become sexually preoccupied. If they have these attitudes and a clear biblical understanding of the meaning of sex and the need for some limits and self-control, they will be able to develop mature and appropriate guidelines for expressing their sexuality before marriage. This will apply to both masturbation and their physical expressions with the other sex.

Before we leave the topic of sexual desire, we would like to point out one other important principle. *All human abilities and attitudes and expressions of desire go through phases of development.* No adult desire magically springs to life at the age of twenty-one or at the time of marriage. Children eat as children, exercise as children, use money as children, and use their brains as children. They also learn to enjoy the companionship of others and to fill many of their God-given desires. These desires mature and change with age, and they are fulfilled differently at different ages, but they exist at every age.

Some parents act as though their teenagers' sexual desires should be the one exception to this rule. They would like to believe that God didn't intend for us to have any type of physical affection or sexual interest until marriage. Before that time, they believe, all desires are sinful. If that were the case, it would be the only area of human existence in which feelings and desires didn't go through a normal progression of development, and the only area in which God implanted a desire that was to be totally ignored. If we couple the complete biblical picture of sexuality with an understanding of normal human development, this viewpoint falls far short. You need to help your teenagers feel good about their developing sexuality, not repress or totally deny their sexual desires!

Manage Your Own Anxiety

For many parents, the most frightening part of letting go of their teenagers is the fear that their sons or daughters will become prematurely sexually active. Some of this concern is normal and expected. You should want your children to avoid the pain that comes from sexual intimacy before marriage. But don't let your worry create more problems. That happened to Ken's mother.

When Ken was seventeen, he started dating steadily. His mother was so afraid of his sexuality that she put up notes in his room reading, "Have you prayed about it?" and "What would Jesus do?" Although Ken thought her notes were crazy, they confused him and made him wonder about himself and his Christian life as much as he did about his mother. Fortunately, the family came for counseling and was able to work out the problem. Ken's mother found out that some of her anxiety stemmed from her own guilt and shame when her younger sister had gotten pregnant as a teenager. That pain and embarrassment was now being brought inappropriately into her relationship with her son. She also realized she was very frightened and confused by her own sexuality as a teenager. Once she understood her fears and talked about her own anxieties, she was able to back away from her guilt-producing intrusions into her son's life.

Some parents are less extreme than Ken's mother, but are still uptight about their adolescents' dating. They don't let their daughters date until they are eighteen, set unrealistic curfews, or quiz their teenagers so thoroughly after a date that they either push them toward premarital sexual intimacies or cause them to shut their parents out entirely. If you are experiencing anxiety over your adolescents' sexuality, you may need to look at your own sexual feelings as an adolescent. Were your parents able to talk openly with you about sexuality? Did you feel guilty or confused about your sexual life—or lack of it? Did you go farther than you wish you had? And how do you feel now about your sexuality? Do you enjoy it and feel comfortable with it or do you still have some anxiety or embarrassment or guilt? If you do, you need to come to a better understanding of your own teenage struggles and feelings so you won't pass your problems on to your teenage sons and daughters.

What About the Pill?

Parents of today's teenagers face several questions their parents didn't face. One is contraceptives. With birth-control methods readily available, you need to decide how you are going to talk to your teenagers about contraception. As one father asked, "Should I assume that everyone is having sex and pass out contraceptives to my kids with their monthly allowances? Or should I act as though they don't exist?"

Neither of these extremes is helpful. You certainly shouldn't assume your teenagers are going to engage in premarital sex and take it upon yourselves to make it as "safe" as possible. One of your responsibilities is to help your teenagers develop a biblical set of sexual values. On the other hand, you shouldn't ignore the realities of sexual experimentation. With nearly three of four teenagers having sexual intercourse, it is naive to think your sons and daughters are beyond temptation. Even though the frequency of intercourse of religiously committed adolescents is approximately 10 to 20 percent lower, the figures are still extremely high. The fact is that the majority of even Christian adolescents and young adults will have sexual intercourse before they marry. Some parents choose to ignore this potential problem and let their teenagers suffer the consequences if they become sexually involved. Most, however, want their children to be prepared.

If you have communicated openly with your children while they were growing up, they will probably know a lot about contraceptives before they reach adolescence. If you use contraceptive pills, for example, you can be sure your children will have asked you what those pills were for, long before they arrived at puberty. And, if you use condoms, it is not unlikely that your children have come across your supply long before they are inclined to use them. Your response to a young child's, "What's that?" should be an honest, "That's a condom." If they ask, "What's it for?" tell them, "It's so mommy and daddy won't have more children just now." And if they seem to want more information and they are old enough to understand, tell them. "Mom and Dad use it when they are having intercourse. It fits on Daddy's penis so that Daddy's sperm won't go into Mommy's vagina and fertilize an egg. If that happened, Mommy would have another baby and we have decided three children is just right for our family now." Most children will just say, "Oh" and be on their way. It's no big deal to them. They just wanted a little information.

Most parents find that easy enough with young children, but by the time their children reach adolescence they become more anxious. With the recent radio and television advertisements for condoms and massive cautions about AIDS and safe sex, however, it is even less possible for children to be unaware of the existence and importance of contraceptives. In spite of this, some parents fear that giving their teenagers information about birth control and sexuality will encourage them to act out their sexual urges. Just the opposite is usually true. Adolescents who don't understand their sexuality are more likely to experiment in order to satisfy their curiosity.

The best approach combines full information presented in a biblical context. You might tell your adolescents, "We believe God made sex for marriage and hope you will wait until then to have intercourse. But if you become sexually active before marriage, don't compound one problem with another one."

Some parents believe this is too explicit, or communicates a lack of trust. Or they are afraid it gives their teenagers tacit permission to become sexually involved. If you feel that way, you can avoid those concerns by talking about other teenagers' needs for contraceptives. After watching a TV program or reading an article on AIDS, abortion, or teenage sexuality you can discuss the use of contraceptives as a broader social issue. Without suggesting that your own teenagers may need to use contraceptives, you can ask them what they think teenagers who are sexually active should do, and share your values and commitments.

Chapter Highlights

Human sexuality is a powerful and beautiful God-given aspect of our lives. It grows out of our total personalities and involves our bodies, our emotions, our relational abilities, our values, and our spiritual commitments. Because of its complexity, sex is subject to serious distortions and your adolescents need a lot of assistance integrating their sexuality into their lives. You can help by enabling them to learn to feel good about this God-given gift, seeing that they understand their bodies and their sexual functioning, assisting them in developing positive attitudes and values about their sexuality, and helping them set appropriate limits.

If your children reach adolescence with good attitudes toward themselves and others, they will find it much easier to integrate their awakening sexuality into their increasingly adult identities while reserving intercourse for marriage. But no matter how emotionally healthy and spiritually mature your teenagers are, they will probably have to struggle at least a little with their feelings about their sexuality, the opposite sex, and their sexual drives. You can help them integrate their sexuality into their lives in a healthy way by:

- being open and direct in discussing sexuality
- affirming their developing masculine and feminine identities
- communicating positive attitudes and values about the human body and sexuality
- letting them know that sexuality is a God-given gift to be engaged in its fullest in marriage
- being aware of their friends and setting some realistic limits on their activities
- fostering inner permission to enjoy their bodies and become increasingly sexual beings
- helping them learn to set limits on their physical expressions of affection.

If you can offer this kind of understanding and support, you will make your adolescents' journey much easier, safer, and more enjoyable. You will also prepare them for the full expression of sexuality in marriage.

NOTES

1. Illustrations are by Dr. Narramore unless indicated otherwise.
2. Genesis 1:28.
3. Song of Solomon 1:15.
4. Genesis 2:24.
5. 2 Timothy 2:22.
6. See, for example, 2 Timothy 3:4 and 1 Thessalonians 4:3-5.

He who gathers crops in summer is a wise son, but he who sleeps during harvest is a disgraceful son.

PROVERBS 10:5

CHAPTER NINETEEN
DELAYED DEPARTURES: THE LIVE-IN YOUNG ADULT

When his Uncle Larry asked twenty-three-year-old Mark why he was still living at home, Mark quickly replied, "Where else can I get free rent, home cooking, cable TV, and free laundry? I'd be a fool to live anywhere else."[1]

Mark summed up the attitude of a large number of young adults. For them the question is not, Why are you living at home? but, Why should I live anywhere else? And can you blame them? With the cost of housing rising out of sight, a new car costing between $10,000 and $20,000, and the typical age of first marriage rising into the mid-twenties, young adults need some good reasons to pass up an offer of free room and board.

For the first time in decades, large numbers of post-high school and post-college young adults are staying at home, and others are returning after a few years on their own. Twenty-two million American youths over eighteen are still living at home. In 1984 over half of all males between twenty and twenty-four years of age were living with their parents.[2]

Earlier generations of young Americans had plenty of reasons to move away. Many were getting married before they turned twenty. Uncle Sam saw to it that a lot of them left home for military service. Others moved out to get away from conflicts with their mothers and dads or to prove they were "grown up." On top of these reasons, society expected it. Leaving home was the normal thing to do. But now several of these reasons are no longer applicable. The military draft is ended. Most people do not want to marry immediately after high school. And society no longer expects young adults to make their own way by the time they hit late teens or early twenties. On top of this, more than 12 million American young adults are enrolled in colleges and universities every year. When you add these changes to the financial pressures of setting up housekeeping, it is easy to see why many young adults are foregoing independence and choosing to stay at home.

Sometimes a few years at home after high school or college works fine. Many moms and dads are happy to have their young adults at home, and the financial savings make sense. It is the attitude and purpose and length of these extended stays that determine whether or not they are good for all concerned. Saving enough money to fund a college education or to make a down payment on a residence can be excellent reasons. So can the desire to give eighteen-year-olds a little more time to mature before striking out on their own. Not all late adolescents are ready to tackle life at nineteen or twenty or even twenty-one. Although they could probably make it if they had to, they could suffer strong setbacks in the process. Instead of forcing them out prematurely, many parents decide to give them a couple of years at home to solidify their personalities and keep growing toward maturity. Continued emotional support can allow these young adults to gradually ease into adulthood and test out their increasing autonomy.

If an extended stay at home has a clear purpose and your young adults are willing to live by a few rules around the house, you should feel free to go for it. But don't jump to the conclusion that this is always—or even usually—the best option for adult children. Many eighteen- to twenty-four-year-olds are staying at home to avoid taking responsibility for their lives. They are abusing drugs and alcohol, refusing to find a decent job, sponging off their parents, or deferring the development of mature relationships outside the family. Instead of employing the convenience of home to ease into new responsibilities, they use it to avoid cutting their cords of dependency on their parents and moving into the adult world. There are no fixed rules for deciding exactly which adults should stay and which should go—and when. As in so many parenting decisions, general guidelines can help, but we parents must ultimately rely on wisdom and intuition. The main principle to keep in mind is this: avoid fostering dependency.

Twenty-one-year-old Scott's parents realized they had fallen into that trap. Following a weekend workshop on parent-teen relationships, they asked if they could talk with me about their son. Three years after graduating from high school, Scott was still living at home. He had taken a few courses at a local community college and held a couple of part-time jobs but wasn't motivated to do much more. He came in at all hours of the night, slept until noon, lounged around the house for a while, and then headed off to spend the day with his friends.

"Scott is basically a good kid," his parents explained, "but we are getting worried. He doesn't seem to know where he's headed, and what's worse, he doesn't care. If we ask him to do anything around the house, he's always 'too busy.' On Saturdays he blares his radio all over the house until we can't stand the noise. If we ask him to turn it down, he slams the door or turns it off completely. We don't want to push him out before he is ready, but we're beginning to wonder if living at home is helping anybody. It seems like we're just giving him room and board so he can do whatever he pleases and he is getting on our nerves. If he had a job, it wouldn't bother us so much, but it seems like he's getting a free ride and we're getting all the headaches."

After a few discussions with a counselor, Scott's parents sat down with him and discussed their concerns. At first, Scott thought this would just be another lecture his parents would soon forget. But when they told Scott he would have to come up with a definite plan for a job or more schooling within a month and implement the plan by the next semester if he was going to continue living at home, he got the message. Within three weeks he had a full-time job, and when I saw them a year later they told me things were going well. "Scott is banking over $300 a month and is much more helpful around the house. Recently, he even started talking about finding an apartment with a friend."

Staying in the Nest

Young adults who live at home tend to fall into four broad categories. First are the normal kids who simply see the wisdom of saving some money or continuing their education while living with mom and dad. This arrangement is temporary and will only last until school is over or until some clear goals such as graduation, a job, or a down payment for a house are met. These young adults aren't dependently trying to avoid the real world and they don't create needless hassles around the home. They are studying appropriately or holding steady jobs and helping pay their own way. It is clear they want their independence and are only delaying certain aspects of that process until they have a better economic foundation. We consider this a healthy and normal arrangement.

A second group of live-in young adults is a bit more problematic. These young men and women are trying to delay entrance into the real world because they don't want the responsibilities that come with being independent. They want to remain in a state of economic dependence and have the privileges of adulthood without the responsibilities. Instead of using their extended stay as a launching pad into adulthood, they use it to prolong their adolescent dependencies. This hinders the process of consolidating their personalities, since a major requirement for maturing the personality is the settled confidence that one can take charge of his or her own life.

Although these live-at-home adults may try to convince themselves or others that they could "leave if they wanted," their confident-sounding affirmations may be mere illusions designed to hide their fears of failing or being alone. They may be children who resolved their middle adolescent rapprochement conflict between dependency and independency by opting for the security of dependency. Instead of consolidating their personalities and taking responsibility for their own economic and physical provisions, they leave responsibility on their parents' shoulders. Letting this type of young adult continue living at home for long can do more harm than good. They may keep developing the social or playful or childish parts of their personalities but not their mature planning and observing and responsible parts.

The third group of live-at-home young adults comprise what two authors call "boomerang kids."[3] These young adults have left the nest, started out on their own, and then encountered setbacks that drove them back to the safety of home. Broken marriage is the most common stressor that creates this dilemma. Each year, nearly half a million young people between twenty and twenty-four are divorced, and many of them return to mom and dad in their time of crisis. Other young adults face the sudden loss of a job or serious accidents or illnesses. A year or two earlier, these young adults may have been coping nicely with adulthood. They hadn't given a thought to coming home and were responsible young adults. But suddenly they are no longer able to cope and have no place else to turn. These boomerang kids present unique problems since they have been used to functioning on their own for a while—and may even return with a grandchild or two. We will talk about their special needs later in this chapter.

The final group of live-at-home young adults might be called the "marginally functional" or "borderline" young adult. These young men and women have serious psychological problems and are not able to cope in the adult world. Some of these young people are borderline psychotic; some have had psychotic episodes while in the military and never fully recovered; others have abused drugs so long they cannot function well in society; and others suffer a variety of serious social and emotional disorders. These young adults pose the most difficult situations because they really cannot cope alone.

The Borderline Young Adult

Twenty-year-old Cindy had run away from home during her senior year of high school. After spending three years on the streets of Los Angeles, she ended up back on her parents' doorstep—a broken and disturbed girl. Cindy had been through drugs, prostitution, and everything imaginable. Severely depressed, in poor health, and with a vacant stare in her eyes, Cindy was a shell of a person.

Twenty-four-year-old Gerald had been an adequate student in high school but he never fit in socially. His ideas were a little "off the wall" and he spent most of his time reading or taking care of his pets. He started college at a local university but dropped out and returned home after two years because he felt out of place and couldn't concentrate. His parents assumed Gerald would settle down, grow out of it, and either go back to college or get a job. But several years later, Gerald was still living at home reading, or listening to music in his room, and occasionally wandering around town. By now, his parents realized Gerald had some serious problems and took him to a psychiatrist.

Due to their severe emotional problems, there is no way Gerald and Cindy can face life on their own at this time. Although neither of them will necessarily have to be confined for long-term institutional care, they both need extended professional help if they are ever to function in society. Actually, mental health professionals are divided over the prospects of young adults like Gerald and Cindy. Some believe they are doomed to live at home or in a "halfway" care facility. Others believe that with excellent long-term medical and psychological therapy they may reach a much higher—and even a healthy—level of adjustment.

In any case, young adults like Gerald and Cindy present problems beyond the scope of any book. Normal young adults can be nudged into adulthood by sensitive parents who are willing to encourage them and set some limits. Borderline adults do not have the ability to function normally in society and need immediate professional help. If you push them out of the house, they will end up on skid row, in a mental hospital, or on the streets.

If you have an adult child like Gerald or Cindy, please don't try to apply the principles of this chapter with the hope that he or she will soon be able to make it on his own. Painful though it is, you need to realize you are in for a long, difficult struggle. These young people must have long-term professional care. Seek out a treatment facility that will provide both thorough medical care and long-term psychotherapy. They may need a period of psychiatric hospitalization. Only in the context of this kind of quality professional care will you be able to find out just what resources your child has and what the future holds.

Arranging an Extended Stay

Fortunately, few parents have to struggle with the chronically severe problems of a marginally functional young adult. For most of us, the questions revolve around how to get along with normal or boomerang young adults who want to live at home for a brief (or extended) period of time. In the rest of the chapter, we will discuss several things you should consider in making decisions about whether your young adults should still be living at home and, if they do stay, some guidelines that can make life easier for all concerned.

Since young adults want to stay home for different reasons you will always need to consider whether staying at home will be best for your specific son or daughter. Young adults have different personalities and needs. The apostle Paul told members of the church at Thessalonica that they should "warn those who are idle, encourage the timid, help the weak, and be patient with everyone."[4] Unruly or idle young adults need to be warned and not protected from the consequences of their actions. Fainthearted or timid young adults need to be encouraged so they can gain the confidence to move out on their own. And the truly weak, those who really cannot cope by themselves, need extra support.

Suppose your high school son indicates he doesn't plan on going to college. He says he will look for a job after he graduates and just "hang around town for a while and see what happens." Or suppose your daughter plans to take a course or two at a local college, live at home, and look for a part-time job. Should you accept that, say nothing, and hope for the best? Or should you sit them down and announce that their days at home are numbered? Like one couple I know, would you inform your recent high school graduate you are selling your four-bedroom home and moving into a smaller one and that he will need to find a place of his own? Hopefully not! But you do need to talk a few things over.

Most of the frustrations reported by parents of live-in young adults stem from failure to establish clear guidelines early with their children. Without any discussions, their young adults assume they can stay at home indefinitely or without sharing the responsibilities of running a household. Worse yet, many late adolescents assume they can come in whenever they please, play their music as loud as they want, and keep the house in any condition they like. Then when their parents start complaining about loud music and messy rooms, they get furious. This sets a vicious cycle in motion.

1. The young adult children fail to live up to their parents' unspoken (or unenforced) expectations.
2. The parents respond by complaining, nagging, or threatening.
3. The adult children accuse parents of "treating me like a child."
4. Both parents and children become increasingly frustrated until someone explodes.
5. Someone withdraws or vows to do better and then the cycle repeats again.

By the time your children graduate from high school you have probably already had a number of conversations about their future. You will know if they plan to go to college, work, marry, or join the military. But you may still need to have a couple of deliberate discussions to make sure you thoroughly understand their plans—especially if they include living at home. A conference with your young adult son or daughter can usually be carried out casually and in an almost offhand way. But several important issues do need to be discussed: Why do they want to stay at home? Have they considered any other living arrangements? What do they see as the pros and cons? How long might they want to stay? And have they thought about what it might be like living at home as a young adult?

You also need to think about the rest of the family. How does your husband or wife feel about your children staying home? Were you planning to use your child's room for a study or an extra bedroom? Does your family's financial situation justify continued financial support to your young adults? Do you and your spouse agree this would not be a step backwards for your son or daughter? Have your other children been planning on a bedroom for themselves or more access to the family car? We aren't suggesting you sit your young adults down and interrogate them about their plans but you do need to understand each other's expectations.

If you decide it is feasible for your adult child to live at home, you will need to discuss more specific questions and work out guidelines to govern the relationship. You will need to come to agreement on questions such as:

- Will your sons or daughters be in college or maintain a full- or part-time job?
- Will they pay rent? If so, how much and when? (When becomes important because many late adolescents assume they can always pay mom and dad last—if they have any money left over).
- Will there be limits on noise, music, smoking, or alcohol use in the home?
- Will regular chores or work around the house be expected?

- What level of tidiness will be expected in their room and throughout the house?
- Will your sons or daughters have access to the family car? If so, will they pay for their gas and insurance? If not, are they prepared to buy their own car or walk or ride the bus?
- Approximately how long do they think they may want to live at home?
- Do they have a game plan or goal to work toward and motivate them?
- If you are going to continue contributing to your adult children financially, how much will that be and until when?

If you haven't trained your children to take responsibility or do much planning for themselves, these questions may come as quite a shock. They may have assumed they could carry on at home as they always have. Ideally, they have been taking responsibility for years and can carry on the same way. Unfortunately, this is often not the case. Some young adults react to even the suggestion of rules or limits with, "Come on, Mom. Don't treat me like a child."

But it is not "treating someone like a child" to expect an adult to pay rent. It is not "parental" to rent out a room to nonsmokers only. And it is not infantilizing to agree with a guest boarder that they will not mess up any of the public rooms of the house. To put it another way, the guidelines you follow with live-in young adult children are agreements between adults. You can avoid a lot of hassle by telling your children, "We would love to have you live here for a while longer. But since you are a young adult now, we need to discuss how this will work. As an adult, you need your privacy and you have the right to run your own life. We also have a few needs. We have no desire to treat you like a child, but if we were renting a room out to a stranger, we would have a few guidelines. We aren't talking about rules that parents set for children. We are talking about guidelines for three adults living in the same home."

If your children have trouble understanding this, don't be surprised. They may think being adult means being able to do anything they please. Listen carefully for their feelings. Are they feeling that you are unfair? Do they feel pushed out? Or do they think you are treating them like children? If so, encourage them to talk about those feelings and try your best to understand. Reassure them of your love and your lack of desire to control them. Then restate your position. You would love to have them live with you but there will have to be a few rules. These are not childish rules to train children. Husbands and wives have rules, roommates have rules, and landlords and tenants have rules. Although you are their parents and probably will have some worries about them, you really want to treat them as adults. Clarifying a few guidelines is the best place you know to start. You want them to have the freedom to run their own lives, but you want the same privilege. They have the option of living with you under a few conditions or finding a place where they like the arrangements better.

Your discussions should include financial arrangements. Requiring partial rent or room and board is one good way to help young adults take responsibility. If they claim they can't afford it, you may need to help them take a look at their life-style. Around us in California, masses of young adults are driving nice cars, wearing designer clothes, spending weekends skiing in the mountains, and telling their parents they can't afford to help with the rent or find their own place. If they are enjoying that kind of life-style and cannot afford to pay their own rent, they may need to change their life-style! Proverbs says "He who gathers crops in summer is a wise son, but he who sleeps in harvest is a disgraceful son."[5] Later adolescents clearly need to take a major responsibility for their own financial needs.

The Boomerang Child

Late one evening, Sam and Joanna received a tearful phone call from their daughter, Glenna. After four years of marriage, her husband had walked out on her, taken their only car, and headed for another state. Glenna was left with two young children, the younger in diapers, and less than $200 in the bank. She had no job and there was no way she could pay the rent that was coming due in a few days. Sam and Joanna got out of bed and drove over to encourage Glenna. They listened to her painful story. She knew that she and Jim had marriage problems but she never believed he would leave her and the children. What was the matter with him? What had she done wrong? Where could she tell Michael his daddy had gone? And how could she pay the rent?

After a couple of hours of tearful and supportive listening, Sam and Joanna assured Glenna they would help in any way they could. Sam said he knew a lawyer that could help her and suggested she cancel all their credit cards immediately so Jim couldn't run up any more bills. Then Sam told Glenna, "We would be happy to have you stay with us until you can get back on your feet. We don't have a lot of room but we can get by for a while."

"Really, Dad?" Glenna replied gratefully. "I don't want to be a burden on you, but I don't know what else to do." "That's what we're here for, honey," encouraged Joanna. "We can talk about the details tomorrow, but you know we're standing with you." Unknown to Glenna, Sam and Joanna had decided on the drive over to her apartment that they would ask her to move in for a while. They didn't have money to pay the rent for Glenna and they knew that she would need their emotional support as well.

Over the next several days, Sam and Joanna and Glenna worked out their arrangements. Joanna was happy to baby-sit the children when Glenna found a job. They wouldn't expect her to pay rent, but they would like her to share the food expenses. She could put away everything else she earned toward a car and, hopefully, a down payment on her own place or at least a few months' rent.

Divorced or widowed young mothers like Glenna present perhaps the most difficult situation. Crushed by a failed marriage or the loss of a loved one, and pressed by financial realities, many young mothers are almost forced to return home even if they are pretty independent and self-confident. And while you want to be helpful in their crisis, there are limits to what parents can and should do for them. You will have to negotiate things like where will the baby sleep, who will handle the baby-sitting, and whose limits (parent or grandparent) will be enforced and who will discipline the child.

You will also need to talk through other issues. If your daughter doesn't have a job, you may not expect her to get one in the next two weeks. But you should expect her to begin actively looking when the immediate shock of the divorce or death has passed. You also need to talk about your role with her finances. Since the major motivating factor for returning home is financial, it is probably unrealistic to ask her for rent. But for her well-being she should be moving toward the time when she will be able to support herself in her own place. To accomplish that, she must reach the point when she is either paying you monthly rent or putting that amount away in savings in preparation for a return to independent living.

After basic questions are settled and things are going better, you need to talk over how long she thinks she will need to stay. Most young adults won't abuse your support and will want to leave as soon as possible. When they are emotionally refueled and on their feet financially, they are anxious to be on their way. The few who are not need to be helped to take that big step again.

What to Do When They Won't Go

Some young adults don't seem to have a clue that they are wearing out their welcome or failing to take responsibility for their lives. After an initial settling period, a boomerang child may start enjoying home a bit too much. Or a post-school young adult may not be making any plans to strike out on his own. Coupled with the problem of prolonging their dependency, these children can also start to get on a parent's nerves or seriously hamper the parents' life-style or emotional environment. If this happens, you may need to help them take another step toward independence. Here are some signals that it is time to have another talk:

- They have lived with you for one to two years after finishing their education
- They have not held a steady job for several months to a year
- They do not seem seriously committed to earning a decent living in the near future
- They are unable to prioritize and handle their finances
- They continue to show early- or middle-adolescent attitudes and characteristics (e.g., they have not yet consolidated their personalities) and they are alternately independent and dependent or resent you and frequently get into quarrels
- You believe they aren't maturing and taking responsibility for their lives
- They have no medium- or long-term plans

If several of these are true in your family, your adult child has either reached the time when he or she should be setting out on his own, or you have failed to establish and carry through on some "house rules." Assuming the problem isn't the house rules, you should raise your concerns, ask them about their plans, and talk things over. At the same time you are sensitive to their needs or fears, you should make it clear you believe it is important for all concerned that they begin thinking about getting their own apartment.

If your young adults keep dragging their feet, you need to have another talk. You might begin by asking how long they think they would like to stay. This puts the responsibility on them, gets them thinking, and lets them know that you are serious. Without giving the impression you want to kick them out, you have started the discussion. If your young adults say they are perfectly happy to stay indefinitely, you may need to be more direct. You can state why (either for your good or theirs) you believe they need to start considering other options.

If your children say they want to stay "until I find a place" or "until I save a little money," ask, "How long do you think it will take to do that?" An "I don't know" reply can be met with the statement such as, "We aren't comfortable with such an indefinite time." If they say "a year or two" you might counter with, "Six months sounds a little more realistic to us. That would give you time to put away a thousand dollars (or find a job or an apartment) but still not rush things too much." A realistic but definite time frame is one of the best ways of telling young adults that you have confidence they can take greater responsibility for their lives. It also draws a realistic boundary that clearly lets them know what they can expect.

If your son or daughter cites a lack of money as an excuse for staying home, say you would be happy to help him or her plan a workable budget. And if they still don't see how they can get started, you might offer to pay their first month or two of rent, but make it clear that after that they are on their own. The issue here, of course, is not whether you can afford to pay for their expenses or not, but their need to take responsibility for their own lives.

Chapter Highlights

Living at home as a young adult can be a necessary, profitable, and enjoyable experience. Given the economic realities in many areas, a year or two at home after completing school is often wise and realistic. As parents, however, you need to be sure these arrangements are good for both you and your adult children. Arrangements that give you time to enjoy an adult relationship with your children and give your young adults a little additional time to consolidate their personalities or to get on their feet financially are fine. But arrangements that perpetuate childhood dependency will actually cripple your young adults and should be modified or terminated for their welfare and your own.

NOTES

1. Illustrations are by Dr. Narramore unless indicated otherwise.
2. Jean Davies Okimoto and Phyllis Jackson Stegall. *Boomerang Kids* (Boston: Little, Brown and Company, 1987).
3. *Boomerang Kids.*
4. 1 Thessalonians 5:14.
5. Proverbs 10:5.

They will soar on wings like eagles; they will run and not grow weary, they will walk and not be faint.

ISAIAH 40:31

CHAPTER TWENTY

LOOKING FORWARD: LOOKING BACK

We began our story of adolescence by comparing our children's journey toward adulthood to two familiar sights: a ship preparing to leave a harbor and a young toddler separating from his mother. In the process we traced the progressive unfolding of teenagers' needs to become increasingly aware of their own distinctiveness from us and others, to gradually cut cords of dependency that have bound them securely to us during their childhood years, and to make initial headway toward developing their own resources and adult identities.

As your teenagers make this trip, two God-given emotional needs propel them forward. The first is a need for love, belongingness, and emotional nurturance—an experience that psychologists call attachment. If that need is met, your children store up ample resources for their long trip. The foundation for their self-esteem and confidence emerges from this attachment. So does their inner sense of strength and depth and wholeness.

Paradoxically, this same attachment process prepares your children for eventual disengagement, their second major need. In order to solidify their own mature identities, children need to move away from you emotionally. They must find out they can do for themselves what you used to do for them. If you help your teenagers meet these two needs, they should be able to successfully navigate their adolescence and prepare for young adulthood. Although no teenagers escape adolescence totally unscathed, a steady supply of loving support and age-appropriate opportunities to separate from you provide the best guarantees that your children will reach adulthood safely.

Once your sons and daughters reach their early twenties, their journey is well underway. Like the ship that has left the harbor, they may occasionally encounter some stormy times as well as many pleasant and exciting ones. Every few months they may pull into your harbor for a brief refueling, but those visits will be fewer and farther between. The results of your initial fueling and furnishing, however, will go with your children wherever they go. They will unconsciously draw on those resources to face each new challenge of their lives.

In order to have a happy, fulfilling relationship in marriage, for example, they will draw from their reservoir of love and independence. Their ability to be close and loving as well as to have minds of their own will be essential for developing happy marriage relationships. When your sons and daughters join the work force, they will call on these same two inner strengths.[1] They will need to be able to get along with others but also make their own decisions and work independently.

When your children have children of their own, these two resources will be needed again. To the degree they can both love their children and encourage their development of separate identities, they will be effective parents. When your children's children eventually leave their home, your children's abilities to be both loving and independent will be tested once more. They will need to have a strong sense of personal identity to enjoy their children's leaving, and a loving relationship with their mate to feel good about entering the next phase of their life. Then, if your children lose their spouse through death, their ability to function healthily and happily as individuals will be tried once more. Throughout the life cycle, these same two abilities and needs will undergird their lives.

As you help your sons and daughters clear the developmental hurdles of adolescence, you help them solidify both of these abilities. You also bestow far more than these emotional supplies. You give them a legacy of freedom to become all that God created them to be. Jesus exemplified this in his ability to be deeply loving and self-sacrificing while also standing for the truth and being willing to go against the grain of an entire society and its leaders. He had a strong, secure identity and he was totally free to be lovingly involved with others. This twin ability to be both loving and independent is a hallmark of personal maturity. The progression from intimate bonding with one's mother, through separation and establishing one's own identity, to entering into loving and productive adult relationships is also at the heart of God's design for every person and family. You have the rich opportunity of helping your sons and daughters in that process.

NOTES
1. Galatians 6:5.